A Brief History of Modern Psychology

2nd Edition

Ludy T. Benjamin, Jr.

WILEY

Vice President and Publisher: *George Hoffman*
Executive Editor: *Christopher Johnson*
Assistant Editor: *Brittany Cheetham*
Editorial Assistant: *Kristen Mucci*
Photo Editor: *Mary Ann Price*
Marketing Manager: *Margaret Barrett*
Senior Production Manager: *Janis Soo*
Assistant Production Editor: *Pauline Tan*
Cover Designer: *Kenji Ngieng*

This book was set in 10/12.5 Palatino by Laserwords Private Limited.

Founded in 1807, John Wiley & Sons, Inc. has been a valued source of knowledge and understanding for more than 200 years, helping people around the world meet their needs and fulfill their aspirations. Our company is built on a foundation of principles that include responsibility to the communities we serve and where we live and work. In 2008, we launched a Corporate Citizenship Initiative, a global effort to address the environmental, social, economic, and ethical challenges we face in our business. Among the issues we are addressing are carbon impact, paper specifications and procurement, ethical conduct within our business and among our vendors, and community and charitable support. For more information, please visit our website: www.wiley.com/go/citizenship.

Library of Congress Cataloging-in-Publication Data
Benjamin, Ludy T., 1945-
   A brief history of modern psychology / Ludy T. Benjamin, Jr. –2nd Edition.
      pages cm
   Includes bibliographical references and index.
   ISBN 978-1-118-20677-5 (pbk. : alk. paper) 1. Psychology–History–19th century.
2. Psychology–History–20th century. I. Title.
   BF95.B438 2014
   150.9–dc23
                           2013027983

10 9 8 7 6 5 4 3 2 1

In memory of Robert Val Guthrie (1930–2005)
American psychologist and historian
who made the invisible people visible

and Darryl Bruce (1939–2011)
cognitive psychologist and historian
and beloved friend

And in honor of Nicholas and Dorothy Cummings
for their extraordinary support of the
Center for the History of Psychology
at the University of Akron

Brief Contents

Contents

Illustrations

Preface

As the title of this book indicates, this is a history of modern psychology. It is a brief history, and we will say more about that later. Today psychology exists in three forms. There is an academic psychology located in secondary schools, colleges and universities, and research institutes. There students can study the field of psychology for preparation for a career in psychology or as preparation for any number of other fields such as medicine, law, the ministry, business, and education. There instructors can teach courses in this fascinating discipline. Psychological scientists can work to answer the complex questions of human behavior and mental processes.

In addition to academic psychology, there is also a profession of psychology that applies the knowledge of scientific psychology to real-world problems. These professionals have studied psychology beyond the baccalaureate level and have earned master's or doctoral degrees. If they work in the mental health fields (e.g., clinical psychology, counseling psychology, or marriage and family therapy), they are required to obtain professional licensure as a condition of being able to practice. These professionals include industrial-organizational psychologists who work with businesses, corporations, and unions on a wide array of issues in the workplace, such as increasing worker satisfaction or selecting effective managers. Forensic psychologists work in the judicial system offering expert testimony about the mental states of individuals, about the advisability of placement of children in child-custody cases, and even about strategies for presenting cases in the courtroom. Sport psychologists work with individual athletes or athletic teams to enhance performance, often helping athletes to overcome mental obstacles that impede performance. School psychologists work with teachers, parents, and children, providing a host of services aimed at seeing that children get the educational and behavioral help that they need. Clinical and counseling psychologists offer psychotherapy to individuals and groups who are experiencing psychological problems from minor adjustment issues to serious psychopathology. These, and other kinds of practicing psychologists, make up the profession of psychology.

The third kind of psychology is the oldest. It might be called public psychology or popular psychology. It comprises public interest in and beliefs about behavior and mental states. It involves practitioners, such as phrenologists and mesmerists from the nineteenth century, and contemporary practitioners who are not trained in psychology, but advertise themselves as persons who can offer psychological help such as reading a person's mind, foretelling the future, or offering some form of therapy that they believe will be effective in treating certain kinds of problems. They can practice in this way as long as they do not advertise themselves as a psychologist. That label is licensed. Contemporary popular psychology is manifested in hundreds of ways, for example, books, television shows, magazines, and radio talk shows. One can buy books on how to have a happy marriage, how to raise optimistic children, how to control ones emotions, how to be an effective leader, and how to overcome depression. These books would be labeled popular psychology if the authors had no educational background qualifying them as experts in these subjects. Of course, this pervasive popular psychology is not always the psychology that psychologists would want to claim as their own. Nevertheless, it is a psychology and is part of the history of psychology.

This public psychology has likely existed since humans first appeared on this earth. However, academic psychology (sometimes called scientific psychology) and the profession of psychology have their roots in the late nineteenth century, only about 135 years ago. This book is the story of the development of the science and profession of psychology. More will be said about the relationship of these to popular psychology in Chapter 1.

One of the sad ironies of the history of psychology is that the first book on the history of psychology to become quite popular was authored by a psychologist named Boring. He published his book in 1929, revised it in 1950, and for nearly 40 years it was considered the authoritative treatment of the history of psychology – required reading for most doctoral students in psychology. Although the juxtaposition of Boring and history is amusing, it is only mildly so. That is because there are actually people in the world who believe that history is boring! But how absurd! How could history be boring? History is the story of fascinating lives in fascinating times. If it were not interesting, why would anyone take the time to remember it? History recounts the drama of our past. It allows us to connect our lives to that past. It helps us make sense of the present. It gives us some basis on which to speculate intelligently about our future.

It helps us integrate our knowledge in a framework of more meaning-ful understanding. It teaches us some humility for our own views and, we hope, some tolerance and understanding of the views of others. Like any good story, history alternately fills us with joy or sadness, hope or despair. For those who would want to understand the human condition, the history of psychology is a good place to begin.

Some histories of psychology focus principally on the history of the science of psychology, which was, in fact, the subject of Boring's history. Such an approach tells only half of modern psychology's history. There is a modern profession of psychology that has grown up as a twin of experimental psychology. The overwhelming majority of psychologists today do not work in research labs or universities. Instead, they serve the public directly as practitioners in numerous professional specialties. This book treats both stories, the science and the practice of psychology, illustrating their roots and their co-development.

The title of this book indicates that this is a *brief* history, and there is a reason for that. It is meant to be an alternative to the typically encyclo-pedic history of psychology textbooks, of which there are many good ones. In writing a smaller book, it is my hope that instructors will find it useful to pair this book with other specialty books in a history of psy-chology course (such as *A History of Psychology in Letters*, 2nd ed., Wiley, 2006), including readers, or to pair the book with the rich collections of online readings that are available on the Internet. It is possible to use this book for the integrative story that it offers and pair it with pri-mary readings by the pioneers of psychology and related fields such as Wilhelm Wundt, G. Stanley Hall, Mary Calkins, E. B. Titchener, and John B. Watson. Readings by these individuals, and hundreds of oth-ers, are available on the Internet at a number of sites. Students can read chapters from Freud's *The Interpretation of Dreams*, Darwin's *Origin of Species*, and James's *Principles of Psychology*, or hundreds of other books and articles critical in psychology's history. A particularly rich site for the history of psychology is *Classics in the History of Psychology*, main-tained by Professor Christopher Green at York University in Toronto (http://psychclassics.yorku.ca).

For the student, my hope is that this book will provide you with a solid grounding in psychology's past, that it will help you integrate your knowledge of contemporary psychology into a more meaningful whole, and that it will help you understand psychology's place in a larger story. Additionally, I hope that it will stimulate your curiosity about the top-ics and individuals discussed in this book, leading you to read some of this earlier work that changed our understanding of human nature. For the general reader, I hope that you will find that the book provides the historical and disciplinary context that will help you better understand the richness and complexity of contemporary psychology in its several forms.

In this second edition, I have benefited from the advice of many users of the first edition. Much new material has been added to this edition, reflecting the growing scholarship on the history of psychology and related fields. To accommodate these additions and still keep the book in its brief form, I have reduced the amount of biographical coverage. As a historian, I favor a personalistic approach to history and so I have maintained the biographical content that I believe is necessary to provide context to understanding the theories, research, and practices described in this book. Such material is essential to the quality and character of the narrative. The great American historian, Henry Steele Commager (1965), reminds us that although history has multiple functions, at its essence, *history is a story*, and few things are more enjoyable than a story well told. The history of psychology is a fascinating story, and my hope is that even in this brief history I have created an account that is both scholarly and informative, and, in the best traditions of good history, interesting reading.

I express my gratitude to John Wiley and Sons for the opportunity to produce this second edition. I am grateful to my former editor, Chris Cardone who invited me to write this book and to my current editor at Wiley, Chris Johnson, for his stewardship on this second edition. I have also benefitted from the help of Wiley assistant editor Brittany Cheetham and editorial assistant Kristen Mucci for handling many of the production issues on this book.

I thank Kerry Buckley whose excellent biography of John Watson gave me the idea for the opening of the chapter on behaviorism. I also thank David Baker, Lizette Royer Barton, Jennifer Bazar, Darryl Bruce, Robin Cautin, Deborah Coon, Paul Craig, Nicholas Cummings, James Deegear, Stanley Finger, James Goodwin, Christopher Green, John Hogan, Alexandra Rutherford, Michael Sokal, Roger Thomas, Karyn Plumm, Peter Frecknall, David Wilder, Thomas Heinzen, and Gwen Murdock for their suggestions on this book and its predecessor. I greatly appreciate the scholarship and sense of history they brought to the task. I thank my undergraduate and graduate students of many years whose comments and questions have shaped the content and structure of this book. Finally, I thank my wife, Priscilla, who has worked with me for nearly 50 years, and who brings her talents as librarian and educator to all of my writing projects.

Ludy T. Benjamin, Jr.

1

Pre-Scientific Psychology

Start with these facts. Psychology is the most popular elective in American high schools today. Further, psychology is one of the two or three most popular undergraduate majors in North American colleges. People cannot seem to get enough of psychology; it is everywhere today. It is the substance of movies, novels, computer games, Facebook, magazines, television shows, tabloid newspapers, radio talk shows, and music lyrics. Clearly, there is no shortage of public interest in psychology. People are interested in behavior – their own, their relatives, their neighbors, their co-workers, and even strangers who they know only through the media of books, magazines, or television shows such as soap operas, courtroom programs, game shows, situation comedies, dramas, and the so called "reality" shows. There seems to be a never-ending fascination with human behavior that is perhaps inherent in human nature. It is likely that such an interest has afforded evolutionary advantages. Psychologists refer to this public interest in psychology as popular psychology. It isn't psychology of the form that would be recognized by most psychologists as scientific psychology. Indeed, many psychologists would be embarrassed by any association with it. However, the public loves it, and it is their psychology.

Surely, psychology has existed from the very beginnings of human history. When hominids first walked erect on the earth, facing a life expectancy of perhaps 30 years, a life beset with hardships and dangers that could hardly be imagined today, these early individuals were no doubt in need of human comfort, of reassurance, of empathy, and of guidance. Moreover, where there is demand, there is supply. There must have been individuals who provided services of a psychological nature to their fellow humans as practitioners. These early humans practiced their craft under a variety of names such as sorcerer, wizard, charmer, shaman, medicine man, enchanter, seer, and priest. Their trade involved a combination of medicine, religion, and psychology. Although they often held positions of authority and respect within their tribes, they could lose that social standing, and indeed their very lives, if they were judged incompetent or ineffective in their healing arts. With the passage of centuries, specialization occurred leading to separate professions of medicine, religion, and psychology, although it can be easily argued that these three remain linked in various ways in modern practice. Thus, the practice of psychology dates to thousands of years ago, but, as we will describe in this book, the science of psychology is a nineteenth-century invention.

As the title of this book indicates, this is an account of *modern* psychology, which means that the story recounted here is a mostly recent one. So having acknowledged that the practice of psychology is thousands of years old, we will fast forward to the era of concern for this chapter, which is the nineteenth century. The term "modern psychology" has come to be synonymous with scientific psychology. Indeed, there is consensus that the dating of modern psychology begins with the establishment of a research laboratory by Wilhelm Wundt at the University of Leipzig in Germany in 1879. The historical significance and salience of that occurrence is underscored by historian James Capshew (1992) who wrote, "the enduring motif in the story of modern psychology is neither a person nor an event but a place – the experimental laboratory" (p. 132).

The new psychological laboratories began their appearance in North America in the last two decades of the nineteenth century, first at Johns Hopkins University in 1883, then at Indiana University in 1887, at the University of Wisconsin in 1888, and at Clark University and the universities of Pennsylvania, Kansas, and Nebraska in 1889. The first of the new laboratories in Canada was established at the University of Toronto in 1891 (Baldwin, 1892). By 1900 there were more than 40 such laboratories in North America (Benjamin, 2000), all seeking to apply the new scientific methods, borrowed largely from physiology and psychophysics, to questions of the basic human processes of seeing and knowing and feeling.

When this new psychology arrived on American soil, there was already a psychology in place. In fact, there were two other psychologies extant in the nineteenth century, the practice of psychology, which, as argued, had been around since the dawn of human history, and another psychology that existed largely within colleges and universities known as mental philosophy.

The practitioners of psychology offered their services under a variety of labels. There were phrenologists who measured the shape of the skull of their clients, looking for bumps and indentations that signified talents or deficiencies. There were physiognomists who studied the contours and features of their clients' faces, making determinations of personality traits and abilities based on such things as the shape of a person's nose, the height of the cheekbones, or the distance between the eyes. There were mesmerists who used forms of hypnosis to encourage changes in their clients' behaviors. There were seers and clairvoyants who could predict the future and thus advise clients about their current and future actions. There were graphologists who made psychological assessments based on the characteristics of their clients' handwriting. In addition, there were mediums, psychopathists, psychics, spiritualists, mental healers, advisors, psychometrists, and even people who labeled themselves psychologists. Mostly self-trained and using methods tenuously based in science, if at all, these practitioners sought to help their clients in much the same way as modern psychologists do. They attempted to cure depression, improve marital relations, teach parenting skills, increase job satisfaction, reduce anxiety, and assist in vocational choices. These individuals represented what the general public understood to be the subject matter and practice of psychology. This kind of psychology, however, did not have credibility within the community of higher learning, that is, within colleges and universities, where the other pre-scientific psychology resided.

Mental philosophy was a subject matter that had been part of America and its university curriculum since the seventeenth century.

Figure 1.1 An advertisement for the Chicago School of Psychology in 1900, a school that taught the use of hypnosis for psychological treatment, an example of the public psychology of that time

Of English and Scottish origins, through the works of such philosophers as John Locke, David Hume, George Berkeley, Thomas Reid, and Dugald Stewart, the subject became a nineteenth-century staple in the education of students who learned this brand of empirical psychology from one of several American textbooks on the subject. Demonstrating the centuries-long influence of British empiricism, the focus of mental philosophy was on sensation and perception, usually referred to as properties of the intellect, although the intellect also included other cognitive processes such as attention, learning, memory, and thinking. In addition, mental philosophy covered the emotions (often called sensibilities) and the will, including debates on determinism versus free will (Fuchs, 2000). This tripartite treatment – intellect, sensibilities, and will – defined the extant academic psychology in America when laboratory experimental psychology arrived from Germany.

It is these two psychologies – one public, one academic – that are the subject of this chapter. They are important for the history of modern psychology because they are part of the historical context for understanding the development of the science of psychology, the profession of psychology, and that brand of psychology that has such broad public appeal, often referred to as popular psychology.

A Public Psychology

The public fascination with behavior today existed in the nineteenth century as well, although the media sources in that century were far more limited. Still, people were exposed to psychology through books, newspaper and magazine stories, and advertisements and signs announcing psychological services, for example, "Sister Helen, Palm Reader." People wanted the assistance that they believed could come from those whose special knowledge or talents could help them identify their strengths and improve their personal weaknesses, help them choose a career wisely, help them find a suitable partner for life, help them overcome specific fears, cure them of their depression, help them communicate with dearly departed friends or relatives, or predict their future. There were many of these pre-scientific public psychologies, too many to cover in this account. In order to understand the landscape that scientific psychology faced when it arrived in North America it is important to understand something about these various psychologies. We will focus on a select few that achieved the greatest followings: phrenology, physiognomy, mesmerism, spiritualism, and mental healing.

Phrenology

In the nineteenth century, "having your head examined" did not refer to suspected mental illness, but meant instead a visit to a phrenologist who would examine the shape of the client's head and, based on various cranial measurements, would make pronouncements about the individual's personality, abilities, and intelligence. It began in the work of German anatomist, Franz Josef Gall (1758–1828), who believed that different parts of the brain were responsible for different intellectual, emotional, and behavioral functions. Some parts of the brain would be overdeveloped, creating a bump on the skull, whereas others parts might be underdeveloped creating a skull indentation. The location of these various functions was specific to a particular area of the skull. Thus, a person's propensity for being destructive was measured immediately above the left ear, whereas the area above the right ear indicated a person's degree of selfishness. Spirituality and benevolence were measured at the top of the head, whereas parental love, friendship, and love of animals were measured at the back of the head.

Gall's phrenological ideas were spread in North America by Johann Spurzheim (1777–1832) and particularly by George Combe (1788–1858) who lectured widely in the United States and Canada on phrenology, promoting his book, *System of Phrenology* (first published in 1825), and establishing phrenological clinics in the cities where he traveled. Combe subscribed to the system of categorization of 35 faculties as originally described by Spurzheim. Combe (1835) wrote:

> Observation proves that each of these faculties is connected with a particular portion of the brain, and that the power of manifesting each bears a relation to the size and activity of the organ. The organs differ in relative size in different individuals and hence their differences in talents and dispositions.... Every faculty is good in itself, but all are liable to abuse. Their manifestations are right only when directed by enlightened intellect and moral sentiment. (pp. 54–56)

What the phrenologist provided was not only the cranial measurements that identified the talents and dispositions, but of greater importance, a plan of action designed to strengthen the weaker faculties and thus provide greater happiness and success in life for the client. As John van Wyhe (2004) has written, "The phrenologist claimed to have an almost mystical power to reveal invisible traits and tendencies.... Phrenology was knowing about others and revealing their secrets" (p. 58).

In the United States, the phrenological market had been cornered by the Fowler brothers, Orson (1809–1887) and Lorenzo (1811–1896),

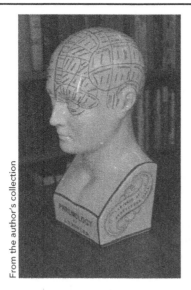

From the author's collection

From the author's collection

Figure 1.2   At left, a replica of the phrenology bust designed by Lorenzo Fowler in the 1840s. It was crafted as an ideally shaped head to be used as a reference point. On the right is the cover of a "Self-Instructor" phrenology manual, also dating from the 1840s. For 25 cents, the client would receive this small book after the examination in which the phrenologist would have recorded his or her measurements in the first few pages, indicating personal strengths and weaknesses. The book included information on how the client could work to improve personal weaknesses

who opened clinics in New York, Boston, and Philadelphia in the late 1830s. They created their own phrenological industry that included books, magazines, phrenology heads, measuring instruments, and phrenological charts. They franchised their business to other cities where they trained examiners and, of course, supplied them with all the necessities to run their clinics. To be trained in the Fowler System was a marketing device, a kind of credential that examiners could use to argue their credibility.

Phrenologists provided examinations or "readings" as they were often called. There were itinerant phrenologists who traveled the country offering their services and carrying the tools of their trade in the carrying cases manufactured by the Fowler brothers for just such purposes. Others operated from their clinics where clients made appointments for their examinations. Some clinics were tied to businesses, serving as a kind of personnel office, testing prospective employees, and sending the results of their examinations to the employer.

Phrenologists provided their clients with a checklist of their faculties, noting those that were over- or underdeveloped. Some faculties were positive, such as sympathy or conscientiousness, whereas others were negative, for example, defiance or secretiveness. Clients would be advised about which faculties required "cultivation" and which ones required "restraint." For example, if the "destructiveness" faculty was shown to be too large, the client was advised:

> To Restrain – Kill nothing; and offset destructiveness by benevolence; never indulge a rough, harsh spirit, but cultivate instead a mild and forgiving spirit; never brood over injuries or indulge revengeful thoughts or desires, or aggravate yourself by brooding over wrongs; cultivate good manners; and when occasion requires you to reprove, do it in a bland, gentle manner rather than roughly; never tease, even children, or scourge animals, but be kind to both, and offset by benevolence and the higher faculties. (Fowler & Fowler, 1859, p. 97)

Many contemporary accounts of phrenology portray its practitioners as charlatans who sought to extract money from their clients by providing services that lacked any scientific basis and were thus worthless. No doubt there were such unscrupulous characters in the phrenological business, yet there were many with honorable motives. Although their science may have been suspect, they likely aided their clients through their powers of observation. In the best empirical tradition, they used their senses to make their diagnoses and inform the counsel they offered their clients. Historian Michael Sokal (2001) has described how this worked:

> After all, they had great opportunities to practice these powers on the individuals they examined. They spent a fair amount of time with their subjects, often in close physical contact. They spoke with these clients – and, especially, listened to them – as they introduced themselves and took in their accents and use of words. They shook their hands and felt their calluses. They observed their dress, and noted its style, cleanliness, and usage. They observed their subjects' carriage as they entered and walked about the examining room and read their "body language." They stood over and behind them as they moved their hands about their heads. And in a less clean age, they especially noted their subjects' odor. (pp. 38–39)

Thus, much could be learned about a client by an observant phrenologist. Such observations could be used to increase the accuracy of the psychological assessment meaning that the client was better served, at the same time raising the client's confidence in the abilities of the phrenologist. That confidence was important in ensuring greater compliance with the directives of the phrenologist and in generating, no doubt, good word-of-mouth advertising for the examiner's services.

Physiognomy

Another of the pre-scientific psychologies popular in the nineteenth century was *physiognomy*, the evaluation of a person's character, intellect, and abilities based on facial features. Physiognomy, also called characterology, began in the eighteenth century, based on the work of a Swiss theologian, Johann Lavater (1741–1801). His book, *Essays on Physiognomy*, was published in 1775 and predated the phrenological ideas of Gall. However, the system never gained the popularity of phrenology. Lavater's system emphasized the eyes, nose, chin, and forehead as the principal indicators of intelligence, sense of humor, sympathy, morality, and other characteristics. About the nose, Lavater (1775) wrote:

> Noses which are much turned downward are never truly good, truly cheerful, noble, or great. Their thoughts and inclinations always tend to earth. They are close, cold, heartless, incommunicative; often maliciously sarcastic, ill-humored, or extremely hypochondriac or melancholic. When arched in the upper part they are fearful and voluptuous. (p. 36)

Sadly, physiognomy, like phrenology, was also used to "validate" ethnic and racial stereotypes. One well-known textbook of physiognomy written by Samuel Wells in 1866 (Wells was brother-in-law to the Fowlers) provided the following analysis of the "Jewish nose": "It indicates worldly shrewdness, insight into character, and ability to turn that insight to a profitable account" (p. 196). The sub-Saharan African nose Wells described as a "snubnose," a nose of "weakness and underdevelopment." He continued, "Such a shortened and flattened proboscis can not…have made any legible mark on the records of the world's progress. Its wearers have never conquered realms and enslaved nations, like the owners of the royal Roman nose, or built magnificent temples and adorned them with works of high art, like the Greek-nosed children of genius" (p. 196).

For a while, physiognomy gained credibility in the field of criminology, largely because of the work of an Italian anthropologist/criminologist Cesare Lombroso (1835–1909), whose work in that field earned him nominations for the Nobel Prize on four occasions. Both before and after Lombroso's writings, there have been many individuals, learned and not-so-learned, who believed in the notion of a "criminal type" identifiable by facial features. Lombroso wrote that criminals were almost never tall, that their heads were over-sized but

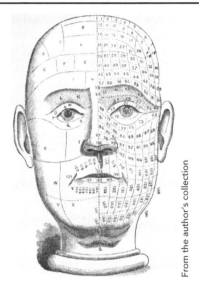

From the author's collection

Figure 1.3   A physiognomy face map from Samuel Wells (1866) showing location of various characteristics such as kindness (2), eloquence (32), sympathy (71), and patriotism (136)

their brains smaller in size, their ears were larger and more protruding, their eyebrows were bushy, and their chins were receding or flat (see Lombroso, 1911; Lombroso & Ferrero, 1899).

Like the field of phrenology, the credibility of physiognomy was seriously diminished at the beginning of the twentieth century; however, it did not disappear and even found its way into employee selection in America in the 1910s through the characterological system of Katherine Blackford. We will discuss her work in Chapter 9, work that proved to be a considerable irritant to psychologists who were trying to establish the legitimacy of their science in the world of business at that time.

Mesmerism

Franz Anton Mesmer (1734–1815) was an Austrian physician who, in 1775, discovered that he could relieve medical and psychological symptoms in his patients by passing magnets over their bodies. He called his procedure animal magnetism, although it would become better known as *mesmerism*. As a physician, Mesmer functioned in a time in which humors, or bodily fluids, such as blood and bile, were viewed as keys to health. Mesmer believed that the fluids in the body were magnetized, and that many conditions of physical and mental illness were caused by a misalignment of these fluids. Mesmer described his treatments as producing a kind of fainting spell that lasted for a brief time. Such spells were likely hypnotic trances. Soon Mesmer found that he could achieve the same results without the magnets by just passing his hands over the patient's body. He reasoned that his constant use of the magnets had transferred some of the magnetic power to him and thus he served as a powerful magnet.

Mesmer became a key figure in Parisian social circles in the 1780s, treating the wealthier citizens of high society. His healing art spread to other practitioners, most of whom had no medical training. This infuriated the French medical community, which asked King Louis XVI to launch an investigation of the validity of Mesmer's methods. The King appointed a blue-ribbon commission, with American Benjamin Franklin as its president. The commission's report was decidedly negative, finding that no animal magnetic fluids existed and there was no evidence of healing due to magnetic forces. However, no formal actions were taken because of the report, and Mesmer and others continued their practice. They emphasized their ties to science, especially medicine and physiology, claiming that mesmerism was a mental science based on scientific experiments. They sought to validate their procedures by demonstrating the links between physiological measures and mental states (Schmit, 2005).

Mesmerism came to the United States in the 1830s and spread throughout the Northeast where mesmerists provided medical healing as well as a psychological program that encouraged self-improvement. Mesmerists also claimed cures for depression and other psychological maladies such as phobias. They did so, relying on hypnotic techniques and the induction of suggestions during hypnotic states. The popularity of mesmerism continued into the early twentieth century in the United States. Some historians have argued that it was the beginning of psychotherapy in America:

> In certain ways, mesmerism was the first secular psychotherapy in America, a way of ministering psychologically to the great America unchurched. It was an ambitious attempt to combine religion with psychotherapy, and it spawned ideologies such as mind cure philosophy, the New Thought movement, Christian Science, and American spiritualism. (Cushman, 1995, p. 119)

Spiritualism

Spiritualism, the New Thought Movement, Christian Science, and mental healing were developments in the second half of the nineteenth century, based largely in the New England states. American *spiritualism* began in 1848 with reports of two adolescent sisters who were able to communicate with a ghost residing in their New York farmhouse. The sisters became mediums, holding séances in which they communicated with the spirits of the dead, for a fee, of course. Spiritualism grew considerably in popularity during and after the United States Civil War because so many individuals were desperate to contact loved ones lost in that war. Belief in spirits and unseen energies was perhaps bolstered by the invention of the wireless telegraph and by the discovery of Roentgen rays (Coon, 1992). Spiritualists provided a number of psychological services including treatments for depression and anxiety disorders, and advice about problems in the workplace, difficulties in marriage, and methods for child rearing. The principal activity of the spiritualists, however, was to facilitate contact with the dead. The chief means of this contact was through participation in a séance.

In the séance, people sat around a table in a darkened room, hands joined with one another and with the individual serving as the medium, typically a woman. The medium was the conduit to people in the afterlife. There would be mysterious sounds – sometimes noises, sometimes voices – and ghostlike forms might appear. The table would begin to move, seemingly on its own, and the windows would rattle. The medium might have what appeared to be a seizure or slump into a trancelike state. Soon she would channel the words of the dead, which were messages for one or more of the participants at the table (Benjamin & Baker, 2004).

These séances were mostly fashionable in the middle and upper classes and were usually conducted in private homes. Some, however, were staged in auditoriums, where they often took on the qualities of live theater. One of the most famous mediums who often used the stage to display her talents in communicating with the dead was an Italian spiritualist, Eusapia Palladino (1854–1918). She performed her séances all over Europe and in the United States. Scientific psychologists, such as Harvard University's Hugo Münsterberg, sought to discredit her and indeed were able to discover a number of instances in which she used deception to create the sensory effects of her séances (Sommer, 2012). Whereas most psychologists regarded spiritualism as chicanery, William James, the noted American psychologist and philosopher and Münsterberg's colleague at Harvard, emphatically did not. James spent many years investigating paranormal claims. He was especially impressed with the séances of Leonore Piper (1857–1950), a famous American medium. He attended her séances for more than 25 years searching for scientific proof that would establish the validity of communication with the dead. Sadly for James, the proof he sought never came.

Spiritualism was not aligned with any particular religion although it may have seemed religious because it was predicated on a belief in an afterlife. Organized Christian religions, however, opposed spiritualism, arguing that belief in spirits was an act of heresy. Leahey and Leahey (1983) have written, "By claiming to produce empirical evidence of survival [after death], Spiritualism denied the need for faith. By claiming that there was no hell, and that a pleasant afterlife was in store for everyone, it denied the fear of God and of hellfire on which organized Christianity depends" (p. 166).

Spiritualism was in decline by the turn of the twentieth century but it enjoyed resurgence in 1917–1918 when there were so many deaths due to the influenza epidemic and World War I. One of the most vocal supporters of spiritualism was Sir Arthur Conan Doyle, author of Sherlock Homes mysteries, who wrote a number of books on the subject and used his considerable wealth to finance the building of a spiritualist temple in London (Lycett, 2008). It diminished considerably in the 1920s, perhaps because so many mediums were exposed as frauds, yet it continues today as an organized religion, primarily in North America and the United Kingdom, and it is still possible to find individuals working as seers, mystics, or mediums who promise contact with the deceased.

Mental Healing

The latter half of the nineteenth century in America was a time of religious liberalism; growth of the cities, particularly in the Northeast; increasing reliance on science; rapid technological changes; and new waves of immigration. It was a time of great social change and many of the pseudoscientific psychologies were allied to that change. *Mental healing* had direct ties to mesmerism and spread across North America in many forms. Its origin was in New England in the 1850s, and is often referred to as the "mind cure" movement or "new thought" movement.

The movement's originator was Phineas Parkhurst Quimby (1802–1866) who had practiced for a decade as a mesmerist before formulating his own theory and method of mental healing. Quimby believed that many diseases had causes that were entirely mental and that other diseases were exacerbated by mental conditions. He was especially critical of physicians, arguing that they often harmed their patients by inducing negative thoughts that prevented or delayed recovery. Quimby saw his task as helping his clients reach a spiritual healing by helping them see how irrationality and negative thinking affected their health. Quimby believed that disease was

> due to false reasoning in regard to sensations, which man unwittingly develops by impressing wrong thoughts and mental pictures upon the subconscious spiritual matter. As disease is due to false reasoning, so health is due to knowledge of the truth. To remove disease permanently, it is necessary to know the cause, the error which led to it. The explanation is the cure. (Anderson, 1993, p. 40)

Thus, Quimby believed that cure resided in the mental powers of the individual and not in the medical practices of physicians. Shown the way to "right thinking," individuals were wholly capable of curing themselves.

Quimby's healing philosophies spread to thousands of mind cure practitioners. One of his early disciples – a woman he had cured of her chronically poor health – was Mary Baker Eddy (1821–1910), who in 1879 founded the Church of Christ, Scientist, better known today as Christian Science, a church headquartered in Boston.

Among the clients for mind cure therapy was psychologist William James whose interest in spiritualism has already been mentioned. James wrote to his sister Alice in 1887:

> I have been paying ten or eleven visits to a mind-cure doctress, a sterling creature, resembling the "Venus of Medicine." Mrs. Lydia E. Pinkham; made solid and veracious looking. I sit down beside her and presently drop asleep, whilst she disentangles the snarls out of my mind. She says she never saw a mind with so many, so agitated, so restless, etc. She said my *eyes*, mentally speaking, kept revolving like wheels in front of each other and in front of my face, and it was four or five sittings ere she could get them *fixed*. (Murphy & Ballou, 1961, p. 8)

Even though Mrs. Pinkham pronounced James cured, he would later write to his sister that he still lay awake at nights.

James was greatly interested in mind cure, spiritualism, and indeed, all paranormal phenomena, and his involvement in these activities was of considerable embarrassment to his colleagues in the new science of psychology. Other prominent psychologists urged James to abandon this work but James responded that he would continue to pursue questions of paranormal phenomena, and that he was dismayed that his colleagues would not keep an open mind on the subject. He argued that psychology was the one science qualified to investigate such occurrences. Although his colleagues did not take up the torch of psychical research, James continued such work until his death. His final publication on the subject appeared in *American Magazine* shortly before his death. In this article, he acknowledged that his lifetime of research had failed to produce the proof that he had sought, but he remained optimistic that such proof would eventually be obtained (James, 1909).

By 1900, the craze of the mind cure movement had largely ended, but mental healing continued, both within organized religion, such as Christian Science, and in private homes and clinics where mental healers practiced. Furthermore, mind cure would play a role in the development of psychotherapy in the twentieth century in what would be called the Emmanuel Movement, a movement that blended religion, medicine, and psychology (see Caplan, 1998; Gifford, 1997).

When the science of psychology arrived in North America in the 1880s to occupy its new laboratories, it found itself in conflict with this public psychology of phrenologists, physiognomists, mesmerists, spiritualists, and mental healers. The new scientific psychologists were using their brass instruments to study the nature of visual and auditory processes, and to measure the speed of mental processes such as the time involved in thinking. Here is how historian Deborah Coon (1992) has described the conflict:

> It is not overdramatizing to say that [psychologists] were self-consciously engaged in a battle for intellectual and disciplinary survival. Psychology had a critical problem in the process of its professionalization and conceptualization, however. It was haunted by a public and by some members of its own ranks [e.g., William James] who thought that the most interesting questions about the mind concerned not the range of perception and the timing of thought, but whether or not people could communicate with each other by direct thought transference, whether gifted individuals could foretell the future, or whether the living could communicate with the dead. (p. 145)

Thus, the new psychology had to battle for scientific respectability, seeking to gain admission into the club of older, established sciences. The new psychologists, as scientists, saw themselves as the arbiters of truth, as the ones who would define psychology, as the sole experts on all questions psychological (Lamont, 2013). The pseudoscientific psychologies represented a significant foe. Yet other opposition came from within the halls of the academy, from within the very university philosophy departments that would house the new psychologists. This opponent was mental philosophy. It was important that if the new psychology was to be recognized as the sole authoritative voice on psychology, then they would have to disparage the old psychology and create disciplinary boundaries to distance themselves from the mental philosophers (Leary, 1987; Rodkey, 2011).

The Road to Mental Philosophy

In reading many histories of psychology, it would be easy to form the impression that there was no academic psychology in North America when the experimental science of psychology arrived in the 1880s. The new experimental psychologists would take up residence in departments of philosophy because there were no departments of psychology. Typical among the extant offerings of those departments was a course on *mental philosophy* that might be a semester or two semesters in duration, typically offered to students in their junior or senior years, sometimes in conjunction with a course entitled moral philosophy (that covered such topics as morality, conscience, virtue, religion, love, justice, and civic duty). Mental philosophy, as taught in North American universities in the nineteenth century, had its origins principally in seventeenth-century England, beginning with the writings of John Locke. Locke's ideas still dominated 200 years later but would be joined by the work of the Scottish realists. These philosophers created an empirical science of the mind that sought answers to many of the same questions that would be addressed by the new experimentalists. Furthermore, they created a home for the new psychology in the university curriculum (Fuchs, 2000).

British Empiricism

In one of the most important books in the history of psychology, *An Essay Concerning Human Understanding*, published in 1690, philosopher John Locke (1632–1704) offered a radical conception of the mind as *tabula rasa*, a blank slate. He wrote:

> Let us then suppose the mind to be, as we say, white paper, void of all characters, without any ideas; how comes it to be furnished? Whence comes it by that vast store, which the busy and boundless fancy of man has painted on it with an almost endless variety? Whence has it all the materials of reason and knowledge? To this I answer, in one word, From experience; in that all our knowledge is founded, and from that it ultimately derives itself. Our observation, employed whither about external sensible objects, or about the internal operations of our minds, perceived and reflected on by ourselves, is that which supplies our understandings with all the materials of thinking. These two are the foundations of knowledge, from whence all the ideas we have, or can naturally have do spring. (Locke, 1849, p. 75)

In his *Essay*, Locke denied the existence of all innate ideas, including the idea that humans were born with innate knowledge of the existence of God. In the passage above, he wrote that all knowledge comes from but two sources: *sensation*, via direct experience with the external world and *reflection*, meaning ideas from an interaction of new sensations and ideas already in the mind from early sensations or from thought processes independent of any new sensations.

> All our ideas are of the one or the other of these. The understanding seems to me not to have the least glimmering of any ideas which it doth not receive from one of these two. External objects furnish the mind with the ideas of sensible qualities, which are all those different perceptions they produce in us; and the mind furnishes the understanding with ideas of its own operations. (Locke, 1849, p.76)

Although Locke placed great emphasis on the importance of the senses for the acquisition of knowledge, the mind was assumed not to know the external world directly but only indirectly through the processes of reflection, an assertion that was strengthened by George Berkeley's mentalistic philosophy. For Berkeley (1685–1753), all knowledge was dependent on the experiencing individual, and qualities of objects of the external world existed only as they were perceived.

These ideas set in motion an empirical approach to the study of the mind that emphasized observations of the senses and especially an understanding of the processes of perception, learning, thinking, and memory. This work guided the ideas of a great lineage of British philosophers that included David Hume, David Hartley, James Mill, and John Stuart Mill (1806–1873). In J. S. Mill's 1843 book, *A System of Logic* he argued that the time had come for an empirical science of psychology. That book was an important stimulus for Wundt's decision, some 35 years later, to press beyond empiricism and pursue an *experimental* science of psychology.

Scottish Realism

Scottish clergyman Thomas Reid (1710–1796) is generally recognized as the founder of *Scottish realism*, a philosophy of the human mind also known as "common sense philosophy." Reid disagreed with the British empiricist view that denied the reality of direct knowledge of objects and events in the world. He wrote:

> If, therefore, we attend to that act of our mind which we call the perception of an external object of sense, we shall find in it three things: – *First*, some conception or notion of the object perceived; *Secondly*, A strong and

irresistible conviction and belief of its present existence; and, *Thirdly*, That this conviction and belief are immediate, and not the effect of reasoning. (Reid, 1785, p. 16)

Reid was author of a series of books that explored the five senses, describing, in considerable detail, the ways in which the senses are used to gain knowledge of the world. Two of his books described the mind in terms of its separate faculties. This taxonomy of mind would grow in popularity, leading to the term Scottish faculty psychology, and, oddly, providing support for the legitimacy of phrenology. Reid's ideas were developed over the next half century by other Scottish intellectuals, especially by Dugald Stewart. These ideas crossed the Atlantic via Scottish immigration to the United States and Canada in the late 1700s and early 1800s, supplanting the philosophies of Locke and Berkeley so that by the 1820s, Scottish philosophy dominated North American college classrooms (Evans, 1984).

With greater trust in the senses and the conviction that the external world was directly knowable via the senses, the Scottish philosophers placed their confidence in *observation*. Scottish philosopher James McCosh (1886) described it this way: "[using observation in psychology] we notice mind as it operates and mark its various states … we also employ experiment, which is a mode of observation in which we artificially place the agents of nature in new circumstances that we may perceive their action more distinctly" (p. 2). Further, there was the issue of a long-standing realization – one that argued against the possibility of a valid science of psychology – that in an empirical science of psychology, the observing and observed were the same, namely the mind. McCosh (1886) wrote that "in psychology we make our observations by Self-Consciousness, which is the power by which we take cognizance of self as acting; say as thinking or feeling, as remembering the past or anticipating the future, as loving, fearing, resolving" (p. 2). This realization would play a role in early twentieth-century American psychology in the debates over introspection as a research method, a topic that will be discussed in Chapters 5 and 8.

American Mental Philosophers

The dominance of Scottish thought in American colleges coincided with the emergence of a new learning device – the textbook. Higher education had always involved reading original sources, for example, Locke or Hume, but now there were authors who were synthesizing and integrating the ideas of multiple scholars into comprehensive texts. Thomas Upham (1799–1872), a professor of mental and moral philosophy at Bowdoin College, is generally considered the author of the first textbook in American psychology, *Elements of Intellectual Philosophy*, published in 1827, and expanded to two volumes in 1831 as *Elements of Mental Philosophy*. There were other American writers of mental philosophy textbooks in the mid-nineteenth century as well, including Elizabeth Ricord of Geneva Female Seminary in New York who in 1840 wrote *Elements of the Philosophy of Mind Applied to the Development of Thought and Feeling* (Scarborough, 1992) and William Lyall, professor of philosophy at Dalhousie University in Nova Scotia, whose 1855 textbook was entitled *Intellect, the Emotions, and the Moral Nature* (Page & Clark, 1982). However, none of these books enjoyed the success achieved by Upham whose delineation of topics would closely mirror the form of the new experimental psychology and the textbooks in the new field (e.g., Ladd, 1887; James, 1890). His textbooks were widely used for more than 50 years.

Upham divided mental philosophy into three realms, reflecting the influence of Scottish faculty psychology: intellect, sensibilities, and will. In his two-volume book, the intellect comprised the first volume and consisted of such topics as the senses, attention, dreaming, consciousness, learning, memory, reasoning, and imagination. The second volume comprised the sensibilities (emotions, desires, moral sensibilities, and abnormal actions and feelings) and will (Upham, 1831). The content of these chapters represented the results of the empirical investigations of the mental philosophers, and they proved foundational for the new laboratory psychology. Historian of psychology Alfred Fuchs (2000) has written that "Although the experimental psychologists thought of themselves as replacing a philosophical discipline with a science, they could be more accurately characterized as adding laboratory experimental procedures to what was already defined as an empirical, inductive science" (p. 9).

Struggles for the New Science

When the first Americans returned home in the 1880s from their studies in the German psychology laboratories to establish the new experimental science on their side of the Atlantic they faced a number of obstacles. They believed that psychology could and should be a natural science and worked toward that recognition. The extant psychologies in America, however, were regarded as problematic. There was already a psychology embraced by the public that was based on paranormal events such as mind reading, fortune telling, conjuring up spirits, and feeling for bumps on the head. In addition, there was an academic field – mental philosophy – that defined psychology in university settings. Psychologists rejected mental philosophy as

Figure 1.4 Thomas Upham, professor of mental philosophy

a valid psychology, both because of its earlier ties to metaphysics and the fact that its knowledge base was not derived in the laboratory.

This conflict with philosophy would shape many of the debates in psychology during its twentieth-century development, especially so with the rise of behaviorism. It has been described as a time when psychology lost its mind and is the subject of Chapter 8.

2

Physiology, Psychophysics, and the Science of Mind

A small painting in the Museo del Prado in Madrid, Spain shows a physician, scalpel in hand, removing something from the head of a seated man. The painting dates from 1490 or later and is by the Dutch artist Hieronymus Bosch. It is titled *The Extraction of the Stone of Madness*. The painting is usually interpreted as an allegory for foolishness or stupidity; indeed an alternative title for it is "the Cure of Folly." Historians view Bosch's brain operation as a fictional event offered as an illustration of how foolishness might be cured, by removing the "stone of madness." Although rare, brain surgeries existed in Bosch's time. Indeed archeological evidence indicates that such operations, called trephining, occurred more than 8,000 years ago when late Stone Age humans bored or chiseled holes into skulls of living individuals, perhaps to release supposed evil spirits, or as a cure for headaches or bizarre behaviors, or maybe for punishment.

Awareness that the brain was an organ of importance is an idea that dates back millions of years in human history. There is anthropological evidence that suggests early hominids knew that head injuries could cause disabilities or death and often inflicted such injuries intentionally on animal prey as well as other hominids. In recent human history, we credit Hippocrates (460–379 B.C.) with the recognition that the brain is the organ of intelligence. Anatomical treatises on the brain and sensory organs (particularly the eyes), including diagrams based on dissections, are more than 2,500 years old.

The Renaissance was an especially productive time for advances in brain anatomy. Leonardo da Vinci (1452–1519) dissected more that 300 cadavers (many of them executed criminals) and made more than 1,500 detailed drawings of the brain. Finger (2000) noted that he "displayed an accuracy regarding the human body and its parts that had not been seen before" (p. 58). Alas, he did not publish his drawings, so few people saw them. One who did publish was Andreas Vesalius (1514–1564) who made significant advances in neuroanatomy

Figure 2.1   *Extracting the Stone of Madness* by Hieronymus Bosch, ca. 1690

and described the human brain "more realistically than ever before, in words and with pictures" (p. 68). Important milestones during the Renaissance included the discovery of cerebrospinal fluid, a differentiation between white and gray matter in the cortex, the naming of many brain areas (such as the pons and hippocampus), and the discovery that the image on the retina was inverted (Finger, 1994).

One critical invention for neuroanatomy and neurophysiology in the seventeenth century was the microscope. Although there were earlier inventors who developed lenses that would magnify objects, it was Anton van Leeuwenhoek (1632–1723) of Holland who created lenses of sufficient magnification to see neurons. Indeed it was van Leeuwenhoek who was the first human to see the "invisible" world of unicellular organisms in a sample of pond water that he studied under his microscope. One can imagine the thrill that such a discovery would have generated. He also used his microscope to study the tissues of the eye, especially the retina. From his descriptions, it is possible that he was the first individual to see the photoreceptors for vision – rods and cones (Finger, 1994). Whereas the understanding of brain anatomy was improving by use of the microscope and by better dissection and preservation techniques, brain function – neurophysiology – was another matter. Significant understanding of the functions of various areas of the brain and nervous system would have to await the technological advancements of the nineteenth century.

Understandably, much of this early neurological work had medical implications. But there were other reasons to study the brain and nervous system as well. Philosophical speculation about the nature of mind had led to increased interest by anatomists and physiologists in the brain, spinal cord, and senses. For the purposes of this book we will join that program, already in progress, in the early nineteenth century. We will begin with a discussion of research on the brain and nervous system and then describe the work done on the various senses. Finally, in the last section of this chapter we will describe the nineteenth-century development of a field known as psychophysics that sought to measure the relationships between events in the physical world and the psychological perception of those events. All of this work in neurophysiology, sensory physiology, and psychophysics proved critical as the building blocks for the new science of psychology that emerged at the end of the nineteenth century.

Brain and Nervous System

Today, neuroscientists have at their disposal a great number of techniques that allow them to examine brain and behavior relationships. Among the most sophisticated of those is the fMRI or functional magnetic resonance imager, a device that provides images of blood flow or other metabolic changes in an intact, functioning brain in a conscious human subject. It allows the comparison of brain activity with ongoing mental activity, for example recording images of the brain's functioning while the subject is solving mental arithmetic problems or reciting words from a memorized list. This technique, and others, is adding considerably to our understanding of the actions and functions of the brain and nervous system. Still, the more we learn, the more we realize how little we really know about the work of the body's most complex system. As much as we have advanced in brain science – and much has been learned – there is still a long way to go.

At the beginning of the nineteenth century there were several key questions in neurophysiology that would be important to a science of psychology. One question concerned the various areas of the brain. The neuroanatomists had shown clearly that there were different areas of the brain, marked by differences in tissue structure, texture, and density (and later, discoveries of cellular composition). Might these different areas serve different functions or were the functions of the brain non-specific and spread across the entire cortex? This was the question of *cortical localization* of function. Another question concerned the possibility of *specificity of the nerves*. Might certain nerves carry information of only one kind or did nerves carry all kinds of information? With regard to nerves, scientists were also concerned about how information was transmitted in the nervous system and particularly about how fast this information traveled. This was the question of the *speed of nerve conduction*. We will begin our discussions of these three areas, starting with cortical localization.

Cortical Localization

The theory of cortical localization was essentially a nineteenth century invention and its initial and most vocal proponent was discussed in the previous chapter, Franz Josef Gall, a distinguished anatomist and the inventor of phrenology. Gall published his ideas on phrenology (which he called crainoscopy) in the early 1800s when he was nearly 50 years old. By that time he was already well known for his work on the cranial nerves, brain stem anatomy, and differentiations of the neural functioning of white and gray matter in the cortex. Gall claimed that his ideas on phrenology began when he was nine years old and noticed that a classmate, who showed an excellent verbal memory, had bulging eyes. He observed this feature in other individuals, each time noting the correlation between the bulging eyes and excellence in verbal memory. Eventually he assumed that growth of the frontal lobes of the brain was excessive in these individuals, thus causing their eyes to bulge. In his career as an anatomist he had occasion to examine a number of clinical cases of individuals who had suffered head wounds and consequently showed certain personality changes or intellectual deficits as a result. These clinical observations were useful, but still secondary, to the discoveries involving bumps on the head. Gall's system of phrenology identified 27 different faculties that resided in the cerebral cortex.

For about a decade, the medical community embraced the phrenological ideas. There was already extant work on nerves that showed specificity of function, so it made sense that the cortex could show such specificity as well. Further, the neuroanatomical studies on the brain, some of it done by Gall himself, showed obvious anatomical differences across the cortex. So why not functional differences as well?! By the 1830s, however, the medical and scientific communities in North

America and Europe had rejected the validity of phrenology. The individual most responsible for this was a French neurophysiologist, Pierre Flourens (1794–1867) who set out to test the claims of the phrenologists. Gall had argued that 19 of the 27 faculties found in humans could also be found in animals. Using animals, Flourens removed brain tissue from those areas of the cortex claimed by the phrenologists to be responsible for certain behaviors. For example, Gall claimed that the cerebellum was the brain area controlling sexual behavior. Yet when Flourens made lesions in that brain area he observed deficits in motor behavior but not changes in sexual activity. Further, as he made larger and larger lesions in the cortex and cerebellum, he noted loss of functioning across many different behaviors, a discovery that led him to conclude, erroneously, that behavior control was spread widely across the brain and not localized in a particular area (Fancher & Rutherford, 2012). Within the scientific community, the work of Flourens and others nailed the lid shut on phrenology's false claims as science. Moreover, it might seem that Flourens' work also ended the theory of cortical localization of function. But the story doesn't end there. Several of Flourens' countrymen disagreed with his position and would eventually provide the evidence to document such brain localization.

As early as 1825, Jean-Baptiste Bouillaud (1796–1881) had made his case for functional locations in the brain, emphasizing an anterior portion of the cortex that was responsible for speech. Simon Ernest Aubertin (1825–1893), the son-in-law of Bouillaud, has been described as the most "ardent" supporter of cortical localization in the mid-1800s (Finger, 2000), and he too believed in a similar anterior location for a speech center in the brain. At an 1861 meeting of the Parisian Society of Anthropology, Aubertin made his forceful case for a speech center noting that it was supported by his own clinical research and would be further solidified pending autopsies on several patients with loss of speech (Thomas, 2007). In attendance at that meeting was Paul Broca (1824–1880), a French neurophysiologist and surgeon working at the Bicêtre Hospital in Paris. In April 1861, Broca encountered a patient in surgery who was suffering from cellulitis, a skin disorder involving spreading inflammation of the tissue. Broca discovered that the man could not speak, other than repeating the same syllable, "tan." He learned that the man could understand anything that was said to him but was incapable of generating any speech, a condition that had existed in him for more than 20 years. Furthermore, 10 years earlier he suffered gradual paralysis in his right arm and leg and for the past seven years had been bedridden. The patient, Leborgne, died a few days after Broca first saw him (see Domanski, 2013 for a history of this

National Library of Medicine

Figure 2.2   Paul Broca

famous patient). Broca immediately performed an autopsy, examining the patient's brain. He suspected damage on the left side of the brain because of the right side paralysis; contralateral projection was already known from a number of clinical cases where head injuries on one side of the brain were associated with paralysis on the opposite side of the body.

What Broca found was a hole in the cortex of the left frontal lobe. This tissue was no doubt deprived of its blood supply 20 years earlier, died, and resulted in the loss of speech. In the 20-year span it had dissolved and been carried away in the cerebrospinal fluid. The body paralysis had resulted from lesions elsewhere on the same side of the brain. Broca reasoned that this area in the frontal lobe was important for language. He presented his findings at the next meeting of the Society of Anthropology acknowledging the support that his case provided for the localization ideas of Bouilland and Auburtin.

Still Broca felt that he needed more evidence to confirm his hypothesis for the location of the speech center. Over the next several years he acquired approximately a dozen more clinical cases, demonstrating frontal lobe damage in each of the cases in virtually the same area of the frontal lobe, and, in almost all cases, in the left cortical hemisphere (Finger, 2000; Schiller, 1992). Today that area of the brain is called *Broca's area*, and it is known to be associated with the production of speech (expressive aphasia), but not the understanding of language (receptive aphasia) which is mediated in the left temporal-parietal cortex known as *Wernicke's area*. Later nineteenth-century work involving electrical stimulation of the brain would illustrate the problem with Flourens' surgeries and provide convincing support for the localization theory.

The earliest of these studies took place in 1870 by two German neurophysiologists, Edward Hitzig and Eduard Fritsch. Electrical stimulation studies of nerves were performed as early as the 1790s, and the electrical nature of nerve impulses was at least marginally understood in the early nineteenth century. Using the exposed cortices of dogs, Hitzig and Fritsch used a very mild electric current to stimulate various points on the cortical surface. Their results showed that a number of different voluntary movements occurred due to the stimulation. Stimulation in one area produced movement in the front leg; stimulation in another area resulted in movement in the hind leg. Other stimulations produced facial movements. These movements were reliably reproduced whenever the electrical probe was placed in a particular cortical area. These findings for voluntary motor specificity in the cortex added considerably to Broca's data in supporting belief in cortical localization (Brazier, 1961; Finger, 2000).

There is some evidence that Hitzig may have been the first individual to electrically stimulate a living human brain, but that claim is controversial (Thomas & Young, 1993). Better known is the work of an American physician, Roberts Bartholow, who in 1874 applied electrical current to the brain of a patient and reported movement in her arms and legs that was contralateral to the stimulation of her brain (Bartholow, 1874; Harris & Almerigi, 2009). Then in 1876, Scottish neurologist David Ferrier published his book, *The Functions of the Brain*, a work based on several years of intensive studies of several animal species, particularly monkeys. Ferrier's surgical and stimulation techniques were excellent, and he produced a level of detail in mapping the sensory and motor functions of the brain that had not been demonstrated before (Finger, 2000). Thus in a little more than a decade and a half after Broca had presented his findings on Leborgne's brain, the evidence for cortical localization of function was convincing. These findings supplemented earlier discoveries of specificity in other areas of the nervous system as well.

Specificity in the Nerves

Accompanying the specificity of function in various brain areas was the knowledge that there was also specificity in the nerves. In 1811, the Scottish anatomist Charles Bell privately published a booklet in which he stated that the spinal cord was made up of two kinds of nerves – sensory nerves in the dorsal portion of the cord and motor nerves in the ventral part of the cord. Eleven years later, Francois Magendie, a French physiologist, published a similar discovery in a French scientific journal, laying claim to the discovery. This pronouncment angered Bell and his supporters who claimed priority for Bell. Magendie responded that he had never read Bell's booklet, which is probably true, given its small printing and private distribution. The dispute was not settled for the two scientists, but with the passage of time the controversy has been resolved to some degree by labeling the specificity of spinal functioning the *Bell-Magendie law*: afferent information from the senses to the brain is carried in the dorsal part of the spinal cord, efferent information from the brain to the motor effectors is carried in the ventral part of the cord. This discovery of separate neural systems for sensory and motor functions would prove important for many areas of neurophysiology and much later for a scientific psychology grounded in stimulus-response experiments.

Johannes Müller (1801–1858), a German physiologist, is known today for his discovery of the *law of specific nerve energies*, published in 1826, the belief that each sensory nerve carries only one kind of sensory information, regardless of how the nerve is stimulated. Müller noted that the same sensation could be produced by two kinds of external stimulation, such as a person reporting "seeing something" when stimulated either by light on the eye or physical pressure on the eye. In each case, the optic nerve was stimulated and the resultant effect was a visual experience. Furthermore, the optic nerve would carry only visual information, the auditory nerves only auditory information, and so forth. In Müller's words, "The nerve of each sense seems to be capable of one determinate kind of sensation only, and not of those proper to the other organs of sense; hence one nerve of sense cannot take the place and perform the function of the nerve of another sense" (Müller, 1848, p. 1073).

In fact, Müller was not the first to propose the idea of sensory nerve specificity. Bell made a similar argument in 1811 (Boring, 1942). Yet it was Müller's work that was widely known in promoting the idea of sensory nerve specificity, providing further evidence of the specificity of the functional organization of the brain.

It might be presumed that the discoveries on cortical localization and nerve specificity added to evidence in support of the scientific validity of phrenology. It is true that the phrenologists were correct about certain areas of the brain having specific functions, but they were wrong about which areas did what, and they were wrong about the possibility of measuring brain growth from the surface of the skull. Whereas these neurophysiological studies added to the fervor of the phrenologists in their beliefs about the correctness of their field, they did nothing to change the mind of the scientific community that had rejected phrenology by the 1830s.

The Speed of Nerve Conductance

There is one other nineteenth-century discovery in neurophysiology that would be of considerable importance to the beginnings of scientific psychology, and that is the answer to the question: How fast is information conducted by the nerves? Johannes Müller had addressed this question in some of his writings, arguing that the transmission was instantaneous, perhaps traveling as fast as the speed of light, thus there was no reason to try to measure it. Müller wrote in 1840: "We shall probably never attain the power of measuring the velocity of nervous action; for we have not the opportunity of comparing its propagation through immense space, as we have in the case of light" (as cited in Finger & Wade, 2002a, p. 150). One scientist who did not subscribe to that belief was one of Müller's students, Hermann von Helmholtz (1821–1894).

Helmholtz is arguably one of the most brilliant scientists of all time, at least judging by his contributions to multiple fields. He was trained in medicine, but his interests carried him in many different directions. His contributions in optics were substantial. As an inventor, he created the ophthalmoscope as a way to observe the retina, a device still used in eye examinations today. He also invented the ophthalmometer, a device to measure curvature of the eye. He devised a stopwatch that measured time in smaller increments than existing devices. He made numerous scientific contributions to vision and audition including the development of a theory of color vision and a theory of pitch perception (which we will discuss shortly). He was one of the developers of the law of conservation of energy in physics. He contributed to musical theory, developed a new geometry, worked on speech synthesis, did important research in meteorology, and prior to the work of Alexander Graham Bell, drew the plans for (but did not build) a workable telephone (Cahan, 1993).

Helmholtz studied medicine at the University of Berlin where, as noted earlier, Johannes Müller was one of his teachers. In 1849, he joined the faculty at the University of Königsberg where he began his work on nerve conductance. This work was stimulated by one of his friends from medical school, Émil du Bois-Reymond, who proposed that the nervous impulse was an electrochemical wave and that its transmission time might be slow enough to measure. Helmholtz was

Figure 2.3 German stamp of Herman von Helmholtz issued in 1994 on the 100th anniversary of his death. The imagery emphasizes his work in ophthalmology and color vision

intrigued by this idea and decided to test it. He worked with the severed leg of a frog, stimulating one end of the nerve and measuring the arrival of the impulse at the other end, as indicated by a twitch of the foot. Perhaps the task sounds simple, but it was a complex study, particularly because of the small time intervals involved. He calculated that the impulse traveled at approximately 90 feet per second. Certainly neural conductance was not instantaneous, or anything near that, and *nerve conductance was clearly measurable* (Cahan, 1993; Finger & Wade, 2002a). Such measures would form the basis of the measurement of reaction time, one of the measures that would be a mainstay in the early scientific psychology laboratory that Wundt would establish in Germany 30 years later (in fact, as a young researcher, Wundt worked in Helmholtz's laboratory). Wundt's earliest psychological research involved the measurement of the speed of mental processes, research that could not have been done without the realization that nerve transmission occurred at a measurable speed.

Sensory Physiology

If the empiricists were right, that all knowledge comes to the mind via the senses, then to understand the mind, one must know everything there is to know about the senses. How many are there? Are they the same for everyone? Are they the same for animals other than humans?

To what stimuli do they respond? What role is played by the various physical components of the several senses? How is sensory information carried in the nervous system? How is it transformed? How are factors of stimulus quality, intensity, and duration interpreted in the brain? What neural pathways connect the senses and the brain? Is there specificity of sensory function in the brain and, if so, which areas of the brain correspond to which senses? These and other questions inspired the research of the physiologists of the nineteenth century. Most of these questions had been answered, at least to some degree, by the end of the nineteenth century.

Physiologists had investigated the organs of sensation. The stimuli were largely known – light for vision, sound for audition, chemicals for taste and smell, and tactile pressure and temperature differentials for touch. The cortical areas for the different senses had been identified and some of the pathways from receptors to the brain had been identified as well. One of the first tasks had been to discover the receptors, those specialized cells that would change energy from one form (e.g., light) to the electrochemical energy that could be transmitted in the neurons, a process known as transduction.

The retina had been described in great detail and by 1851 was known to contain rods and cones. It was known that color perception differed across different retinal areas. Visual acuity studies had demonstrated that acuity was better for images on certain parts of the retina than others (the famous Snellen eye chart invented in 1862, with its horizontal rows of block letters of differing sizes, is still used today to assess visual acuity). There were excellent descriptions of color vision, depth perception, afterimages, optical illusions, movement perception, brightness contrast, color blindness, and dark and light adaptation. In audition the conduction process was well understood as were the components of sound – frequency, intensity, and timbre. The basic tastes had been identified and the structure of taste buds described. Similar progress had been made on smell and touch. Again, this work was so important because of the role the senses played in writing on that blank slate known as mind. We will briefly describe two areas of this sensory work, one from vision – the perception of color, and one from audition – the perception of pitch.

Color Vision

Work on color vision intensified after 1850, partly because of advances in sensory physiology and partly because of advances in optical technologies. In 1852, Helmholtz revived a theory proposed originally by Thomas Young in 1801. Named the *trichromatic theory* or

Young-Helmholtz theory of color vision, it proposed three kinds of fibers in the retina that were differentially sensitive to red, green, and blue light. It was known that any spectral hue could be reproduced by some combination of those three colors. Helmholtz described his theory as an extension of Müller's doctrine of specific nerve energies, noting that in this case there were three different kinds of nerve fibers, each of which would conduct sensory information of only one color.

Whereas the Young-Helmholtz theory could explain a number of color phenomena, such as color blindness and color mixture, it was not good at explaining color afterimages, complementary colors, black-white perception (achromatic colors), or the phenomenological importance of yellow as a primary color. It was not surprising to see an alternative theory offered.

Ewald Hering (1834–1918) proposed his theory of color vision in 1874. It is called the *opponent process theory* or *Hering theory* of color vision. It proposes the existence of three color receptors, in this case three different chemical substances in the retina that can be either built up (an anabolic process) or broken down (a catabolic process). One of these substances was responsible for blue-yellow perception, another for red-green perception, and the third for black-white perception. This theory included yellow as a primary color (along with red, blue, and green) and grouped colors via complementary pairs. Thus, it accounted well for the color phenomena that could not be explained by the Young-Helmholtz theory. For virtually a century, these two competing theories were debated with each of them accumulating a body of supporting scientific evidence. Eventually research in the 1960s found that the Young-Helmholtz theory explained color vision at the retinal level, whereas the opponent process theory better accounted for the way color information was processed in the lateral geniculate body of the thalamus, a major relay station from the eye to the visual cortex of the brain.

Pitch Perception

A similar debate was also taking place in the latter half of the nineteenth century regarding the nature of sound frequencies. How are differences in auditory frequency (the psychological term would be pitch) perceived? Eventually two theories competed for authority. The first was the *resonance theory* of Helmholtz that is more commonly called *place theory*. Helmholtz proposed his theory in 1863, a theory that E. G. Boring (1942) labeled "a scientific achievement of the first importance" (p. 404). Helmholtz based his theory on his knowledge of the basilar membrane in the cochlea of the inner ear. The membrane was wide at one end and narrow at the other, leading Helmholtz to draw an analogy between its operation and that of a piano keyboard. He argued that different frequencies would have their greatest impact at different places on the membrane. Helmholtz believed that the basilar membrane was composed of a series of transverse fibers (like the strings on a piano), each of the fibers tuned to a separate frequency. The brain would be able to discern whether a sound was low or high in frequency by information carried from different regions of the membrane (Finger & Wade, 2002b).

Ernest Rutherford (1861–1937), who argued that the firing of the impulses from the basilar membrane would match the frequency of the incoming sound, proposed an opposing theory, called *frequency theory*, approximately 20 years later in 1886. A tone of 1,000 cycles per second would cause the membrane to produce a train of impulses at the rate of 1,000 per second that were sent to the brain. With new discoveries about the electrophysiology of the auditory system, both of these theories were found to have problems and were subsequently modified by later research. In addition, both theories remain valid today in accounting for the major aspects of auditory perception, although they are modified from their original versions.

Space does not permit discussions of the groundbreaking research in the sensory processes that occupied the last half of the nineteenth century. Research involved all five senses as well as related processes, such as time perception, sometimes referred to as the time sense. Research involved an explication of the anatomy of the sensory structures and then physiological research to demonstrate the role of the various structures, for example, the iris, the cochlea, and the tympanic membrane. Other research focused on a number of special topics as noted earlier for the visual sense. This work by physiologists would be continued by psychologists in the new field of scientific psychology, a field initially called *physiological psychology*. As we will see in the next chapter, research on sensation and perception was the mainstay of Wundt's psychological laboratory, making up at least 50% of the studies published in the first 20 years of the laboratory. Those topics would dominate American psychology as well, as will be evident in subsequent chapters.

Psychophysics

The German philosopher and physicist, Gustav Fechner (1801–1889), awoke on the morning of October 22, 1850. It was a Tuesday. What was special about the day, and the reason he remembered it so precisely, was that he had an important insight. To say that it was an incredibly significant insight is to understate its importance. He had an insight that in effect could be said to have created the field of psychology. What was this insight? – [drum roll] – Fechner realized that *it was possible to measure, with great precision, the relationship between the physical and psychological worlds*. It was nothing short of an attempt to solve the mind–body problem. Perhaps you are not impressed. Read on.

Answer this question. Which weighs more, a pound of lead or a pound of feathers? Likely, you said that they both weigh the same. You would be right, and you would be wrong. You would be right from a physical point of view. That is, if you put a pound of lead on a scale and weighed it, and then put a one-pound bag of feathers on the same scale and weighed it, they would weigh the same. That is, their physical weights are the same. However, if you held the lead in one hand and the bag of feathers in the other, you would notice immediately that their weights are quite different. The lead would feel much heavier; in fact, many people would say that it was two to three times heavier than the bag of feathers. The experience of the objects on your hands is a psychological experience. In other words, the two items weigh whatever your brain tells you they weigh and your brain will tell you (because of density differences) that the lead is much heavier. I have done this demonstration with students in many of my classes and it is a very dramatic demonstration of the difference between the physical and psychological worlds. *They are not the same.* If they were, there would be no need for psychology as a separate discipline.

What is out there in the world is not necessarily what we perceive. For example, you might go to a movie and notice that the movement on the screen looks quite real. Yet you know that *nothing is moving* on that screen. All that is appearing on the screen is a succession of still photographs being projected at about 24 images per second. Therefore, the physical reality is that of a succession of discrete images; but the psychological reality is of movement that appears quite real. Again, the physical and psychological worlds are not the same. They are related, and they are related in some meaningful and lawful ways. Psychologists have spent roughly the last 140 years trying to understand those relationships. This is what the field of psychophysics is about – measuring the relationships between stimuli in the external world (physical events) and the person's perception and experience of those stimuli (psychological events).

Ernst Weber's Research

Ernst Weber (1795–1878), was a professor of physiology at the University of Leipzig when he began his work in the field that would become known as psychophysics. His principal area of research was somatosensory perception, that is, the sense of touch, and he published his first work in that field in 1834. Although he made a number of important contributions to sensory physiology and psychophysics, he is important to psychology for two discoveries: the two-point threshold and a psychophysical relationship that specified the perceived differences, known today as Weber's Law.

Weber's interest in touch perception included questions about the relative sensitivity of different areas of the skin. To test this sensitivity he used a compass-like device (the kind of compass that is used to draw circles) with two points. The distance between the two points could be varied from almost adjacent to several centimeters apart. Subjects were typically blindfolded and the experimenter would touch them on the skin with the two points, beginning with the points close together. Subjects were asked to respond as to whether they felt one or two points. The compass points would be moved farther apart in small increments in repeated trials until the subject responded "two." That distance was the *two-point threshold* for touch sensitivity in that particular area of the skin, meaning the distance required between the compass points for the subject to discriminate reliably between one and two points of touch. Weber believed that the skin consisted of a mosaic of sensory circles, each of which was linked to a single touch nerve. In some areas of the skin, such as the face, the circles were smaller, meaning the nerve endings were denser and the sensitivity greater. In other skin areas, the circles were larger leading to poorer touch sensitivity.

Weber's second contribution, and arguably the more important one, emerged from his work on the perception of pressure on the skin. He used weights to measure pressure, giving one weight (called the standard) to the blindfolded subject, removing it, giving the subject a second weight (the comparison weight), and asking the subject if the second weight was lighter, heavier, or the same. The point at which the subject can reliably discriminate between two stimuli – weights in this case – is called the *difference threshold* or *just noticeable difference* (jnd). That difference is not a constant value but varies in terms of the absolute magnitude of the stimulus. Weber (1834) wrote, "In comparing objects and observing the distinction between them, we perceive not the difference between the objects, but the ratio of this difference to the magnitude of the objects compared" (p. xvi). For example, suppose that a person can discriminate between a weight of 30 ounces and 31 ounces. Then the jnd for a standard weight of 30 ounces would be one ounce. But that would not be true of a standard weight of 60 ounces. Because the jnd is a ratio function, the jnd for a standard weight of 60 ounces would be two ounces. Expressed as Weber's Law it would be $\Delta S/S = K$, where ΔS is the comparison weight (62 ounces), S is the standard weight (60 ounces) and K is the ratio (1.033) specifying the increase or decrease in the stimulus that must occur for the subject to report a just noticeable difference. Thus *Weber's Law* expresses the amount of change necessary for the subject to perceive a stimulus as different (e.g., heavier, brighter, louder, sweeter). Weber found that the ratio relationship applied to other sensory modalities as well, for example, vision, although the value of K changed across sensory systems and sensory properties. The law was not perfect. It did not predict performance well at the extremes of the stimulus dimensions, but it worked well in the midranges.

Fechner's Psychophysics

Fechner knew about the work of Weber, but he didn't understand the significance of it until his insight on that October morning in 1850. It wasn't just that the jnds represented a quantitative difference; they represented a psychological difference! For example, the jnd for the 30-ounce standard weight was one ounce whereas it was two ounces for the 60-ounce weight. Quantitatively those jnds are different; one is twice the weight of the other – two ounces versus one ounce. But

Courtesy of Ralf Endres

Figure 2.4 Gustav Theodor Fechner painted in 1848 by his brother, Eduard Clemens Fechner

what Fechner realized was that psychologically, the experience was the same. That is, the perceived *difference* in the two sets of weights was identical for the subject. This insight led to a reformulation of Weber's Law into a logarithmic version written as S = k log R in which S equals the perception of the stimulus, its perceived magnitude or intensity k is a constant, and R equals the actual physical value of the stimulus. This law has become known as *Fechner's Law*, although some books refer to it as the Weber-Fechner Law.

Fechner's insight led to a decade of research in psychophysics, measuring the *absolute threshold* (the smallest value of a stimulus that can be detected) and the *difference threshold* (the smallest difference between two stimuli that can be detected). He used several psychophysical research methods (methods that are still in use in psychology today), one of which he invented called the method of average error (also called the method of adjustment) to measure difference thresholds. One of the methods he used to measure absolute thresholds was the *method of limits*, described in the next paragraph (Heidelberger, 2004).

Consider an auditory task in which the experimenter wants to determine what the minimal intensity of a particular sound must be to be heard. The experimenter chooses a tone of particular frequency (say 256 cycles per second, which is middle C on a piano) and presents it in a series of trials, beginning with a sound intensity that is too low to be heard. With each trial, the intensity is increased until the subject says, "I hear the tone." That represents an ascending trial. Now the experimenter might begin a second trial series with the tone clearly above threshold, decreasing the intensity with each trial until the subject says, "I can no longer hear the tone." That would be a descending trial. In a threshold experiment, perhaps 20 or more of these ascending and descending trials would be conducted and the threshold values averaged across the trial series to determine the absolute threshold for intensity for that individual for that particular tone.

The language in audition and the other senses reflects the awareness that the physical and psychological worlds are not the same. Psychologists use different terms to indicate whether the value is physical or psychological. For example, a light will have a particular wavelength but the perception of wavelength is called hue (a psychological term, meaning the person's perception of the wavelength). Light intensity, a physical term, has as its psychological counterpart, brightness. Frequency means the physical wavelength of sound; pitch is the psychological term. Sound intensity is physical, loudness is psychological, and so forth. All of this was embodied in Fechner's insight, that the psychological and physical worlds are not the same, that the relationship of these two worlds is lawful and can be measured.

In summary, the neurophysiology, sensory physiology, and psychophysics of the nineteenth century set the stage for an experimental psychology, providing the new science with the tools it needed to answer its questions of sensation, perception, thinking, memory, and learning. Brain areas were found to be linked to specific behaviors, nerves were found to have specific functions, and nerves were found to conduct their messages at a measurable speed. The anatomy and much of the basic physiology of all five senses were known. Fechner's insight and seminal book, *Elements of Psychophysics* (1860) proved to be the watershed event that truly convinced the would-be psychologists that an experimental science of psychology was possible. Wilhelm Wundt, Herman Ebbinghaus, and the other early German psychologists all acknowledged the key role of Fechner's book in their own work. Their stories and the birth of a new science are the subject of the next chapter.

3

Germany and the Birth of a New Science

At the age of 47, Wilhelm Maximillian Wundt (1832–1920) occupied the professorship in philosophy at the University of Leipzig, one of Germany's great universities. Trained in medicine and philosophy and having worked with Johannes Müller and Herman Helmholtz, Wundt had long been interested in psychological topics. Like others of his generation, he pondered the question of whether psychology could be a science, a question that most of his contemporaries had answered with a resounding "no." As mentioned in Chapter 1, he was familiar with John Stuart Mill's belief that psychology could be an empirical science. He was influenced by Fechner's 1860 book that suggested the possibility of psychology as an experimental science. Wundt considered those issues for nearly 20 years before he took a bold and risky step in his career. He decided to establish a laboratory to pursue experimental research in psychology. He assembled a rich collection of extant scientific apparatus and then designed new equipment to meet his needs when no such instruments existed. He welcomed students from all over the world to work in his laboratory and thus trained many of the first generation of psychologists. He wrote perhaps the most important psychological textbook of his time and he founded a journal to publish the new experimental work coming from his laboratory. It is principally for these reasons that Wundt is recognized as the founder of the science of psychology.

American students have been journeying to European universities since the 1700s. European study afforded a cultural richness that was synonymous with being well educated. Americans went for exposure to the art, music, architecture, and history of many centuries and, in the nineteenth century, to Germany for the science. The prestigious universities at Heidelberg, Leipzig, and Göttingen were several hundred years old when the University of Berlin, founded in 1809, instituted a philosophy of *Wissenschaft* that would change the face of university education. Its curriculum promoted an active epistemology, particularly with regard to science, and a freedom of teaching and inquiry that had not been characteristic of universities. The University of Berlin established well-equipped laboratories where professors were encouraged to conduct research and to involve their advanced students in that work, teaching them the methods of original inquiry. Professors were given a great deal of freedom to teach what they wished and to research questions of their own choosing. *Wissenschaft* also extended to the curriculum; students were given considerable freedom in selecting courses toward their degrees. Soon other German universities adopted a similar model; as a result, Germany would achieve international prominence in science and preeminence in the fields of chemistry, physics, and medicine by the end of the nineteenth century.

The beginnings of laboratory science in American universities lagged behind Germany by about 40 years; laboratories in physics and chemistry were founded in the 1840s. Most of these early laboratories were established by Americans who had taken their advanced study in Germany (Bruce, 1987). That pattern was repeated for the founding of the American psychology laboratories at the end of the nineteenth century. This chapter will focus on Wilhelm Wundt's laboratory, where many Americans studied, but will also describe briefly some of the alternative psychologies that could be found among Wundt's contemporaries in Germany.

Wundt's Leipzig Laboratory

Wilhelm Wundt graduated from the University of Heidelberg in 1855, finishing at the top of his medical school class. After a short time in Berlin where he worked as an assistant to Johannes Müller, he returned to Heidelberg to serve as an assistant to Hermann Helmholtz for six years (Bringmann, 1975). There he published his first book in 1858, a book on muscular movements and sensations. In 1862, he published his second book, *Contributions to the Theory of Sensory Perception*, which described his hopes for an experimental science of psychology. By 1867, Wundt was teaching a course entitled "Physiological Psychology," and out of the lectures for that course emerged what is perhaps his most important book for psychology, *Principles of Physiological Psychology* (1874), a book that went through six editions. In the preface to this book, Wundt wrote that it was his intention to establish psychology as a new science:

> The book which I here present to the public, is an attempt to mark out a new domain of science. I am well aware that the question may be raised, whether the time is yet ripe for such an undertaking. The new discipline

rests upon anatomical and physiological foundations which, in certain respects, are themselves very far from solid; while the experimental treatment of psychological problems must be pronounced from every point of view to be in its first beginnings. At the same time the best means of discovering the blanks that our ignorance has left in the subject matter of a developing science is, as we all know, to take a general survey of its present status. (Wundt, 1904, p. v, originally published in 1874)

Wundt's volume was a comprehensive treatment of the existing scientific research drawn from anatomy, physiology, neurology, and psychophysics and, as such, represented the first true compendium of the state of the new field.

After 17 years at Heidelberg, Wundt joined the faculty at Zurich University in 1874. The following year, however, he was offered the professorship in philosophy at the University of Leipzig, and he accepted that position beginning in 1875. He initiated his famous laboratory there and remained at the university until his retirement in 1917 at age 85. He died three years later.

Earlier we listed the accomplishments that have garnered Wundt the designation as psychology's founder. But why not include Helmholtz or Fechner, also? Thomas Leahey (1991) has written, "Wundt is the founder because he wedded physiology to philosophy and made the resulting offspring independent. He brought the empirical methods of physiology to the questions of philosophy and also created a new, identifiable role – that of psychologist, separate from the roles of philosopher, physiologist, or physician" (p. 182). John O'Donnell (1985) has referred to Leipzig as the place where psychology was manufactured and argued that Wundt's central role in the development of modern psychology "derives not from any scientific discovery that bears his name eponymously but rather from his heroic propagandizing for experimentalism" (p. 16). In Chapter 1, we noted the importance of the laboratory as "the enduring motif in the story of modern psychology" (Capshew, 1992, p. 132). It should be noted that the birth year of the science of psychology is usually given as 1879. That date does not correspond with the year of publication of Wundt's book on physiological psychology (1874), nor with his arrival at Leipzig (1875). Instead, it marks the publication of the first research from his lab.

Wundt did mark out a new science. In doing so he built one of the best research laboratories in psychology in the world, trained more than 180 students who earned doctoral degrees in psychology or philosophy, established the first experimental psychology journal in 1881 (*Philosophical Studies*), and published a large number of books and articles covering diverse areas of psychology. In fact, it has been noted that Wundt wrote more in his lifetime than most people read in theirs. One count of his published work puts his total output at 53,735 total pages over a career of 68 years; that is 2.2 published pages a day, every day for 68 years! (Boring, 1929).

Wundt was nominated three times for the Nobel Prize in Medicine and Physiology. One of his nominators, Hugo Münsterberg, wrote to the Nobel Committee: "I propose him as the man who through sixty years of indefatigable work has furthered that part of psychology of which he is practically the creator, physiological psychology" (Benjamin, 2003, p. 734). Although Wundt was one of six finalists for the award in 1916, he never received a Nobel Prize.

Wundt's System of Psychology

To describe Wundt's psychology in a brief space is an impossible task as one might imagine when someone's career has produced more than 50,000 published pages. Wundt had two psychologies: one he labeled *voluntarism*, an experimental psychology that guided his work in the laboratory, and one he considered nonexperimental, his *Völkerpsychologie*, which is often translated as cultural psychology (which is covered in a later section of this chapter).

Wundt (1912) said that the goal of psychology was to discover "the facts of consciousness, its combinations and relations, so that it may ultimately discover the laws which govern these relations and combinations" (p. 1). And what was consciousness? Wundt wrote, "It consists of the sum total of facts of which we are conscious" (p. 1). Influenced by Fechner's work, Wundt acknowledged that every conscious experience has two factors. One is the content of the experience, that is, the objects or events that are present for the observer. The other is what the observer makes of that content, or what Wundt called apprehension, meaning how the experiencing individual interprets the content. This was about *process* and not about content, and it was largely where Wundt's interests lay and what his psychology was about (Blumenthal, 1975).

For Wundt, this division of experience described the differences between the research approach of the natural sciences and the research approach of psychology. Thus "the natural sciences ... concern themselves with the objects of experience, thought of as independent of the subject, [whereas] psychology ... investigates the whole content of experience in its relations to the subject and also in regard to the attributes which this content derives directly from the subject" (Wundt, 1902, p. 3). This distinction also clarified for Wundt the difference between mediate experience, which is the domain of the natural sciences, and *immediate experience*, which is the domain of psychology. This distinction is an important one.

A physicist would study experience independent of an observer, probably via a device that measures the experience. For example, a physicist might evaluate changes in the intensity of a sound by using a sound-level meter. The "experience" assessed by the physicist is mediated by the measuring device and is, in fact, a product of that device. On the other hand, a psychologist who would study changes in the intensity of a sound would want to know how a listening human being perceived those changes. The human listener would make judgments about the sounds based on how loud (or soft) the sounds appeared to that individual. This is immediate experience. It is experience as felt by the individual and not mediated through some other entity. Recalling our example from the previous chapter, the scales of the physicist would say that the lead and feathers weighed the same, but the "scales" of the psychologist would say that the two objects were very different in their relative weights. Physicists try to study their objects of interest without becoming a part of their experiments; that is, they try not to affect, personally, their experiments. However, psychologists can't do that. Psychologists are studying the experience of an experiencing person, and the real meaning of their studies comes not from an analysis of objects in the external world but from an understanding of how those objects are or are not part of the individual's experience. Conscious experience exists in the experiencing person. Recall the riddle asking, 'If a tree falls in the forest and there is no one there to hear it, does it make a sound?' If by sound you mean the propagation of sound waves which the tree would generate when it falls, then yes, the sound occurred. However, if by sound you mean the act of hearing when sound waves fall on a human ear, then no sound occurred.

Wundt (1902) recognized that any experience was a complex entity made up of sensations, associations, and feelings: "The actual contents of psychical experience always consist of various combinations of sensational and affective elements, so that the specific character of a given psychical process depends for the most part, not on the nature of the elements, so much as on their union into a composite psychical compound" (p. 33). An immediate goal of his psychological research was to analyze experience in terms of its component elements and compounds. He wrote, "All the contents of psychical experience are of a composite character. It follows, therefore, that psychical elements, or the absolutely simple and irreducible components of psychical phenomena are the products of analysis and abstraction" (Wundt, 1902, p. 32).

One of the goals of Wundt's psychology was to identify the most basic elements in conscious experience and to understand how those elements were organized into psychical compounds or aggregates. Some of the studies in Wundt's lab were designed to do just that, particularly a number of studies on vision. Yet, as noted above, Wundt recognized that consciousness was more than a tally of its elements; it was more than its elements and more than its compounds. For Wundt the mind was an active entity that organized, analyzed, and altered the psychical elements and compounds of consciousness, creating experiences, feelings, and ideas that were not evident in any study of just the components. Wundt called his psychological system *voluntarism* to indicate the voluntary, active, and willful nature of the mind. The key concept in this voluntaristic psychology was *apperception*. Apperception was an active intentional process, that is, one involving will, in which parts of consciousness would have a greater focus or clarity. Apperception was not only important for bringing some part of conscious experience to maximal clarity, it also was the principal process by which psychical elements and compounds were synthesized into new conscious experiences, a process that Wundt labeled "creative synthesis." Wundt (1902) wrote, "As a result of this voluntary activity [apperception] the product of this synthesis is a complex in which all the components are derived from former sense perceptions and associations, but in which the combination of these components may differ more or less from the original forms" (p. 291). In Wundt's experiments, observers were expecting some stimulus occurrence; they were listening or looking for it. When it occurred, they would focus attention on it, largely ignoring the rest of the stimulus array. This focal clarity of attention is apperception.

Wundt's Research Methods

Earlier we quoted John O'Donnell's remarks about Wundt, lauding his "heroic propagandizing for experimentalism." This is a critically important point. Wundt's psychology was about using scientific methods to answer psychological questions, and one did that through experiments that emphasized the systematic manipulation of variables and employed methods of precise observation. For Wundt, experiments were needed to determine causality, and for psychological experiments that meant providing causal explanations of psychological processes in psychological (not physical or psychophysical) terms. He emphasized that psychological processes were always mental

Figure 3.1 Wilhelm Wundt (center) in a simulated reaction-time experiment in his Leipzig laboratory in 1912 with some of his colleagues and former students

processes; "psychological experimentation was to test explanations of how mental processes interacted" (Danziger, 1980, p. 115).

How did Wundt study consciousness? How did he study the immediate experience of his subjects? He used a method that has been called introspection, but is more accurately labeled *experimental self-observation*. More will be said about this distinction in Chapter 5 in discussing one of Wundt's students, Edward Titchener. For his self-observation studies, Wundt trained his observers, who typically were his doctoral or postdoctoral students. These observations were set up in the way an experiment would normally be conducted. The observer was presented with some stimulus condition (e.g., a visual stimulus, a tactile stimulus). The observer was instructed to be in a state of readiness and was told when the stimulus would be presented. Stimuli were typically of short duration, and the observer's job immediately at the end of the stimulus presentation was to give an account of what the observer experienced. That constituted one experimental trial, and any investigations would typically involve multiple trials. The stimulus itself would often be changed in value to determine how such changes altered the self reports. Such a procedure had most of the components of a modern experiment: training of an observer, presentation and manipulation of an independent variable, and measurement (via self report) of the effect of the stimulus (the report representing the dependent variable).

In his laboratory, Wundt also used the psychophysical methods developed by Fechner and methods borrowed from physiology. One of those from the latter category was the *reaction time method*, a method that had been used by Helmholtz in measuring the speed of nerve conduction and by others in physiology and astronomy. Of particular influence on Wundt was the work of Dutch physiologist, Franciscus C. Donders (1818–1889) who used the reaction time method to measure the speed of mental events. His reasoning was that if thinking involved neural transmission, then one could measure the speed of certain mental problems by measuring reaction time and subtracting out the time required for the sensory (afferent) and motor (efferent) components. Wundt used this method in his own lab. For example, one of his American students, James McKeen Cattell (who is discussed in the next chapter) used the procedure for his dissertation research. He wrote home to his parents in January, 1884, about that work:

> We work in a new field, where others will follow us, who must use or correct our results. We are trying to measure the time it takes to perform the simplest mental act – as for example to distinguish whether a color is blue or red. As this time seems to be not more than one hundredth of a second, you can imagine this is no easy task. (as cited in Sokal, 1981, p. 89)

One variant of the reaction time method was to test subjects using a simple reaction time task, for example, having a subject press a key as soon as a light was turned on. After multiple trials, the experimenter could average the values for an average reaction time. Then the same subject could be tested in a choice reaction time task, which required the subject to press one key if the light was red and another key if the light was green. In this choice task, the sensory and motor components are identical. That is, the time required for the subject to see the light and move her/his finger to press the key were the same in both tasks. What differed was the mental processing time. In the simple task the subject had no decision to make; just press the key as soon as possible after the light came on. But in the choice task the subject had first to judge the color of the light and then think about which key was to be pressed. In these choice tasks the reaction times were slower. To determine the actual time of the mental task, the value calculated from the simple task was subtracted from the value of the choice task. That difference defined the speed of the mental event. Although this method proved popular in Wundt's lab for nearly a decade, it was eventually abandoned because it was demonstrated that changes in the experimental conditions changed the nature of the tasks qualitatively as well as quantitatively, making the subtraction procedure invalid. The reaction time method was fine for certain kinds of experiments though, and it is used today in cognitive psychology, typically referred to as mental chronometry.

The Research in Wundt's Laboratory

Much of the research in Wundt's laboratory was conducted by his students (discussed later). And most of that work was published in the journal that he founded. About half of the research was on topics related to the processes of sensation and perception, mostly on vision, including depth perception, color vision, negative aftereffects, visual illusions, and color blindness. There was also research on auditory phenomena, such as tone perception; on touch, including two-point thresholds and other studies of tactile pressure; and on time perception. In the 1880s the reaction time studies were popular but they declined after about a decade as noted earlier. They were replaced in the 1890s by research on emotions, stimulated in part by Wundt's development of what is usually called his *tridimensional theory of feeling* that placed all emotions on three separate continua: pleasant-unpleasant, tension-relaxation, excitement-depression. Additional studies focused on attention and association.

Wundt's Völkerpsychologie

In the 1890s, when Wundt was in his 60s, he began an ambitious project that resulted in a 10-volume work entitled *Völkerpsychologie* (published between 1900 and 1920). The word doesn't translate well into English. It has variously been translated as social psychology, as folk psychology, and as cultural or ethnic psychology. Most authorities recognize the last two terms as coming closest to describing the content of the 10 volumes. These books have been described as an extensive study of the relationships among religion, art, language, custom, morality, myth, and culture – fields that embodied what Wundt regarded as higher human mental processes. Wundt argued that these processes could not be studied by experimental methods (although some scholars dispute that claim) and were thus destined to be understood through other non-experimental methods from fields such as cultural anthropology, sociology, and social psychology.

Very little of this massive work has been translated into English and most historians of psychology have largely ignored it, either because they don't know what is in the 10 volumes or because it doesn't fit with the story of a history of the science of psychology. But this work is seen as an important precursor to several contemporary fields in psychology such as linguistics, cultural psychology, social psychology, and personality. It has been called the second psychology, "a psychology to complement laboratory-based psychology ... [that] would address aspects of human mind and behavior that emerged from cultural life" (Cahan & White, 1992, p. 224). It has been noted that Wundt saw "his second psychology as an essential complement to his experimental psychology" (Cahan & White, 1992, p. 227). For information on this aspect of Wundt's work see Danziger (1983) and Wong (2009).

Wundt's Students

If you wanted to get involved in psychological research in 1879, the University of Leipzig was the only game in town, although that would not be true for very long. Wundt's reputation spread quickly and far, and a large number of students from around the world came to study. Wundt served as the major advisor for more than 180 doctoral students in his years at Leipzig; more than 100 of those came from Germany and Austria, but there were students from England, Canada, France, Poland, Denmark, Romania, Russia, and several other countries as well (see Tinker, 1932). There were 33 Americans who took their degrees with Wundt, 13 of whom did doctoral research in experimental psychology (the others studied philosophy), and there were other Americans who studied or visited the lab but did not earn degrees there (Benjamin, Durkin, Link, Vestal, & Acord, 1992). By all accounts, Wundt was an excellent mentor, open to his students' ideas for their own research, generous in the time he gave to them, supportive of their work by providing the necessary equipment and books, and assisting them in publishing their work in the journal he founded.

The first of the American psychology students to visit the lab was G. Stanley Hall who arrived there in 1879. Hall had earned his doctoral degree in psychology with William James the previous year. The first American to earn a doctorate in psychology with Wundt was James McKeen Cattell, mentioned earlier, who finished his degree in 1886. The second was Harry Kirke Wolfe who finished four months after Cattell. Hall returned to found the first psychology laboratory in America at Johns Hopkins University in 1883. Cattell founded laboratories at the University of Pennsylvania in 1889 and Columbia University in 1891. Wolfe founded a laboratory at the University of Nebraska in 1889. James, Hall, and Cattell, arguably the three most important American psychologists of their time, will be discussed in detail in the next chapter.

With the first American psychology laboratory opening only four years after the Leipzig laboratory, it is not surprising that psychology spread quickly to other universities in Germany as well. The psychologies developed at these other German universities differed from Wundt's, often in radical ways. In the remainder of this chapter we will briefly discuss some of these pioneering German experimental psychologists.

Hermann Ebbinghaus and the Study of Memory

The research of Hermann Ebbinghaus (1850–1909) is well known among psychologists today, especially so among cognitive psychologists. Even psychologists who have little knowledge of their field's history seem to know about Ebbinghaus. There are good reasons for his continued celebrity. At the age of 29 he began a research program on human memory that was nothing short of remarkable for its time. The studies culminated in a book in 1885. William James (1885) called the studies heroic. In their book on the history of modern psychology, Schultz and Schultz (1987) wrote that Ebbinghaus'

> book represents what is perhaps the single most brilliant investigation in the history of experimental psychology. In addition to beginning a whole new field of study, which is still vital today, it provides a striking example of technical skill, perseverance, and ingenuity. It is not possible to find in the history of psychology any other investigator working alone who subjected himself to such a rigid regimen of experimentation. The research was so exacting, thorough, and systematic that it is still cited in contemporary textbooks. (p. 73)

That is high praise indeed, and the sentiment is shared by many other historians of psychology and contemporary researchers in memory as well.

Unlike Wundt who had a well-equipped laboratory of many rooms and many doctoral students to engage in his research program, Ebbinghaus worked by himself. He had received his doctorate at the University of Bonn in 1873. In 1879, he began his memory studies and used them in 1880 to gain an unsalaried position at the University of Berlin. He continued his memory research there, again, by himself, eventually publishing his famous book as *Über das Gedächtnis* (*Studies on Memory*) in 1885.

Ebbinghaus got the idea for his memory studies after reading Fechner's book, *Elements of Psychophysics*. He reasoned that he might

Figure 3.2 Hermann Ebbinghaus. At right is the cover of Ebbinghaus's 1885 book, *Über das Gedächtnis* (*Studies on Memory*) autographed by Ebbinghaus and presented to Gustav Fechner. Fechner would have been 84 years old at the time

be able to use procedures similar to the psychophysical methods described by Fechner to investigate higher mental processes such as learning (association) and memory. Wundt, Johann Friedrich Herbart, and others believed that it was not possible to investigate the higher mental processes because of the interference of language, learning, and memory – factors that would bias the self observations. But Ebbinghaus (1913/1885) decided he would try. In the preface to his book on memory he wrote:

> In the realm of mental phenomena, experiment and measurement have hitherto been chiefly limited in application to sense perception and to the time relations of mental processes. By means of following investigations we have tried to go a step farther into the workings of the mind and to submit to an experimental and quantitative treatment the manifestations of memory. (p. v)

You will recognize his references in this paragraph to the work of Wundt on sensation and the speed of mental processes.

To begin his studies, Ebbinghaus needed subjects. He had none, and so he used the one he did have, himself. To test his memory under a variety of conditions, he needed to be able to learn something. Yet because he was both the experimenter and the subject, it was important that he not be familiar, in advance, with the material he was going to be learning. Furthermore, he decided not to use words as the information he would memorize. Words carried meaning. Any word could conjure up a number of different associations. The word milk might make one think of cow or bottle or baby or mother or white or cold or cream, and so forth. Ebbinghaus viewed such associative baggage as a detriment to his research, and he wanted to find a way to eliminate it. The solution he arrived at was to create a series of *nonsense syllables*, many of them constructed as three-letter syllables of the consonant-vowel-consonant form that would be meaningless, such as XAJ or CIH or BEQ. Ebbinghaus generated more than 2,300 of the syllables and printed each one separately on a card. He placed the cards in a box and thus could draw out a random sample of nonsense syllables for any of his studies.

There had been earlier investigations of associations, for example by empiricist philosophers. The typical form of these studies was to generate a list of words, present the words one at a time to a subject, and then ask the subject to generate as many associations as possible. Of course these investigations were studying associations that had already been formed. Ebbinghaus wanted to study associations *as they were being formed*. No one had done that before because anyone with language skills already had associations to virtually any word that could be used. But the nonsense syllable largely eliminated that problem. E. B. Titchener (1928) called Ebbinghaus' invention of nonsense syllables the most significant advancement in the study of memory since the work of Aristotle.

Ebbinghaus had an excellent sense of experimental design issues and worked hard to eliminate any confounds that might bias his data. Because he was the only subject, he tried to keep his life conditions reasonably constant. For example, he tested himself at the same time each day, he maintained constancy in the testing environment, and as best he could, given that the studies were conducted over many months, he tried not to vary his activities in the hour or so before the tests. When reciting the syllables, he used a metronome to keep his timing constant, and he tried to say each syllable with the same voice inflection. The studies raised important questions about memory that are still important today, and that is one of the reasons his work has remained of interest. Yet there is no doubt that part of the equation for his continued currency is that he conducted his research with such skill and care that the results have stood the test of time.

Ebbinghaus' book contains the results of 20 studies that he conducted over several years. The breadth of such a program of study is beyond our coverage here. He did research on the course of forgetting over time in which he discovered the now-famous forgetting curve which shows that most forgetting occurs in the first few hours after learning and then levels off at a slower forgetting rate. He investigated how the length of a series affected the number of trials needed for learning and found that it was not a linear relationship. He studied how retention is affected by relearning. He investigated how the number of repetitions affects forgetting. He even compared the ease of learning of meaningful material (using poetry) compared to an equivalent amount of non-meaningful material (nonsense syllables) and how, after mastery of the material, the courses of forgetting differed. To get an idea of how time-consuming and thorough some of his studies were, consider that in a study of repetition, he used 420 series of 16 syllables each, with each series being repeated as much as 64 times, an investigation that required more than 15,000 recitations (Roediger, 1985)!

Ebbinghaus left Berlin in 1894, apparently because he had published little since his memory studies. For the last 15 years of his life he was a faculty member at two other universities. He made a few additional contributions, including developing a testing procedure that influenced the development of intelligence testing, but there was nothing to match the quality of his memory work (Fuchs, 1997). And he had only a few doctoral students to aid his research or carry on his legacy. He died of pneumonia at the age of 59. A few years before his death, Ebbinghaus published a book entitled *Fundamentals of Psychology*. It was dedicated to Fechner whose book had started Ebbinghaus on his remarkable research. In the dedication, Ebbinghaus wrote, "I owe everything to you."

Franz Brentano's Act Psychology

Wundt opened his laboratory in 1879; Ebbinghaus began his memory studies in the same year. Scientific psychology was clearly in the air. Another convert to the new science was Franz Brentano (1838–1917), a German who spent most of his academic life in Austria (at the University of Vienna) and Italy. Brentano's version of psychology is called *act psychology*. It is a molar psychology that called for a larger unit of analysis in looking at consciousness. For example, with respect to vision, Brentano argued that it was important to study the act of seeing itself and not to focus on what was seen. Thus he would have opposed that portion of Wundt's psychology that focused on an analysis of psychical elements and compounds. Brentano's major contribution was a book entitled *Psychology from an Empirical Standpoint* (1874), a book that spelled out his act psychology.

Act psychology postulated intentionality in conscious acts. Individuals intended to do things, to see things, to experience things. There was thus a purpose to consciousness. For Brentano it meant that psychology should not study the contents of consciousness but the actions of consciousness. His ideas in this vein would foreshadow American functional psychology and Gestalt psychology, both of which will be discussed in Chapters 5 and 11.

Brentano also differed from Wundt in the way that he thought science should be conducted. Brentano advocated an approach known as *experimentum crucis* (crucial experiment) meaning that he felt science was best served by a few grand experiments that tested big questions, with a few studies smaller in scope to round out the edges. Wundt believed in a systematic series of small studies that would build a science, small step by small step. Finally, Brentano opposed the use of introspection as a research method; he believed that it was impossible for observers to report with accuracy on their own states of consciousness (Rancurello, 1968).

Carl Stumpf and the Psychology of Music

Carl Stumpf (1848–1936) played the violin at age seven, and at age 10 wrote his first musical composition, an oratorio for three voices. Music would be of great importance to him all of his life. He studied with Brentano at the University of Würzburg before getting his doctorate at the University of Göttingen in 1868 at the age of 20. At Göttingen he worked with Rudolph Hermann Lotze, famous today for his work in perception, and he had some contact with the psychophysicists, Ernst Weber and Gustav Fechner. In 1873, he joined the faculty at the University of Würzburg where he did important work on depth perception.

In modern terms, Stumpf like many of his German contemporaries would be classified as a cognitive psychologist. His emphasis was on the study of sensation and perception, particularly the perception of tone. He performed a number of classic experiments on audition, including studies of overtones (harmonics), combination tones, beats (inter-tones), and especially pitch perception. But his first love was the psychology of music, and that is the field of his greatest contributions. At Würzburg he began a massive project involving years of study on the *psychology of tones*, which resulted in two volumes that are considered classics in the history of the psychology of music. This work on tone, published in 1883 and 1890, was highly regarded in the scientific world, and was often compared to the auditory work of Helmholtz (Langfeld, 1937). In these volumes he described his work on tonal fusion, the common experience of hearing a single tone when two different tones were played together. He argued that the principal reason for this was the degree of consonance of the tones, for example two notes an octave apart or notes at particular intervals that were more consonant, for example, the interval described as a perfect fifth. He also studied the psychological nature of melodies.

In 1894, Stumpf accepted the chair in philosophy at the University of Berlin, the most prestigious philosophy chair in Germany. There he also served as Director of the Institute of Experimental Psychology, an institute that Ebbinghaus had begun. Stumpf expanded the scope of

Figure 3.3 Map of Germany and surrounding area, showing founding and reestablishment dates of the major universities

the institute, greatly enlarged its quarters, and built it into a force to rival the Leipzig laboratory. He continued his work on music, collecting records of primitive music from many cultures over a span of 20 years, amassing an incredible international library of more than 10,000 records. These were used as research for his 1911 book *The Origins of Music*, a book that theorized about the earliest musical sounds in human culture and the development of music over the centuries. Because of this work, Stumpf is considered one of the key pioneers in what is called comparative musicology or ethnomusicology. The importance of this book for contemporary researchers in this field is evidenced by the fact that an English translation of the book was published in 2012.

Finally, Stumpf's many students included Wolfgang Köhler and Kurt Koffka, who would be instrumental in the founding of Gestalt psychology; Kurt Lewin, who was also part of the Gestalt group and was a key figure in the development of experimental social psychology in America; and Oskar Pfungst who, along with Stumpf, would be involved in investigating the famous case of *Clever Hans*, the horse that supposedly could count. Stumpf and Pfungst used controlled experimental procedures to demonstrate that the horse's owner was giving subtle cues to the horse indicating when he should cease tapping his hoof on the pavement (see Fernald, 1984; Pfungst, 1965). When Stumpf retired from the University of Berlin in 1921, he was succeeded by his student Wolfgang Köhler.

Georg Elias Müller and Memory

Whereas Ebbinghaus spent a few years investigating memory, G. E. Müller (1850–1934) spent much of his lengthy career working on that topic. Müller was a productive scholar, a member of the faculty at the University of Göttingen where he received his doctorate, and director of the psychology laboratory there for 40 years (Krohn, 1893). He made contributions to a number of psychological topics including sensation, color vision, learning, attention, and psychophysics. His principal work was in memory. He replicated much of Ebbinghaus' work but extended it considerably as well. In addition to similar experiments, Müller also asked subjects what they were thinking in the various memory tasks. That is, he asked them to report on any strategies they were using in trying to memorize the lists. As a result, he learned that there were a number of cognitive strategies, including the assignment of meaning to stimuli that were meant to be meaningless and the chunking of syllables into units to give them meaning. Müller did much original work in this field as well. He invented the memory drum which was a boon to research in that it systematized the presentation of stimuli for memory tasks. Indeed the memory drum proved to be a staple in psychology laboratories all over the world for decades. Müller wanted to go beyond Ebbinghaus' discovery of the rate of forgetting and understand why forgetting occurred. To that end he pioneered work in interference theory, and conducted studies on both proactive and retroactive inhibition. Moreover, he did important studies showing under what conditions information from one task would transfer to another.

Müller's laboratory opened only two years after Wundt's lab. It attracted a large number of excellent students from Germany and nearby countries, yet it never attracted very many American students. Of the few who studied there, the best known was Christine Ladd-Franklin (1847–1930), who became an important contributor to the field of vision, especially color vision (Furumoto, 1992). Few of Müller's articles or books were ever translated into English, which meant that most American psychologists knew little of his work (Behrens, 1997). In his history of experimental psychology, written in 1929 when Müller was still alive, E. G. Boring described Müller's contributions to experimental psychology. His summary statement was that "As a power and an institution he is second only to Wundt" (Boring, 1929, p. 369).

Oswald Külpe and Thinking

Oswald Külpe (1862–1915) earned his doctorate with Wundt in 1887. He had taken his first course in psychology from Wundt, but had then gone to Göttingen to study with Georg Müller before returning to Leipzig. He remained at Leipzig after his graduation for seven years, serving as chief assistant in Wundt's laboratory. Eventually the chance came for him to establish his own laboratory and his own brand of psychology. He moved to the University of Würzburg in 1894. On his own, Külpe was able to pursue his beliefs about psychology. He was interested in investigating the higher mental processes, especially thinking, that were off limits in Wundt's laboratory. Perhaps that was the influence of Müller. He also developed an introspection procedure that involved retrospection, a tactic that Wundt believed compromised the validity of the observer reports (Lindenfeld, 1978).

Külpe's method of introspection is usually referred to as *systematic experimental introspection*. Observers would experience whatever stimuli or events they were supposed to experience – often more complicated events than were typical of the Leipzig work – and then provide a comprehensive account of the mental processes involved. It was retrospective because the reports were taken at the end of the stimulus event. To get around the problem of memory in such a procedure and to systematize the introspective accounts, Külpe and his students divided the tasks into meaningful components, requiring introspective accounts after each component, a method called fractionation. These introspections would be repeated several times to ensure reliability.

Külpe was interested not just in the report of the conscious experience of the event but in the mental activities associated with thinking about that event. This procedure led to some interesting discoveries about thought processes. One was that when observers were given instructions for a task, such as being asked to add pairs of numbers that they would see, their introspective accounts of the addition indicated that the instructions were incorporated before the task such that they did not play a role in the task itself. That is, when the number pair appeared, the subject did not have to think, "I must add these numbers," rather the process just occurred to generate the solution. This phenomenon was called *mental set*, a concept that would have great importance in cognitive psychology.

Another finding from the thinking studies was especially controversial. Wundt and his student Titchener believed that all thought was composed of either sensations or images. Yet in some of Külpe's studies, observers gave introspective accounts of thoughts that involved no such imagery. For example, in a study by one of Külpe's students, Karl Marbe, subjects lifted pairs of weights, one at a time, and at the end made a judgment of which weight was heavier. Observers reported forming images of each of the weights when they lifted them but reported that there was no sensory or imaginal content present when they made the judgments. This phenomenon was called *imageless thought*, and it created a great rift between the Würzburg and Leipzig laboratories. Wundt argued that the introspections were not valid because the judgment task was too complex to be introspected. The controversy was never resolved.

It should be obvious that although Wundt is credited with the founding of scientific psychology in 1879, within a few short years, the science of psychology could be found in many leading German universities. Ebbinghaus, at Berlin, had developed his psychology independently at about the same time. Brentano (who was at the University of Vienna in Austria) had developed his act psychology independently, writing his important book in 1874, the same year that Wundt published the first edition of his major work. Stumpf was a student of Brentano and began his psychological work at Würzburg in the 1870s, although it would be

1883 before he published the first volume of his magnum opus on tone. Georg Müller opened his exceptionally productive laboratory at Göttingen in 1881, only two years after Wundt's lab. And Külpe, Wundt's student, would take over the Würzburg laboratory in the 1890s. Americans would study with each of these individuals, although the preponderance would be trained at Leipzig. Experimental psychology was not only spreading across Germany but was being imported to North America which could boast of more than 40 psychology laboratories by 1900, more than any country, including Germany. But American psychology would have a very different look as we will see in the next chapter that explores the beginnings of scientific psychology in America.

4

Origins of Scientific Psychology in America

The 400th anniversary of Christopher Columbus's "discovery" of America was fast approaching and workers in Chicago were completing preparations for the World's Columbian Exposition, also known as the Chicago World's Fair, scheduled to open in 1892 on a 600-acre site on the shore of Lake Michigan. Construction delays prevented the Fair's opening until May 1, 1893. The feature attraction of the Fair was a marvel of engineering, a giant wheel that towered 27 stories above the fairgrounds. It was what everyone was talking about. It had been designed by an engineer, George Ferris, and it marked the beginning of the Ferris wheel. Passengers on the wheel sat or stood in cars almost the size of railroad boxcars, 36 of them, each carrying up to 60 people. The wheel proved to be an enormous draw, no doubt the reason that many of the more than 27 million visitors attended the Fair during its six-month run. The Fair was a great economic success, but it had meant much more to the people of Chicago than money; it was a chance for the revitalized city to show the world what it had made of itself since the disastrous fire of 1871 that had leveled much of Chicago.

Tucked away in one of the 200 buildings at the Fair was a small exhibit of two rooms labeled The Psychology Laboratory and organized by Joseph Jastrow, a psychologist at the University of Wisconsin. One room displayed scientific apparatus used in psychological experiments as well as photos of apparatus and subjects being tested. In the other room, visitors would be given a clipboard and laboratory score sheet. There they could move among a number of experimental stations to measure their accuracy of movement, reaction time, color vision, sensitivity to pain, judgment of weights, memory, and so forth, recording their measurements on their scoresheets. The exhibit marked scientific psychology's first attempt to display its new science to the general public. It was part of a public education campaign to convince Americans that the answers to psychological questions resided within the laboratories of the universities and not

Bettmann/CORBIS

Figure 4.1   The Court of Honor of the Chicago World's Fair in 1893 as seen from the roof of the Manufacturing Building. The Fair was often referred to as "The White City" because of the white stucco covering most of the buildings

in the hands of mesmerists, spiritualists, or phrenologists. No doubt, The Psychology Laboratory did not attract the crowds drawn to the Ferris wheel. However, the meager display served notice that the new scientific psychologists intended to be the voice of authority in matters psychological.

With Americans going to Germany to study with Wundt and his contemporaries, the stage was set for the seeds of the new science to be planted in American soil. Many of America's first generation of laboratory psychologists took their training abroad, some were "home" schooled, and at least one was self-taught. This chapter tells the story of the emergence of American experimental psychology at the end of the nineteenth century, focusing on the contributions of three individuals: William James, G. Stanley Hall, and James McKeen Cattell. James is the self-taught psychologist in this group, remarking once that the first psychology course that he took was the one he taught at Harvard University in 1875. G. Stanley Hall, although only two years younger than James, was James's doctoral student at Harvard. Cattell began his graduate work with Hall at Johns Hopkins University but finished his doctorate in Leipzig with Wundt. Although it appears that there are three academic generations here, they actually functioned together in American psychology in the 1880s and 1890s.

William James as Psychologist

William James was born in New York City to a family of privilege and wealth. In addition to schools in the United States, he attended schools in France, England, and Switzerland. His home was a place of important guests such as Ralph Waldo Emerson (his godfather) and Henry David Thoreau. The James family was well educated and well traveled, exposed to art, literature, music, and architecture. For a time James considered a career as a painter and exhibited considerable talent in that regard (Leary, 1992). His younger brother, Henry became a famous novelist and lived in London for many years. Henry became one of only a few Americans who have been honored with burial in Poet's Corner in Westminster Abbey.

James earned a medical degree from Harvard in 1869. In 1872, he was hired by Harvard to teach courses in physiology, establishing a physiology laboratory in 1875 to supplement his new course on physiological psychology. Some historians have argued that this laboratory was the first psychology laboratory in America (Harper, 1950). However, it is better viewed as a demonstrational lab and not a research lab.

In the 1870s, publisher Henry Holt was producing a series of books entitled the *American Science Series*. He wanted a volume to cover the new science of psychology, and in 1878, he signed James as his author, which was a bit of a risk because James had never written a book. Holt

Houghton Library, Harvard University

Figure 4.2   The William James house at 95 Irving Street near the Harvard University campus

wanted the book in a year, but James asked for two years to complete the task. At the end of the two years, however, James had made almost no progress on the book. Reading James's letters, which are in the archives at Harvard University, it would appear that he began writing in earnest on the book in 1885. Although Holt must have wondered if the book would ever appear, the manuscript finally arrived in late summer of 1890, 10 years overdue! It was published that fall in two volumes and 1,400 pages as *The Principles of Psychology*. This book has no rival for importance in the history of American psychology. It has never been out of print and continues to sell today to new generations who discover James's extraordinary prose and his wonderfully illustrative examples.

James's Principles

James's *Principles* was the American version of Wundt's *Principles of Physiological Psychology* in that both were meant to be compendia of the extant work in the new science. James's book wasn't the first such book in America. Three years earlier, a psychologist at Yale University, George Trumbull Ladd (1842–1921), had published *Elements of Physiological Psychology* (1887). That book had some impact on the new field, but nothing like the influence that would be enjoyed by James. James was a popular teacher at Harvard, a fact that was related to the success of the book. Historians of psychology Raymond Fancher and Alexandra Rutherford (2012) wrote, "The book succeeded for the same reasons his teaching succeeded: it stressed the personal utility and relevance of psychological ideas, and used an unself-conscious frankness and naturalness in discussing them" (p. 316).

The chapters of James's book would have looked familiar to the mental philosophers. There was coverage of consciousness, sensation, perception, association, memory, attention, imagination, reasoning, emotions, and will. But the content was quite different, drawing from the decades of work in neurophysiology, sensory physiology, and psychophysics, and the psychological work of the previous decade.

One of the key concepts of James's psychology was the *stream of consciousness* and its linkage to *selective attention*. Pre-scientific definitions of psychology had emphasized it as the study of the soul or the study of the mind. Common in the new psychology – variously called experimental psychology or physiological psychology to distinguish it from the psychology of mental philosophy – was a definition that emphasized the study of consciousness. In a clear attack on the reductionistic portion of

Wundt's psychology (and a rebuke that could be applied to the especially atomistic psychology that Titchener developed a few years later,
which will be discussed in the next chapter), James (1890) wrote:

> Most books start with sensations, as the simplest mental facts, and pro-
> ceed synthetically, constructing each higher stage from those below it. But
> this is abandoning the empirical method of investigation. No one ever
> had a simple sensation by itself. Consciousness, from our natal day, is of
> a teeming multiplicity of objects and relations, and what we call simple
> sensations are results of discriminative attention, pushed often to a very
> high degree. (v.1., p. 224)

James noted that consciousness did not exist in bits or discrete units,
rather it flowed like a stream. Thus, elemental analyses of consciousness
made no sense; they created an artificial psychology.

James, like many scholars of his generation, was greatly influenced
by the ideas of Charles Darwin (discussed in the next chapter). Darwin had brought attention to concepts of adaptation and survival value.
James sought to discover the role of consciousness in human survival.
Surely, consciousness had evolved. What were its purposes? What were
its functions? In the earlier quotation, James talked about consciousness
as "a teeming multiplicity of objects and relations." At many moments
in life we exist in a world of sensory overload from which we must
extract some information, make sense of it, and act on it. Processes such
as habit and selective attention help us navigate successfully in such
a world. The following lengthy quotation illustrates the role of selective attention in consciousness and the role of consciousness in human
progress and survival. "Illustrates" is the right verb because although
James abandoned his career as a painter, he continued to paint with his
words, as this passage makes evident:

> ... we see that the mind is at every stage a theatre of simultaneous possi-
> bilities. Consciousness consists in the comparison of these with each other,
> the selection of some, and the suppression of the rest by the reinforcing
> and inhibiting agency of attention. The highest and most elaborated men-
> tal products are filtered from the data chosen by the faculty next beneath,
> out of the mass offered by the faculty below that ... The mind, in short,
> works on the data it received very much as a sculptor works on his block
> of stone. In a sense that statue stood there from eternity. But there were
> a thousand different ones beside it, and the sculptor alone is to thank for
> having extricated this one from the rest. Just so the world of each of us,
> howsoever different our several views of it may be, all lay embedded in
> the primordial chaos of sensations, which gave the mere matter to the
> thought of all of us indifferently. We may, if we like, by our reasonings

unwind things back to that black and jointless continuity of space and moving clouds of swarming atoms which science calls the only real world. But all the while the world we feel and live in will be that which our ancestors and we, by slowly cumulative strokes of choice, have extricated out of this, like sculptors, by simply rejecting certain portions of the given stuff. Other sculptors, other statues from the same stone! Other minds, other worlds from the same monotonous and inexpressive chaos! My world is but one in a million alike embedded, alike real to those who may abstract them. How different must be the worlds in the consciousness of ant, cuttle-fish, or crab! (v. 1, pp. 288–289)

For James, consciousness was thus about making choices. For humans as an animal species largely freed of instincts, actions become matters of personal responsibility. In a world of chaos, something that has evolved to aid the species in making good choices has important survival value, and that something was consciousness.

One of James's most important chapters in his *Principles* was the one on habit. Just as consciousness was important for the survival of the individual, *habit* was a key force in the maintenance of social order. He wrote, "Habit is thus the enormous fly-wheel of society, its most precious conservative agent. It alone is what keeps us all within the bounds of ordinance" (James, 1890, v. 1, p. 121). James theorized that habits became engrained because of neural pathways that began to fire automatically in appropriate situations. Because habits were neurally based, they were difficult to change once established. Thus James wrote about the importance of avoiding the establishment of bad habits and ensuring the development of good ones, part of his message of personal utility as noted above by Fancher and Rutherford.

One of James's original contributions in *Principles* was his *theory of emotion*. The common view of emotion in James's time was that the perception of a situation gave rise to a subjective feeling that was followed by a series of bodily changes. James turned this idea around, arguing that the bodily changes result from the perception of the situation, and that recognition of the bodily changes subsequently produces the subjective feeling we label emotion. A similar theory was published about the same time by the Danish physiologist Carl Lange (1834–1900) and is today referred to as the *James-Lange theory of emotion*. The theory was controversial in its day and remains so today but has not been discarded as a potential explanation of some emotional experiences. These ideas, as well as James's conceptions of learning, motivation, and attention would prove especially important in the development of an American school of psychology known as functionalism, a psychology that sought to understand the functions of consciousness. That school will be discussed in the next chapter.

Although James's *Principles* was an especially influential book, both in its shaping of psychological thought as well as recruiting a generation of young scholars to the new science, James never developed a career as an experimental psychologist. He wrote a book on the psychology of religion (*The Varieties of Religious Experience*, 1902) and another on the relation of psychology to teaching. The rest of his written work, which was substantial (once he got the hang of writing a book he was able to write many of them), was in philosophy, especially his philosophy of pragmatism (see James, 1907). James didn't like laboratory work, but thought that Harvard should have such a lab if it was to excel in psychology. To that end, he recruited Hugo Münsterberg (see Chapter 6) from Germany in 1892, one of Wundt's doctoral students, to head the Harvard lab. Today, approximately 125 years after writing his *Principles*, James continues to enjoy the reputation of one of America's greatest psychologists and philosophers.

James's Student: Mary Whiton Calkins

Because he was not involved in laboratory research, James did not have many psychology students, but the few he had were excellent. In 1890, Mary Whiton Calkins (1863–1930), a professor at Wellesley College was asked by her college to offer a course on the new psychology. She had very little background in the subject so she approached William James about taking some courses at Harvard. In the fall term of 1890, she took William James's beginning psychology course. She was the only student in the class so they met in James's home (see Figure 4.2) as they sat in his parlor on either side of a fireplace discussing psychology, especially his *Principles*, which had just been published. There had been four other students in the class, all males, but they dropped the class, perhaps because they heard that a woman had enrolled. Such was the nature of higher education for women in the nineteenth century. Indeed, women were not allowed to enroll officially at Harvard in the time Calkins was there. So although she took the requisite coursework for a doctorate, completed her doctoral research, and passed her oral doctoral exams, she was never granted her PhD even though James and other faculty petitioned the university on her behalf (Furumoto, 1991; Scarborough & Furumoto, 1987).

Calkins returned to Wellesley where she had established a psychology laboratory in 1891, the first psychology laboratory founded by a woman. She would go on to a career of considerable accomplishment. Between 1894 and 1898, she published four articles on memory, each of them describing multiple studies (see, for example, Calkins, 1894, 1896).

Figure 4.3 William James (left) and Mary Whiton Calkins in 1889, about the time that she began her studies at Harvard University

To carry out her work she invented a technique that is still a mainstay in memory research today, the *paired associates method*, a technique in which items (words, nonsense syllables, pictures) are presented in pairs in the learning trials and then one item of the pair is used to cue the other in the memory trials. Calkins was especially interested in primacy and recency effects, that is, studying memory for items presented early in a list and those at the end of the list. Her work showed how the recency effect could be reduced or eliminated by insertion of some kind of distractor task between presentation of the list and recall of the list. That technique is a common research procedure today. Further, she also did important work on what today would be called retroactive interference, a principal cause of forgetting. Summarizing her legacy for the fields of association and memory, Madigan and O'Hara (1992) have written, "[her writings] constitute a truly remarkable legacy, as they represent important, basic, replicable phenomena that are fundamentally important to our current conceptualization of human memory" (p. 174).

As a psychologist, Calkins found it possible to embrace not only the new experimental psychology but also the mental and moral philosophy that preceded it. She spent most of her career advocating for what she called *self psychology*, her system of what psychological science should be (see Calkins, 1900). She argued that psychology should be a science of selves and not a science of consciousness or behavior. Her self psychology has been described as an introspectionist psychology that sought to study the several selves of an individual – the self that doesn't change, the self that changes, the unique self, the social self. It proved to be a losing battle, fought at a time when her colleagues were distancing themselves from philosophy and, in most cases, from a reliance on introspection as a method of study. She persisted throughout her life in promoting this unique vision of psychology (Wentworth, 1999).

As evidence of the respect her colleagues held for her, Calkins was elected president of the American Psychological Association in 1905, the first woman to hold that office. Further, she was elected president of the American Philosophical Association in 1918. More than a decade after she completed her work at Harvard, the Dean of Radcliffe College (Harvard's new women's college) contacted her to say that Radcliffe wanted to give her a PhD degree. Stating that her coursework and research were at Harvard, *not* at Radcliffe, Calkins politely declined.

G. Stanley Hall and the Professionalization of Psychology

G. Stanley Hall (1844–1924) was 30 years old, teaching philosophy at Antioch College in Ohio when he obtained a copy of Wundt's *Principles of Physiological Psychology*. He was captivated by the book and wanted to get training in the new experimental psychology, but he was from a farm family of modest means in Massachusetts, and the savings from his Antioch salary could not support study in Europe. Hall went to Harvard University instead in 1876 for his doctoral work with philosopher–psychologist William James (1842–1910). At the time, James was offering the only course in America on the new scientific psychology, a course he had begun teaching in 1875. Hall graduated in June of 1878 with a PhD degree in philosophy, the first awarded by the Harvard Philosophy Department. Eventually Hall was offered a faculty position in psychology and pedagogy at Johns Hopkins University in Baltimore. There he opened the first psychology laboratory in America in 1883 (Ross, 1972).

In his illustrious career, Hall not only founded the first psychology laboratory, but also founded the first psychology journal in America; founded the first professional organization for psychologists in 1892, the American Psychological Association; began the Child Study Movement, a nationwide effort to use psychology to enhance education; and started the first journal of applied psychology and the first journal of religious psychology. He brought Sigmund Freud to the United States in 1909 for his only visit (see Chapter 7); and wrote several important books, including the first book on the psychology of aging and a major two-volume work on adolescence.

While at Johns Hopkins, Hall began publication, in 1887, of North America's first psychology journal, the *American Journal of Psychology*. He stayed at Hopkins only a few years before becoming president of a new university in Worcester, Massachusetts, Clark University. He remained in that position for 31 years until his retirement in 1920. Hall established a second psychology laboratory at Clark in 1889 with Edmund Sanford as lab director; Sanford had earned his doctorate with Hall at Johns Hopkins (Goodwin, 2006).

Although Hall was more at home in the laboratory than was James, his research productivity was really quite modest. It was clear that he preferred a role that was more administrative and entrepreneurial. He was a forceful speaker who had the ability to inspire others to his causes, which is nowhere more evident than in the field of child study as the foundation for education and parenting (Brooks-Gunn & Johnson, 2006). His interest in education was long-standing and covered the years from kindergarten through doctoral education. An article that he published in 1882, entitled *The Contents of Children's Minds*, would take his psychological work in a different direction.

The Child Study Movement

The end of the nineteenth century was a time of rapid social change in America. Industrialization, growth of the cities, child labor laws, compulsory schooling laws, and thousands of new immigrants resulted in exploding school enrollments. There were national calls for school reforms that would educate the mixed citizenry for a productive life. There were renewed concerns about raising children of good moral character. Parents demanded information about teaching children and better parenting techniques. Organizations such as the National Education Association (NEA) were particularly involved in these issues. Hall's 1882 article on children's minds led him into this arena where he was asked to address these issues in national conferences. The duties of getting a new university underway delayed him for a while, but in 1891, he addressed the NEA at its annual meeting in Toronto on the need to study children scientifically. The *Child Study Movement* was born, and Hall was its appointed leader. Hall would make Clark University the national center for this work. He established a new journal – *Pedagogical Seminary* – in 1891, where much of the child study research would be published. He also established a clearinghouse at Clark that was to facilitate research on a national scale and to collect the data from those far-flung studies.

The broad goal of child study was to discover all that could be known about the child, such as sensory capabilities, physical characteristics, humor, play, memory, religious ideas, and attention span. With this new knowledge, education would be based on science. Hall reinforced this belief with an article he wrote for a national magazine in 1893 entitled *Child Study: The Basis of Exact Education.* He concluded that article "The one chief and immediate field of application for [psychology] is its application to education, considered as the science of human nature and the art of developing it to its fullest nature" (p. 441).

Hall's preferred method of study was the questionnaire, and he and his colleagues at Clark generated approximately 200 of them. Through state child study societies and other means, Hall enlisted the help of public school teachers, college educators, and parents. There was no theory that guided this research; whatever individuals wanted to study, they were encouraged to study, for example, ideas about Santa Claus, responses to tickling, understanding of clouds, and perception of rhythm. The belief was that if they collected enough data, it could be aggregated in some way that would meet the goals of the movement to improve education and parenting. Many psychologists were critical of the movement, such as William James and Hugo Münsterberg, who argued that the research was suspect and the goals too ambitious. Hall persisted in this work until about 1905 when his interests turned to other subjects. By 1910, the movement had essentially collapsed.

The child study movement was never successful in fulfilling its grandiose ambitions; psychologists searched for laws of human behavior, university administrators looked for better ways to train teachers, educators desired better measures of children's school performance, and parents needed information on child rearing. In the end, the data proved of little use in any kinds of reforms. Despite its failure on its own agenda, the movement had some positive outcomes. It spawned the fields of developmental and educational psychology and made evident the need for physical, behavioral, social, and intellectual norms for children. It led to a true science of the child and applications to education and parenting that were tied to that science. Perhaps of greatest importance, despite the lack of success, child study served notice that the new scientific psychology could be applied for the public good (Davidson & Benjamin, 1987).

Adolescence and Hall's Genetic Psychology

Hall's greatest contributions, as a psychologist, were in the fields of education and development. His magnum opus was surely his two-volume work, *Adolescence: Its Psychology and Its Relations to*

Physiology, Anthropology, Sociology, Crime, and Religion (1904), a book that is generally credited with establishing adolescence as a distinctive stage in human development and introducing the term into popular usage (Arnett & Cravens, 2006). The book reflected Hall's massive amounts of child study data, his devotion to the ideas of Darwin, and his fears of impressionable youth in a society that had lost its controls. It is interesting to read the preface of this book, written more than a century ago, and recognize how similar Hall's sentiments appear to statements one can readily hear today. Consider this passage lamenting the dangers facing adolescents:

> Never has youth been exposed to such dangers of both perversion and arrest as in our own land and day. Increasing urban life with its temptations, prematurities, sedentary occupations, and passive stimuli just when an active, objective life is most needed, early emancipation and a lessening sense of both duty and discipline, the haste to know and do all befitting man's estate before its time, the mad rush for sudden wealth and the reckless fashions set by its gilded youth – all these lack some of the regulatives they still have in older lands with more conservative traditions. (Hall, 1904, v.1, pp. xv-xvi)

Hall had hoped his book would become a handbook for educators and social workers everywhere, but the frank discussions of adolescent sexuality proved to be especially problematic. He published a less sexual version of the adolescence volumes in 1906 as *Youth: Its Education, Regimen, and Hygiene*, a book intended as a textbook for normal-college students (normal colleges existed principally to train teachers). In this book he defended his views on a number of controversial topics such as corporal punishment, tolerance for male misbehavior as natural and acceptable ("boys will be boys"), separate educational curricula for women, opposition to coeducational high schools, the "unfortunate" predominance of women as school teachers, the belief that education should be reserved for those who could intellectually profit from it, and a call for education to include moral and religious training.

Hall's *Adolescence* laid out his system of psychology, which is generally called *genetic psychology*, as noted earlier, heavily influenced by Darwin's ideas. In his descriptions of physical and psychological development from utero through adolescence, Hall described what he believed were the evolutionary benefits of those developments, for example, the development of "sexual organs make[s] procreation surer, less wasteful, and probably far more hedonic as we ascend the scale of being" (Hall, 1904, v. 1, p. 413). Hall adopted biologist Ernst Haeckel's *theory of recapitulation*, which stated that ontogeny recapitulates phylogeny. That is, the evolutionary developments in one's animal ancestry are repeated in the development of the individual from conception through adolescence. Hall believed that recapitulation was indicated in both physiology (for example, in fetal development) and in psychology.

The theory of recapitulation was in serious doubt in scientific circles at the time Hall wrote his adolescence book, and by 1915, the theory had been largely discredited. Hall's biographer, Dorothy Ross (1972), has argued that although Hall got the theory wrong, what he generated in terms of his evolutionary explanations for human development were quite sound.

Psychoanalysis, Religion, Aging

Not only was Hall unusual for his time in his frank treatment of sex in his books, he also was outspoken about sex, arguing in 1907 that sex education classes should be offered in the schools. Drawing on his interest in psychopathology from his postgraduate visits to mental asylums in Europe and from his interest in sex, Hall became fascinated by the ideas of an Austrian neurologist named Sigmund Freud (1856–1939), whose views complemented some of Hall's beliefs. When Clark University was celebrating its twentieth anniversary, Hall invited Freud to speak at Clark, promising him an honorary doctorate from the university. It was a controversial invitation, given Freud's writings about sex and the nonscientific nature of his theories, and some of Hall's psychology colleagues criticized him for it. What followed was the most famous psychology conference ever held in North America. Freud came, his only visit to America, and gave five lectures that were published later in Hall's journal. Because of that visit, psychoanalysis enjoyed enormous growth in America over the next decade, a subject to be discussed in Chapter 7.

We noted earlier that Hall started a journal on religious psychology. He also mentored several students (e.g., Edwin Starbuck, James Leuba) at Clark who received their doctoral degrees in the psychology of religion and are credited with starting the field of the scientific study of religion (Vande Kemp, 1992). Hall, like James, also published a book on the psychology of religion entitled *Jesus the Christ in the Light of Psychology* (1917), a two-volume work that sought to define Jesus Christ in psychological terms, or as Hall wrote, "What were the attributes of His personality generally … in what did Jesusissity consist?" (p. 3). It was, perhaps for good reason, Hall's least successful book. Finally, it should be noted that at the age of 78, Hall published what is usually regarded as the first book on the psychology of aging, entitled *Senescence* (1922), a book based on extensive questionnaire studies of older adults (Cole, 1984).

Figure 4.4 G. Stanley Hall (*left*) and James McKeen Cattell at age 32

Hall is best remembered today for his establishment of components essential to a new discipline (journal, national organization, doctoral programs), for his promotion of applied psychology, and for a number of his doctoral students who went on to stellar careers. He was the mentor of Francis Cecil Sumner, the first African American to get a PhD in psychology in 1920 (discussed in Chapter 11). Hall also played a role in training several psychologists, including Henry Herbert Goddard and Lewis Terman, who were key figures in the development of intelligence testing (discussed in Chapter 6). In generating students who founded the early psychology laboratories in America, Hall was second only to Wundt. Arguably, key among Hall's many contributions was the impetus he gave for the study of development, in childhood, adolescence, and old age, and the legacy of that work for modern lifespan developmental psychology (White, 1992).

James McKeen Cattell: Psychology's Ambassador

James McKeen Cattell (1860–1944) came from a reasonably prosperous family. His father was president of Lafayette College in Easton, Pennsylvania for 20 years; there was family wealth on his mother's side. Cattell graduated from Lafayette College at the age of 20. He began his graduate studies with Hall at Johns Hopkins, but left after a dispute with Hall. He traveled to Leipzig where he earned his doctorate with Wundt in 1886, completing his studies on the speed of mental processes. His real mentor, however, was Francis Galton, a polymath and first cousin of Darwin, who at the time of Cattell's visit to his lab in England in 1888, had developed anthropometric tests, that is, measures of human cognitive, sensory, and motor abilities. This work would make a profound impression on Cattell and guide his research for many years.

Cattell assumed a fulltime faculty position at the University of Pennsylvania in 1889 where he established a psychology laboratory. His laboratory at Penn extended his Leipzig research, and he added a mental testing program based on Galton's anthropometric tests but more focused on psychological measures.

Cattell's Mental Tests

Cattell described his testing program in an 1890 article in the journal *Mind*, entitled "Mental Tests and Measurements." It represented the coining of the term *mental test*. Cattell's 10-test battery included difference threshold for weights, a measure of the least amount of pressure that would cause pain, a test of two-point threshold, dynamometer pressure (strength of hand grip), reaction time for sound, speed of movement of the arm, time for naming colors, bisection of a 50 cm line, number of letters that could be recalled after hearing them once, and judgment of 10 seconds of time. Note that the first three were psychophysical measures. Five of the tests involved sensory measures, and those were included because of the influence of British empiricism. If all knowledge comes via the senses, then it was reasonable to assume that the most capable people would be those with the most acute senses. The others tests were measures that would today be called psychomotor or cognitive.

What was the purpose of these tests? Cattell (1893) wrote, "Tests of the senses and faculties concern the teacher ... such tests give a useful indication of the progress, condition, and aptitudes of the pupil" (p. 257). Moreover,

> In conjunction with the ordinary school examination such tests would show whether the course of study is improving or blunting the fundamental processes of perception and mental life. Tests made at the beginning and end of the day, week, and session would show whether the student is exhausted by the required curriculum. They could be used in comparing different systems of education, different schools ... They would show whether girls are able, without injury to health, to follow the same courses of study as boys. (p. 258)

Certainly, those were very substantial claims to make. In his article, Cattell (1893) not only claimed that the tests could identify the aptitudes of students but could identify those who were gifted and whose "valuable qualities may be early discovered and developed" (p. 258). In essence, Cattell claimed he had developed an intelligence test, although he did not use that label.

In 1894, Cattell convinced the administration at Columbia to allow him to test all of the incoming students, a procedure that he followed for nearly a decade. Cattell was not clear about what purpose the testing program would serve, but he argued for its exploratory nature with the hope that it would bear some kind of pedagogical fruit. Although Cattell was accumulating a great deal of data, he had no way to assess the validity of his tests. That situation would change, however, when his mentor, Galton, and Karl Pearson invented the correlation coefficient that allowed the measurement of the statistical relationship between two variables. Therefore, Cattell, with the aid of a graduate student, Clark Wissler (1901), used the correlation measure to test the relationship between Cattell's tests and grades students were earning in their Columbia classes. The results were zero correlation values! That is, there was no predictive relationship between how students would do on any of Cattell's mental tests and their performance in college courses. Historian Michael Sokal (1982) wrote, "Wissler's analysis struck most psychologists as definitive and, with it, anthropometric mental testing, as a movement, died. ... Cattell ... abandoned his career as an experimental psychologist ... " (p. 338).

Although anthropometric mental testing was largely dead, mental testing was not. Indeed, if any word characterized American psychology in the twentieth century it was *testing*. Intelligence tests of the Binet variety were in vogue by the 1910s. The chief product of psychologists' involvement in World War I was the development of the Army Alpha and Army Beta tests, in essence intended to be intelligence tests. Tests became commonplace in industry after that war, promoted by psychologists, especially in the area of employee selection. Mental testing virtually defined the activities of clinical psychologists in the first 50 years of their profession from assessments of intelligence to tests of personality to tests of psychoses and brain damage. Testing was important for many reasons; paramount among them the notion that it provided a way to verify individual differences, and that was an interest of Cattell's that resulted from his reading of Charles Darwin and his studies with Galton. American psychology was obsessed with the study of individual differences. Although Cattell was not the only early psychologist involved in mental testing, his program was a very visible one and there is no discounting its effect on a psychology that desperately wanted to be able to quantify mental traits (Sokal, 2006).

Cattell as Editor of Science

Cattell founded two psychology laboratories by 1891, one at the University of Pennsylvania and the other at Columbia University; founded (with James Mark Baldwin) one of psychology's most important journals, *Psychological Review*; coined the term "mental test"; founded the Psychological Corporation which would later become the major publisher of psychological tests; and founded and edited the *American Men of Science* volumes. In addition, he mentored a number of doctoral students who made important contributions to psychology, most notably, Edward L. Thorndike and Robert S. Woodworth (both of whom will be discussed in later chapters; Thorndike in Chapter 8 and Woodworth in Chapter 5). Yet arguably, Cattell's greatest contribution to psychology is not in that list.

In 1894, the journal *Science* was failing after being essentially abandoned by its former owners, Thomas Edison and Alexander Graham Bell. Backers of the journal were looking for someone who might revive it, and Cattell, at age 34, ended up as both owner and editor of the scientific weekly. He would continue in that post for an amazing 50 years until his death in 1944! For individuals who have done any journal editing, they know how time consuming such activities are, even for a journal that comes out four times a year. But *Science* appeared 52 times a year, and for 20 years of his editorship of that journal, Cattell also edited one other weekly (*School and Society*) and two monthly journals (*The Scientific Monthly* and *The American Naturalist*). Such is truly an amazing feat!

Within a year after taking over the journal, Cattell had made it viable. He used his broad connections in the scientific community and his entrepreneurial skills to enhance the currency of the content. In January 1896, he scored a journalistic coup with a lengthy article on Wilhelm Conrad Röentgen's discovery of x-rays. The subject was an exceptionally important one, certainly the hottest story in the scientific world. Other stories followed such that *Science* soon became the leading journal worldwide for news about x-rays (Sokal, 1980). Indeed, *Science* quickly became one of the two most important scientific publications in the world, where scientists, still today, vie to get their best work published (the rival journal is the British publication, *Nature*).

Cattell's editorship of *Science*, it can be argued, was a singularly important contribution to the science of psychology, because he welcomed publications from his colleagues in the field. As a result, psychology attained a visibility within the broader scientific community, and within the educated lay community that regularly read the journal, that would never have been obtained with an editor from another scientific field. Cattell gave psychology scientific visibility at a time when it was still struggling to establish itself in the community of sciences. It was a gift to the field that could not have come any other way.

Getting the Word out about a New Science

In Chapter 1, we described the two psychologies in place when the psychology laboratories began to be established in America in the 1880s and 1890s. To be established, to get customers, new businesses have to advertise. The new psychologists found themselves in that position. They were working in a scientific enterprise where few thought any kind of real science was possible, or where people equated psychological science with phrenology or mesmerism or some similar pseudoscience. Consequently, psychologists looked for ways to get their message out to the public.

One of the methods used was to write articles for the popular press – for newspapers and magazines – touting the new psychology. James, Hall, and Cattell all wrote such articles, as did their contemporaries, especially in popular magazines such as *Harpers* or *Atlantic Monthly*. Hall, for example, published the results of some of his child study investigations in popular magazines. Public addresses before civic groups and other organizations were a common activity. Cattell's exposure of psychology in the pages of *Science* was certainly helpful in educating the broad scientific public.

We mentioned Joseph Jastrow (1863–1944) at the beginning of this chapter as the organizer for the psychology exhibit at the Chicago World's Fair. Jastrow was greatly involved in promoting scientific psychology to the general public through a series of popular books and a newspaper column on psychology that was syndicated, appearing in more than 150 newspapers (Behrens, 2009). Jastrow had broached the idea for the exhibit at the Fair at a July 1892 organizational meeting for what would become the American Psychological Association. Hall had organized that meeting and it was held in his home. William James was not much in favor of the Chicago exhibit, but Hall was and he agreed to supply apparatus and photographs to be used at the Fair.

The final decade of the nineteenth century was one of considerable growth for psychology. In 1892, in addition to the founding of the American Psychological Association, there were some very significant figures arriving on the American scene. Edward Titchener, an Englishman, had just finished his doctorate with Wundt and arrived in the United States in 1892 to head the psychology laboratory at Cornell University. He would prove to be one of the major forces in American psychology over the next three decades. William James convinced another Wundt doctorate, Hugo Münsterberg, to leave Germany where he headed the lab at the University of Freiburg, to assume the same duties at Harvard. Münsterberg would also become one of the major figures in American psychology, playing a key role in the development of applied psychology, especially industrial and forensic psychologies. Edward Scripture, another Wundt student, arrived at Yale University to take charge of the laboratory there. Finally, Lightner Witmer restarted Cattell's psychology lab at Penn in 1892. He had been an undergraduate with Cattell at Penn and, at Cattell's suggestion, had gone to Wundt for his doctorate. Four years after returning to Penn, he started the first psychology clinic in America. It was a heady time for the science of psychology and for the application of psychology to real world problems in schools, clinics, and the workplace.

As the various labs took shape, the diversity that existed in German psychology began to be mirrored in America, partly because of differences in European training, but also because of differences in the personalities of the American psychologists, personalities that were shaped by American culture. American psychologists were about to take sides, defining themselves in schools of psychology, initially structuralism and functionalism. Those schools are the subject of the next chapter.

5

The Early Schools of American Psychology

We will start our story of the American schools of psychology in a house in a small village about 25 miles south of London, England. Down House was a frequent recipient of mail because the man who lived there carried on a voluminous correspondence with individuals all over the world. June 18, 1858 perhaps seemed like any other day. It was a Friday, and the postal carrier arrived with his deliveries including an envelope mailed several months earlier from the Malay Archipelago. The owner of Down House, Charles Darwin, opened the envelope, and what he read turned his world upside down. Darwin (1809–1882) had been working on the development of his theory of species change by natural selection for almost 20 years, a fact known only to a small circle of friends. He had yet to publish his ideas, perhaps because there were still some problematic issues that he wanted to work out. Now in his hands was a brief manuscript from a young naturalist, Alfred Russel Wallace (1823–1913), which described a theory almost identical to Darwin's. Darwin was concerned that the receipt of Wallace's manuscript would prevent him from publishing his own work. Friends encouraged him to let them read Wallace's paper and a paper from Darwin together at a scientific meeting. Historians today recognize both men as independently developing a theory of natural selection as the mechanism for species change, but Darwin has received the lion's share of credit for the theory, primarily because of his 1859 book, *On the Origin of Species*, which documented his decades of painstaking work to develop and support his theory. The book appeared in an initial printing of 1,250 copies, and every copy was sold on the first day. Copies of that edition sell today for approximately $225,000.

No scientific theory has had a greater impact on the broad community of sciences than Darwin's ideas about natural selection and sexual selection. Indeed one would be hard pressed to find a science that has not been affected in significant ways by Darwin's theory, including, as just a few examples, pharmacology, genetics, biochemistry, forensics,

From the author's collection

Figure 5.1   The backside of Darwin's home, Down House, showing part of the garden view Darwin would have had from his study

anatomy, botany, anthropology, and psychology. In contemporary science, evolution is regarded as fact. That evolution occurs is not debated; what is debated is the mechanism by which it occurs. In that debate, no theory has seriously challenged Darwin's theory of natural selection. Today his theory continues to have enormous explanatory power.

We have already seen in the previous chapter that Darwin influenced the beliefs of James, Hall, and Cattell, each of whom contributed to the formation of the school known as functionalism, one of the two schools that we will describe in this chapter (the other is structuralism). Darwin's influence initially came from the writings of American philosopher Chauncey Wright (1830–1875) who was among the earliest of American converts to Darwin's theory of species change by natural selection. Wright had a great influence on James who, in turn, influenced Hall, Jastrow, and others (Green, 2009).

The Early North American Psychology Laboratories

Experimental psychology in America spread quite rapidly after G. Stanley Hall established the first laboratory in 1883. Laboratories were an expensive investment because of the various pieces of apparatus needed for research and teaching [see Sturm & Ash (2005) for a discussion of the role of research instruments in psychology]. As mentioned earlier, there were more than 40 psychology labs in the United States and Canada by 1900, five of them established by women. Besides Hall's lab, there were six others established in the 1880s. The ones at Nebraska and Pennsylvania were established by Wundt's students, the ones at Clark, Indiana, and Wisconsin by Hall's students. In the 1890s, Hall's students established labs at Iowa, Texas, and Bryn Mawr. Wundt's students opened labs at Columbia, Catholic, Cornell, Harvard, Yale, Minnesota, Stanford, and California. There were other labs established by students of students, the academic grandchildren of Wundt and Hall.

One of the issues that was prominent at the beginning of experimental psychology is an issue that can be found in the histories of all sciences – the debate over "pure" science versus application. The notion of "pure" science is research that is done without regard to any practical benefits; it is the search for knowledge for knowledge's sake. The adjective "pure" is meant to signify the sanctity of the basic research enterprise. It is contrasted with applied research, which is seen by some as tainted because it is designed to have some practical application. This distinction describes a hierarchy that exists in all sciences in which the "pure" researchers are viewed as superior to the applied ones. The only thing worse than doing applied research is doing no research at all and working as a practitioner. Of course, not everyone holds these prejudices in science, but many do. This prejudice has been part of the fabric of American psychology since Hall opened his Hopkins laboratory. We will see the impact of this issue again in discussing professional psychology in subsequent chapters. It is raised here because it was one of the important issues in the structuralist–functionalist debates.

Wundt's psychology had nothing to do with application, whereas Hall's psychology actively promoted application, most evidently in the child study work. Americans were drawn to Leipzig, and later to American psychology programs, because of an enthusiasm for the prospects of a science of psychology. Cattell wrote that psychology would be *the* science of the twentieth century, the science in which the greatest progress was made. Other early American psychologists, such as Harry Kirke Wolfe and Lightner Witmer, made similar claims. In the beginning, Leipzig was the place to learn the methods of this new science. Not surprisingly though, Americans arrived with their own agenda for that science, one that often emphasized application. Wundt was aware of that fact, and no doubt a bit exasperated by it, describing the pragmatic and materialistic bent of the Americans as "ganz Amerikanisch" – typically American.

Table 5.1 The Founding of North American Psychology Laboratories: 1883–1900

Year	Laboratory	Founder
1883	Johns Hopkins University	G. Stanley Hall
1887	Indiana University	William Lowe Bryan*
1888	University of Wisconsin	Joseph Jastrow*
1889	Clark University	Edmund Clark Sanford*
1889	University of Kansas	Olin Templin
1889	University of Nebraska	Harry Kirke Wolfe**
1889	University of Pennsylvania	James McKeen Cattell**
1890	University of Iowa	George T. W. Patrick*
1890	University of Michigan	James Hayden Tufts
1891	Catholic University	Edward Aloyius Pace**
1891	Columbia University	James McKeen Cattell**
1891	Cornell University	Frank Angell**
1891	University of Toronto	James Mark Baldwin
1891	Wellesley College	Mary Whiton Calkins
1892	Brown University	Edmund Burke Delabarre
1892	Harvard University	Hugo Münsterberg**
1892	University of Illinois	William Otterbein Krohn
1892	Trenton State Normal College	Lillie A. Williams
1892	Yale University	Edward W. Scripture**
1893	Princeton University	James Mark Baldwin
1893	Randolph-Macon College	Celestia S. Parrish
1893	Stanford University	Frank Angell**
1893	University of Chicago	Charles Augustus Strong
1894	Amherst College	Charles Edward Garman
1894	Denison University	Clarence Luther Herrick
1894	Pennsylvania State University	Erwin W. Runkle
1894	University of the City of New York	Charles B. Bliss
1894	University of Minnesota	Harlow Stearns Gale
1894	Wesleyan University	Andrew C. Armstrong, Jr.
1894	Western Reserve University	Herbert Austin Aikins
1895	Smith College	William George Smith
1896	University of California	George M. Stratton**
1896	Wilson College	Anna Jane McKeag
1897	Ohio State University	Clark Wissler
1898	Bryn Mawr College	James Henry Leuba*
1898	University of Texas	Alexander Caswell Ellis*
1899	University of Oregon	Benjamin J. Hawthorne
1900	New York University	Charles Hubbard Judd**
1900	Northwestern University	Walter Dill Scott**
1900	University of Maine	M. C. Fernald
1900	University of Missouri	Max Frederick Meyer
1900	University of Wyoming	June Etta Downey

*Studied with G. Stanley Hall.
**Studied with Wilhelm Wundt.

In Leipzig, and in the laboratories that would follow, Americans learned research methods, and of greatest importance, a scientific attitude (O'Donnell, 1985). The methodological training taught the students how to answer the questions of the mind. They transposed those techniques to their own questions, both in and out of the laboratory. Wundt imbued his students with a scientific attitude that allowed them to frame questions in ways that created a science of mind where most skeptics had argued that such a science was not possible. That scientific attitude was spread widely in the psychology laboratories of America, and arguably, no one did it better than E. B. Titchener.

Structuralism

Edward Bradford Titchener (1867–1927) was barely 25 years old, fresh with his doctorate from Wundt, when he arrived at Cornell University in Ithaca, New York, to head the psychology laboratory there. Titchener was British, from Chichester, England, and earned a master's degree from Oxford University. He studied with John Burdon-Sanderson (1828–1905), a distinguished physiologist who had worked with Darwin on studies of insect-eating plants. He learned the rigors of experimental method from Burdon-Sanderson and experimental psychology from Wundt. Titchener had his own ideas about what a science of psychology should look like. He labeled it structural psychology or *structuralism* because its emphasis was on discovering the structure of consciousness. It would soon be contrasted with another brand of psychology, one that focused instead on the functions of consciousness. This school came to be known as functional psychology or *functionalism*. Indeed, Titchener gave both schools their names. In an article evaluating the two approaches to the science of psychology, Titchener (1898) left little doubt about which one he believed held the greater promise:

> ... I believe as firmly that the best hope for psychology lies to day in a continuance of structural analysis, and that the study of function will not yield final fruit until it can be controlled by the genetic and, still more, by the experimental method. ... (p. 465)

Titchener also was clear on which approach was the better science: "It cannot be said that this functional psychology ... has been worked out either with as much patient enthusiasm or with as much scientific accuracy as has the psychology of mind structure. ... the methods of [functional] psychology cannot ... lead to results of scientific finality." (p. 450)

When Titchener died of a brain tumor in 1927 at age 60, his structuralist school had been isolated for more than a decade, first in opposition to the functionalists who objected to his narrow agenda for psychology and then by the behaviorists who opposed his psychology as mentalism, as embodied in the words of behaviorist John Watson (1913): "The time seems to have come when psychology must discard all reference to consciousness; when it no longer delude itself into thinking that it is making mental states the object of observation" (p. 162). In 1892, when he arrived at Cornell, "making mental states the object of observation" was exactly what Titchener planned to do.

Titchener (1910a) began by distinguishing between *mind* and *consciousness*: "we shall speak of mind when we mean the sum-total of mental processes occurring in the life-time of an individual, and we shall speak of consciousness when we mean the sum-total of mental processes occurring *now*, at any given 'present' time" (p. 19). Like James, Titchener recognized the ever-changing nature of consciousness: "we can never observe the same consciousness twice over; the stream of mind flows on" (p. 19).

The object of study for Titchener was consciousness, and although one could not study the same conscious experience twice, it was possible by training observers, by keeping conditions as constant as possible, and by multiple replications of the observations, to have a science of psychology. The secrets of mind would be revealed through a laborious and systematic investigation of consciousness. That investigation would begin by discovering the elements of consciousness by reducing conscious experience to its atoms, to those components that are irreducible. Titchener (1910a) believed that the problem facing psychology was, in fact, the same problem that faced all sciences:

> Science seeks always to answer three questions in regard to its subject-matter, the questions of what, how, and why? What precisely, stripped of all complications and reduced to its lowest terms, is this subject matter? How then does it come to appear as it does; how are its elements combined and arranged? And, finally, why does it appear now in just this particular combination or arrangement? (p. 36)

Thus structuralism was about (a) identifying the *structure* of consciousness by first identifying its elements, then (b) by discovering how they became grouped and arranged, and then (c) to determine the causes of the particular arrangement of elements – Why this arrangement? Why now? Why not some other arrangement?

The first task, Titchener said, is analysis, whereas the second is synthesis. Those two activities produce a purely descriptive science. Science wants to know more than just description; science wants to be able to answer "why." Science wants to explain cause. Titchener did not believe that one mental process could be used to explain another, but that explanations for mental phenomena lay in the nervous system. Thus, the final task of a science of psychology was to make connections between the elements of consciousness and their underlying physiological conditions. This was structural psychology; this was scientific psychology according to Titchener. Functionalism, on the other hand, he argued, was not science, it was technology (Evans, 1985).

Introspection

Titchener summed up the scientific method in one word "observation." For Titchener, observation had two components: attention to the phenomenon and making a record of the phenomenon. The method for psychology he labeled *introspection*, a "looking within." In Titchener's lab, students and colleagues were trained in his method of introspection, his sole method for psychological investigations. Thus, "introspective psychology" became another name for structuralism.

Consider the following possible experiment in Titchener's lab. A trained introspector will be presented with words, one at a time. The words will be printed on a card that is handed to the introspector. The task is to observe the mental processes (consciousness) that are stimulated by that word presentation. Maybe the observer will recall another word in response to the stimulus word, or maybe the observer might have some kind of an emotional reaction to the word, for example, sadness or happiness or surprise. In Titchener's use of the method, the mental processes might be allowed to run their course and then the observer would respond, describing the mental events in as much detail as possible, or the observer might interrupt the mental processes at any point to give an introspective report. Titchener recognized that interruptions affected the remainder of the mental process, but felt that such breaks were important to get the most accurate introspections. Because the stimulus events could be repeated, it was possible to study later parts of the mental process in subsequent introspections. Titchener (1910a) was adamant about the training required to use the introspective method well and about the attention required during the task if the accounts were to be valid ones. He wrote:

> The attention must be held at the highest possible degree of concentration; the record must be photographically accurate. Observation is, therefore, both difficult and fatiguing ... To secure reliable results, we must be strictly impartial and unprejudiced, facing the facts as they come, ready

to accept them as they are, not trying to fit them to any preconceived theory; and we must work only when we are fresh and in good health, at ease in our surroundings, free from outside worry and anxiety. If these rules are not followed, no amount of experimenting will help us. ... But all this care is of no avail, unless the observer himself comes to the work in an even frame of mind, gives it his full attention, and is able adequately to translate his experience into words. (pp. 24–25)

One of the sources of controversy between Titchener's lab and other labs when differing conclusions were reached for the same phenomena was Titchener's claim that the other introspectors were not properly trained.

Titchener trained his introspectors to produce what he called the "introspective habit," arguing that it allowed his observers to function automatically in making their inner observations without unduly disturbing the ongoing mental processes. It also allowed observers to avoid what Titchener labeled the *stimulus error*, in which the observer would confuse what was being observed (for example, a book) with the basic elements of that stimulus (for example, color, texture, shape). So if you were trying to get a job in Titchener's lab and he laid a book in front of you and asked what you saw, answering "a book" would ensure that you would continue to draw unemployment. Avoiding the stimulus error was something trained introspectors did. Titchener recognized the subjectivity of consciousness, but he sought to ensure objectivity in his experimental psychology by use of well-trained introspectors in highly controlled laboratory experiments (Green, 2010).

Studies of Sensation: Psychology's Periodic Table

Titchener's elements of consciousness were three: sensations, images, and feelings. Although Titchener investigated all three, his focus was on sensations. Sensations were said to have four attributes: *quality* (cold, red, loud, salty), *intensity* (brighter or dimmer, louder or softer), *clearness* (distinct vs. indistinct, dominant vs. subordinate), and *duration* (time course of the sensation). Some sensations could have additional attributes, for example, extent in a touch sensation referring to the amount of skin area experiencing the touch. Yet most investigations of sensations focused on the primary four attributes. Indeed, those same four attributes existed for images, but feelings could only be described in terms of three: quality, intensity, and duration.

To some extent, the attribute of quality was the most interesting, as it was "the attribute which distinguishes every elementary process from

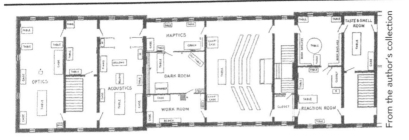

Figure 5.2 The floor plan of Titchener's psychology laboratory at Cornell University, evidencing his emphasis on the study of sensations

every other … it gives a sensation its special and distinctive name" (Titchener, 1910a, p. 53). Titchener sought to develop psychology's own periodic table. In the way that chemists were identifying the basic elements of the physical world, he wanted to do the same for the psychological world. It isn't likely that Titchener's chart could have fit on the wall. By 1896 he had identified 32,820 distinctive visual sensations and 11,600 separate auditory sensations – more than 44,000 separate, distinctive sensory experiences for vision and audition alone! While he was accumulating this exhaustive listing of distinctive sensations, psychologists in the other camp wondered for what reason. What would such an elemental analysis eventually be able to say about the workings of the mind? The criticisms did not dissuade Titchener from his goals, and he pursued his elemental analysis, convinced that is was the one way to gain a scientific understanding of consciousness.

The Laboratory Manuals

Between 1901 and 1905, Titchener published four volumes entitled *Experimental Psychology: A Manual of Laboratory Practice*. These books were often referred to as *The Manuals*, and some historians have identified them as his greatest contribution to American psychology. They grew out of Titchener's desire to develop a set of instructional aids that would teach students the methods of psychological science. Two of the volumes were labeled qualitative experiments and two were labeled quantitative experiments. In each pair, one volume was intended for the student and one for the instructor. The instructors' volumes were written because Titchener realized that many instructors who were teaching the basic laboratory course in psychology had little laboratory experience themselves.

Almost from the day a psychology laboratory was begun in a college, a course was added to the curriculum that taught psychology laboratory methods. On most campuses, this evolved into a two-semester course, usually reserved for graduate students, but eventually offered to undergraduate students as well. It was not a course for original research; rather it was an opportunity for students to repeat a number of the classic experiments in psychology (often called drill exercises), such as measuring the cold and warmth spots on the skin or determining the absolute threshold for a tone. In these laboratory exercises, students were encouraged to work in pairs as observer and experimenter and then reversing their roles. The observer would make the introspections, and the experimenter would manipulate the instruments and keep a record of the observer's reports (Titchener, 1901). The qualitative experiments "were essentially descriptions of conscious experiences by means of introspection, in which questions of 'what' or 'how' are asked. Quantitative experiments assumed that the mental process as such were already familiar from prior examination, and the task was to gather a long series of rather simple observations, which were then expressed through mathematical shorthand in which questions of 'how much' were asked" (Watson & Evans, 1991, p. 395). These *Manuals* dominated laboratory instruction across colleges for 30 years, and they were popular with instructors, even when the instructor would not have identified with Titchener's narrow brand of psychology. We will say more about the legacy of Titchener's psychology at the close of this chapter.

The Experimentalists

Titchener was one of the 31 charter members of the American Psychological Association, arriving in America shortly after the July 1892 organizational meeting in Hall's study. He soon lost interest in the APA as a scientific organization because its membership was open to nonscientists (for example, philosophers) and its annual programs contained presentations that clearly were not scientific. In 1904, he established his own organization, although never an entirely formal one. In fact, it didn't have an agreed-upon name. It was variously called "The Experimentalists or Titchener's Experimentalists." It met once a year in the spring at one of the psychology laboratories in the Northeast. Attendance was by invitation only, and only men were permitted. Titchener wanted it that way because he felt the presence of women would harm the kind of frank discussion that he wanted to have among "laboratory men." Christine Ladd Franklin, who had an excellent record as an experimental psychologist (recall that she studied with Georg Müller at Göttingen), with many published articles in vision, asked Titchener on several occasions to be invited but was always turned down. After Titchener's death, the organization became more formal, changed its name to the Society of Experimental Psychologists (SEP), and they agreed to invite women, although their numbers have never been very large. This kind of "collegial exclusion" was one more example of the barriers that hindered women in their advancement in psychological science (Goodwin, 1985; Furumoto, 1988; Scarborough & Furumoto, 1987). The SEP continues today as an organization of about 200 distinguished scientific psychologists.

Titchener's First Doctoral Student: Margaret Floy Washburn

From the previous section, it would seem easy to label Titchener a misogynist. He is said to have later regretted his decision to exclude women from his experimentalists meetings. Yet Titchener was a strong supporter of women and trained more women psychologists than any psychologist of his generation. Of his more than 50 doctoral students, almost half of them were women (Watson & Evans, 1991).

In the previous chapter, we described some of the struggles of Mary Whiton Calkins to pursue advanced study in psychology. At about the same time, Margaret Floy Washburn (1871–1939) decided to study psychology as well. She began work with Cattell at Columbia but, like Calkins at Harvard, could only audit his courses. Cattell encouraged her to apply to Cornell, which accepted women students, and so in 1892 she found herself in Ithaca with the newly arrived Titchener. She graduated in 1894 as Titchener's first doctoral student and the first American woman to receive a PhD in psychology. Titchener was so pleased with Washburn's thesis that he sent it to Wundt who published it in his journal, a rare honor for students outside of his laboratory. That contact apparently led to Washburn's invitation to be the translator for the second volume of Wundt's *Ethics* (Scarborough & Furumoto, 1987).

Washburn eventually accepted a faculty position at Vassar College in 1903, a women's college in New York where she had been an undergraduate. She remained at Vassar until her retirement. Washburn established an active program in experimental psychology, publishing scores of articles with her undergraduate students (Viney & Burlingame-Lee, 2003). Her position at Vassar and Calkins' position at Wellesley were typical for women PhDs of that time. Most universities would not hire women

From the Collection of Rand B. Evans

Archives of the History of American Psychology,
The Center for the History of Psychology,
The University of Akron

Figure 5.3   E. B. Titchener and Margaret Floy Washburn

as faculty members, and so their opportunities were usually limited to women's colleges. Because of that, many women doctorates in psychology in the early years of the discipline found employment outside of universities in jobs that were typically applied. We will discuss this issue further in Chapters 6 and 9 treating applied psychology.

Washburn is best known for her book *The Animal Mind,* a treatise on animal cognition first published in 1908. It is an odd subject, coming from a Titchener student, because Titchener did not value animal work (although he had done such work as a graduate student at Oxford). But Washburn clearly did. This book went through four editions, the last one in 1936. It was the last of the comparative psychology textbooks that included data using the controversial method of *introspection by analogy,* a method developed by the English naturalist George John Romanes (1848–1894), in which human observers of animal behavior inferred the actions and motives of those animals by analogy to an awareness of their own mental processes. With the advent of American behaviorism in the 1920s, this technique fell into disfavor. Still, Washburn's book was the standard textbook in her day in comparative psychology courses (Dewsbury, 1992).

Washburn was elected president of the American Psychological Association in 1921, the second woman to hold that office (recall that Calkins had been the first in 1905). The next woman president of APA would not be elected until more than 50 years later, Anne Anastasi in 1972.

Functionalism

Functionalism has been called the first uniquely American school of psychology, even though it was heavily influenced by the ideas of Darwin and Galton. That statement would mean that Titchener's structuralism was an imported psychology, even though it was carried out fully in the United States. Some books still portray Titchener's psychology as an extension of German psychology, especially the psychology of Wundt. However, that is a mistake. As you have seen, Titchener's reductionistic approach embodied only a small piece of Wundt's research agenda, and a relatively minor one at that. His psychology is better viewed as a British import, an outgrowth of the mental chemistry of John Stuart Mill and others from his Oxford education. Whether functionalism was uniquely American does not matter. What is important is that it offered a competing view of psychology that was broader conceptually and methodologically and thus took American psychology in several different directions that would shape the field in important ways for both the science and the profession.

Functionalism was never the coherent school that structuralism was. It never had a sole leader, its definition of psychology was broad, its methods were diverse, and its subject matter covered everything from animal behavior to clinical psychology, from advertising to the psychology of law, from learning to intelligence testing. Functionalism, or more accurately, several functionalisms, characterized much of American psychology in the early part of the twentieth century. Although it lacked the focus of structuralism, its impact was much greater.

British Influences

Functionalist psychologists sought to understand the utility of consciousness. What was it for? What exactly did it do? They were also intrigued by the question: how did it come to be? A foundation for these questions and their answers originated in the work of Charles Darwin, as we have written earlier. The theory of evolution was not original with Darwin. There were already existing theories on the evolution of the earth and evolution of plant and animal species. What was unique about Darwin was that he offered a very plausible and very well-supported theory of how evolution worked – *natural selection*. Darwin recognized that animals and plants always competed for limited resources, competition that threatened their survival. Conditions could change at any moment due to climate changes, introduction of a predator or another competitor, disease, and so forth. In these changing times, certain species might die out. Those species or those members of a species, which would survive these changes, would be those with adaptations that were well suited to the changes. Genetics was not known in Darwin's time, so he could not have known about that as a mechanism for variation. He understood that variations occurred, that some of them were beneficial for the organism, in terms of survival, and some were not. Variation meant that some species or members of species would be "selected" by nature as being better suited for new environmental conditions. The critical importance of variation in Darwin's theory led to a rising scientific interest in measuring individual differences – physical differences, and, as psychologists became interested in natural selection, mental differences as well. Functional psychology would be built on a study of individual differences and their role in adaptation. Functionalism was about understanding how consciousness enabled the organism to interact with and adapt to its environment. Thus Darwin's ideas are the very basis for both the scientific and applied work of the functionalists (see Browne, 1995, 2002 for her superlative treatment of the life and work of Darwin).

Recall that William James, G. Stanley Hall, and James McKeen Cattell were all significantly influenced by Darwin's ideas, and each of them incorporated evolutionary ideas into their psychologies. These individuals are all antecedents to the birth of functional psychology in America, a school that developed, in part, in opposition to structuralism. Functionalism was evident in Cattell's mental testing program and its search for individual differences. It was also manifested in Hall's recapitulation theory and in much of his writings. We will say more about some of the several functional psychologies in the next chapter, treating specifically the applied psychologies that grew out of the movement. In this chapter, we will describe American functionalism as it existed around the turn of the twentieth century at the University of Chicago under James Angell and at Columbia University under Robert Woodworth.

Chicago: Angell's Functional Psychology

James Rowland Angell (1869–1949) studied with both William James and John Dewey (1859–1952). Dewey is often viewed as a functional psychologist. Indeed, his 1896 article on the *reflex arc* is typically seen as the official starting point of the functional view in psychology. In that article, he took issue with the reductionistic analysis of the reflex arc into component parts of sensation, thinking, and motor action. Instead he argued that the reflex should be viewed as a whole, as a circuit, not an arc, noting that the three-component sequence did not typically occur in that order but evolved into what today would be called multiple instances of top-down and bottom-up processing, drawing on experience as well as the stimulus events of the moment. Reflexes were seen thus as integrated actions that served an adaptive function.

Dewey brought Angell to the philosophy faculty at the University of Chicago in 1894, placing Angell in charge of the psychology laboratory. When Dewey left for Columbia University, Angell became head of the department. In his tenure at Chicago, he supervised approximately 50 doctorates in psychology, one of whom was John Watson, the founder of behaviorism (Dewsbury, 2003).

Angell became the chief spokesperson for the functional view in psychology. In 1906, he was elected president of the American Psychological Association, and he used the occasion of his presidential address to attack structuralism and to describe the tenets of a functional psychology. Angell (1906) began that address: "Functional psychology is at the present moment little more than a point of view, a program, an ambition. It gains its vitality primarily perhaps as a protest against the exclusive excellence of another starting point for the study of the mind ... " (p. 61). The other "starting point" that claimed "exclusive excellence" was, of course, structuralism.

Angell (1906) identified three conceptions that described functionalism: (a) functionalism studies *mental operations* not mental elements, (b) functionalism seeks to identify the *fundamental utilities of consciousness*, that is, the ways in which consciousness helps the organism adapt to the environment, and (c) functionalism is a *psychophysical psychology*, acknowledging the significance of the mind-body relationship. The first of these conceptions identifies the essential structure–function difference. Both schools made consciousness their object of study. The structuralists, however, were interested in knowing the fundamental elements of consciousness, whereas the functionalists wanted to discover how and why consciousness works, to identify the mental processes by which it operates. In the second conception, functional psychologists want to identify the adaptive role of consciousness. Adaptation implies the organism's ability to change, and that is accomplished by learning. In the third, there is recognition of the relationship between mental and physical processes, that they are the same, again, in the service of adaptation.

From the author's collection

Archives of the History of American Psychology,
The Center for the History of Psychology,
The University of Akron

Figure 5.4   Functional psychologists James R. Angell (*left*) from a painting made when he was president of Yale University and Robert S. Woodworth

In closing his address, Angell spoke to the issue of "certainty" that seemed to characterize Titchener's views, the belief by Titchener that his goal for psychology was the one true way. Angell (1906) said:

> [Functionalism] seems at present a convenient term, but there is nothing sacrosanct about it, and the moment it takes unto itself the pretense of scientific finality its doom will be sealed. It means to-day a broad and flexible and organic point of view in psychology. The moment it becomes dogmatic and narrow its spirit will have passed and undoubtedly some worthier successor will fill its place. (p. 91)

Columbia: Woodworth's Dynamic Psychology

Robert Sessions Woodworth (1869–1962) received his PhD in psychology with Cattell at Columbia in 1899 and soon joined the faculty there. He remained in that department for the rest of his career, teaching part time into his eighties and writing into his nineties. Woodworth never labeled himself a functionalist in the way that Angell did. Still, we have placed him in this chapter because his psychology is regarded as fitting most closely with functional psychology. Woodworth's psychology showed an eclecticism, both in the topics he studied as well as his willingness to incorporate different theoretical viewpoints. He avoided what he considered the extreme positions in psychology, first, structuralism with its narrow definition of psychology and its insistence on introspection as the only valid method, and then behaviorism, with its insistence that mental states could not be studied because they could not be directly observed. He considered his approach a middle-of-the-road psychology.

In his 1918 book, *Dynamic Psychology*, Woodworth took issue with both structuralism and behaviorism. He argued that psychology did not proceed from a definition nor from a method, but from the questions that it sought to answer. The problem for psychology, he said, was to "understand the workings of the mind ... to be informed how we learn and think, and what leads people to feel and act as they do ... [psychologists are] interested, namely, in cause and effect, or what may be called dynamics" (Woodworth, 1918, p. 34). It was the last part of that statement that interested Woodworth the most – "what leads people to feel and act as they do." In a word, he was interested in motivation, a key part of human action that was clearly not directly observable. He wrote:

> Once the point of view of a dynamic psychology is gained, two general problems come into sight, which may be named the problem of 'mechanism' and the problem of 'drive.' One is the problem of how we do a thing, and the other is the problem of what induces us to do it. (p. 36)

These are the questions of "how" and "why" that dominated a functional approach.

By the time that Woodworth wrote his 1918 book, there were psychologists (in the behaviorist camp) who called for a strict S-R psychology that focused on observable stimuli and the subsequent observable responses, trying to draw cause-and-effect relationships between them. Yet, Woodworth argued that such an analysis was not valid if it left out the mental and biological states that intervened between stimulus and response. Instead of an S-R psychology, he proposed an *S-O-R psychology* in which the O stood for *organismic variables*. These variables were part of the organism – the person – and unique to that person. Organismic variables are the emotions, motives, personality traits, prejudices, ambitions, attitudes, that is, all of those personal variables that not only affect which stimuli are selected from what James called that "teeming multiplicity of objects and relations" but determine what responses will occur. Of these variables, Woodworth was most interested in motives, as evidenced in the earlier quotation – "the problem of drive." Woodworth popularized the concept of *drive* in psychology, particularly tied to biological states. Some historians have written that he introduced the term drive into psychology, but that distinction goes to John Watson and John J. B. Morgan who wrote about it in a 1917 article, predating Woodworth's usage.

In his 1918 book, Woodworth concluded that "A dynamic psychology must utilize the observations of consciousness and behavior as indications of the 'workings of the mind' ... " (p. 43). That eclectic viewpoint changed very little in his long career in psychology. When he revised his 1918 book in 1958, he was forced to abandon his title *Dynamic Psychology*, because that phrase had become associated with unconscious motivation through the influence of psychoanalysis. So the new book was entitled *Dynamics of Behavior*. The title did not mean that Woodworth had joined the behaviorist camp, but that most of the research literature cited in the book came from behavioral observations as opposed to introspective accounts. This book continued to reflect Woodworth's interest in motivation but also gave much prominence to learning and perception, processes that are greatly tied to motivation.

Woodworth's Textbooks

Woodworth published an introductory textbook in 1921 entitled *Psychology: A Study of Mental Life*, a very successful book that continued through five editions. In the 1920s and 1930s, it was the book psychology students were most likely to encounter first. It was in the third edition of this book that Woodworth introduced terminology that is familiar to any psychology student today. He described the psychology experiment in terms of *independent* and *dependent variables*. The independent variables, which are under the control of the experimenter, were viewed as the potential cause of the behavior as measured by changes in the dependent variables. Woodworth did not invent the terms nor was he the first in psychology to use them. He popularized them and provided the definition of what constitutes an *experiment*, as the ability to manipulate one or more independent variables while holding all other variables constant and measuring the effect of the manipulation on the dependent variable(s). For Woodworth the experiment was the one way to investigate cause-and-effect relationships (Winston, 2006).

Woodworth produced another textbook that would be his most influential work. Historian of psychology Andrew Winston (2006) has called it "the book that most clearly influenced generations of new psychologists" (p. 59). The book circulated for years in mimeographed form among the Columbia graduate psychology students where it was referred to as "the bible" (Winston, 1990). Eventually Woodworth published it in 1938 as *Experimental Psychology*. In this book he clearly laid out the domain of experimental psychology, excluding, for example, work on mental testing because it did not involve experiments. He made clear the distinction between experiments and correlational studies, noting again that only the former allowed one to make cause-and-effect judgments. This book gave rise to a phrase that all psychology majors know by heart: "correlation does not indicate causation." For more than 20 years, this book was the standard text for experimental psychology courses (Winston, 2006).

The Psychological Work of the Functionalists

There is not much coherent in a description of functional psychology outside of the three conceptions expressed by Angell that were described earlier. Functionalists were diverse in the methods they used and in the subjects they studied. They used introspection, but not typically in the way Titchener did. Instead, their method more closely resembled the experimental self-observation of Wundt. They used questionnaires, made prominent by Hall and others involved in the child study movement. They used mental testing methods pioneered by Cattell, and altered when intelligence testing changed by introduction of the Binet intelligence tests in America by Henry Herbert Goddard, a student of Hall's. They used such tests to measure personality; in fact, in 1919, Robert Woodworth published what may have been the first paper-and-pencil test to measure personality. They used the psychophysical methods that had been instrumental in Fechner's studies. They used animal subjects in studies in order to generalize from those studies to human behavior, in a field that came to be called comparative psychology, a field that was possible only because Darwin's work linked humans with the rest of the animal kingdom and demonstrated a continuity of mental processes (Darwin, 1872). They performed physiological studies, looking at biological processes underlying behavior. In addition, they performed experiments in which they manipulated independent variables and measured their effect on dependent variables.

The functionalists studied sensation and perception, child development, intelligence, sex differences, motivation, abnormal behavior, animal behavior, personality, and other topics as well. Whereas the research focus for the structuralists was on sensation and perception, the functionalists devoted much of their energies to the study of *learning*. The reason for that was quite clear. If consciousness aided adaptation, then that adaptation would occur through learning.

The functionalists spread their psychology far beyond the laboratory. They studied children in schools. They began applying their psychology to business with studies of advertising and personnel selection. They developed an industry of mental testing that involved both researchers and practitioners. They began a forensic psychology that examined a number of relationships between psychology and the law. They were interested in clinical psychology and aided the development of that area in both research and practice. Indeed, applied psychology, which was so adamantly opposed by Titchener (see Evans, 1991; Titchener, 1910b, 1914), was a product of American functionalism.

The Legacies of Structuralism and Functionalism

When Titchener died in 1927, his system of psychology died with him. Although he had produced more than 50 doctoral students, they were not especially loyal to his narrow vision of psychology. They were exceptionally well trained in the laboratory and committed to that as the foundation of good science in psychology. Like so many of Wundt's students, they learned the scientific attitude and the techniques but applied them to agendas of their own choosing. In the last years of his life, Titchener was working on a revision of his system. He was moving away from his focus on elements and, instead, placing greater emphasis on his attribute dimensions, for example, quality, intensity, duration, and clarity (Evans, 1972). A portion of this new system, albeit incomplete, was published after Titchener's death as *Systematic Psychology: Prolegomena* (1929).

Among descriptions that Titchener's contemporaries would have given him, even those who were opponents of his system, would be the phrase "man of science." Probably no other American psychologist during his time was as closely identified with laboratory psychology. He embodied scientific psychology, both in his everyday behavior and in his writings. Nowhere is that more apparent than in the *Manuals*. His insistence on the priority of laboratory studies has remained a part of contemporary psychology. Methods courses, similar to those for which the *Manuals* were written, remain commonplace in both graduate and undergraduate psychology curricula today. Titchener worked diligently, arguably more so than any psychologist of his generation, to establish psychology as a science. Evans (1991) has argued that Titchener did not oppose applications per se, rather he objected to application being mixed with science. For Titchener, educational psychology belonged to the educators, legal psychology to the lawyers, and medical psychology to the physicians. Keeping the science of psychology pure was, for Titchener, the only way that the science would progress.

We have emphasized the influence of Darwin's ideas on functional psychology. Historian of psychology Christopher Green, however, would characterize the relationship in much stronger terms. He has written that "Darwin's theory of evolution by natural selection was not merely an influence on the development of American functionalism … [it] was the very foundation of functionalism" (2009, p. 81). According to Green, the functionalists chose to emphasize evolutionary theory in their psychology as a way to appeal to American pragmatism and "to facilitate the application of psychology to domains outside of the psychological laboratory" (2009, p. 75).

Functional psychology, like structural psychology, would disappear as psychology evolved. In the case of the functionalists, however, much of what they espoused was usurped in modern psychology, although perhaps, in some cases, under different labels. Their emphasis on the study of *learning* would dominate American experimental psychology through the eras of behaviorism and neobehaviorism well into the 1970s. Similarly, the animal research model that they pioneered would also define the prototypical psychologist (white lab coat, white rat) for decades, well into the 1960s. The functionalists were responsible for the growth of applied psychology, which so dismayed Titchener. They pioneered work in so many areas such as child psychology; abnormal psychology; mental testing, including intelligence and personality testing; clinical psychology; industrial and organizational psychology; and other fields as well. Their pragmatic spirit – an influence of James and Dewey – was what led to their work on application, as Green has noted. The modern profession of psychology no doubt owes much to the vision of the functionalists. Several of the applied areas that they pioneered are the basis for the next chapter.

6

The Birth of the New Applied Psychology in America

In the early evening of October 20, 1909, agents of the U.S. government lay in wait in Tennessee, just across the border from Georgia. They were waiting for a truck coming from Atlanta, Georgia, that they had been instructed to seize. The truck was carrying a cargo that would result in a lawsuit from the federal government against the company. The company was Coca-Cola, and the truck carried a shipment of 40 barrels and 20 kegs of Coca-Cola syrup from the plant in Atlanta intended for the bottling plant in Chattanooga. The Coca-Cola Company was being sued for marketing a beverage containing a "deleterious ingredient," namely caffeine. The suit was initiated under the authority of the Pure Food and Drug Act, which had become law in 1906.

As the Coca-Cola Company prepared for a trial set to begin in April 1911, they realized that almost all of the extant research on caffeine was with animals other than humans. They needed some human data, and they needed it quickly. They searched for a psychologist to do the work. Cattell turned them down, but one of his recent doctoral students agreed to do it. Harry Hollingworth (1880–1956) had finished his PhD in 1909. He was an instructor at Barnard College in New York City, recently married, and in need of money. In 40 days, he conducted three major experiments for the Coca-Cola Company that showed few, if any, harmful effects from caffeine for humans, even in doses much greater than would have been consumed by drinking many bottles of Coca-Cola daily. The federal government lost that trial, but won eventually at the Supreme Court. By that time, Coca-Cola had voluntarily reduced the caffeine content in its beverage. We will say more about Hollingworth later in this chapter. His caffeine research is significant for several reasons. First, it was excellent science in terms of methodology, perhaps no surprise because he studied with Woodworth as well as Cattell. Second, it was one of the earliest studies of psychopharmacology in humans. Third, it was perhaps the first research undertaken by a psychologist for a major corporation. And

Figure 6.1   An advertisement for Coca-Cola circa 1910. Although this one does not, some of the ads at the turn of the century emphasized the stimulant properties of the beverage noting, for example, that Coca-Cola "relieves mental and physical exhaustion." It was these claims that the U.S. government found particularly objectionable

fourth, it was one of the earliest examples of a psychologist testifying as an expert scientific witness in a trial, a field that would be labeled as forensic psychology today (Benjamin, Rogers, & Rosenbaum, 1991).

You will recall from Chapter 1, there has always been an applied psychology. But at the close of the nineteenth century, there was a new science of psychology and some psychologists wondered – Will it prove useful outside of the laboratory? It didn't take long before there were psychologists attempting to answer that question. One who wasn't involved was, of course, E. B. Titchener. Addressing the Clark University conference in 1909, Titchener (1910b) told his audience that he stood for pure science without regard to utility. His talk reflected on the past decade of psychology in America, a decade that was very disturbing to Titchener, a decade in which he lamented that psychology was too heavily involved in projects of application. He wrote, "the diversion into practical channels of energy which would otherwise have been expended in the service of the laboratory must be regarded as a definite loss to pure science" (p. 407). Practical diversions, however, were a way of life in 1890s America that was being reshaped by automobiles, motion pictures, dial telephones, portable typewriters, color photographs, and zippers.

Histories of American psychology written a few decades ago indicated that applied psychology in America emerged after the First World War. That simply isn't true, and recent historical research has corrected this erroneous view. Earlier we described G. Stanley Hall's work in leading a national Child Study Movement. Hall had argued that if scientific psychology was applicable to any field, it was certainly applicable to education. That movement can be dated either from Hall's NEA address in 1891 or from the article he wrote in 1883 on the contents of children's minds. The year doesn't really matter; the point is that by 1891 psychological scientists had decided that they had a product to sell to the public. Their claim was that the product – psychological science – offered benefits to that public. Ventures by psychologists into other applied areas would follow quickly – clinical psychology and school psychology, business psychology, vocational guidance, intelligence testing, and forensic psychology. Thus, the science of psychology and the practice of psychology (presumably based on that science) proceeded hand in hand into the twentieth century.

The Beginnings of Clinical Psychology

Questions of abnormality were not uppermost in the minds of the early experimental psychologists. They were interested in understanding the mind, not a "diseased" version of it. Someone with a mental disorder would not have been, of course, able to introspect. Besides, psychological abnormality was already the domain of two medical specialties: psychiatry and neurology. Indeed, the profession of psychiatry emerged in North America as part of the mental asylum movement – the American Psychiatric Association is the former Association of Medical Superintendents of American Institutions for the Insane.

As cities grew and families were packed into more densely populated areas, home care of mentally disturbed family members became more of a problem, especially as people in the community felt threatened by these individuals. The first North American "lunatic asylums" appeared in the United States in the late 1700s in New York, Virginia, and Pennsylvania. Canada, which was more agrarian, had its first asylum in Quebec in 1845 and its first provincial asylum in Toronto in 1850. The mental asylums emerged to deal with psychological cases and to offer the hope of cure of mental illness through a program of *moral therapy* – a program of occupational therapy, exercise, religious training, recreation, personal hygiene, and participation in activities such as gardening, painting, music, or carpentry. Such a program likely provided some help as long as patient populations remained small. However, chronic cases soon became the norm and insane asylums (later called state and provincial hospitals) grew from the recommended patient population of 250 to, in some cases, more than 6,000 patients, becoming warehouses of hopeless humanity. This fascinating

From the author's collection

Figure 6.2 Postcard from 1910 of the "Watertown Insane Asylum" in East Moline, Illinois. It opened in 1898 with 336 patients. By 1935, it consisted of 43 separate buildings and housed more than 2,000 patients. It was closed by the state in 1980

and tragic story is told in several excellent histories (see Dowbiggin, 1997; Grob, 1994). What is important to understand for this chapter is that when psychologists began to show an interest in insanity, it had already been the domain of psychiatry for one hundred years. This issue of priority and ownership would prove especially problematic in the twentieth century as the profession of clinical psychology evolved. There were a few psychologists who did research in mental hospitals in the late nineteenth century, for example, Boris Sidis, a student of William James, who established a research laboratory in the New York Pathological Institute and William Krohn who set up a research lab at the Eastern Hospital for the Insane in Kankakee, Illinois, but they were an anomaly for their time (Popplestone & McPherson, 1984).

Lightner Witmer's Psychological Clinic

In March of 1896, a schoolteacher visited Lightner Witmer (1867–1956) at the University of Pennsylvania, bringing with her a boy of 14 who had difficulty spelling. (Witmer had reopened the psychology laboratory at Penn after returning from Leipzig with his doctorate in 1892.) The teacher had been a student in one of Witmer's classes. She had decided that the boy's problem was a mental one and, if so, then because psychology purported to be the science of the mind, she reasoned that psychology ought to be able to help him. Here is how Witmer described this case:

> At that time I could not find that the science of psychology had ever addressed itself to the ascertainment of the causes and treatment of a deficiency in spelling. Yet here was a simple developmental defect of memory; and memory is a mental process of which the science of psychology is supposed to furnish the only authoritative knowledge. It appeared to me that if psychology was worth anything to me or to others it should be able to assist the efforts of a teacher in a retarded case of this kind. (Witmer, 1907, p. 4)

Witmer evidently treated the case successfully, leading to additional cases being brought to him as word of his successes spread in the educational community. Those instances led Witmer in 1896 to found what was perhaps the first *psychological clinic* in the world. Witmer was so enthused by the successes in his clinic that he discussed his therapeutic program at the annual meeting of the American Psychological Association that year. He urged his colleagues to use psychology "to throw light upon the problems that confront humanity" (Witmer, 1897, p. 116). He hoped that his field would establish training programs that would develop a "psychological expert who is capable of treating the many difficult cases that resist the ordinary methods of the school room" (p. 117).

For the first few years of the clinic, Witmer saw all of the cases himself. They were mostly children, brought to the clinic because of learning disabilities or behavioral disorders. As the case demand grew, Witmer hired additional staff, including some of his own doctoral students in psychology. He decided that the case records might be useful to others who would be interested in opening a similar clinic or just those who wanted evidence of psychology's utility in the domain of human psychological difficulties. Therefore, in 1907, after more than a decade of treating patients in his clinic, he founded a new journal entitled *The Psychological Clinic*. The journal consisted largely of Penn's case studies, detailing the diagnoses made and the treatments rendered. In the first issue of the journal, Witmer described a program of education and training to prepare psychologists to do clinical work and he named the field "clinical psychology." This marked the first suggestion of a specialized graduate curriculum to prepare psychologists for this practical work.

In the clinic, Witmer developed what he called the "clinical method." This involved a team approach, typically employing both a physician

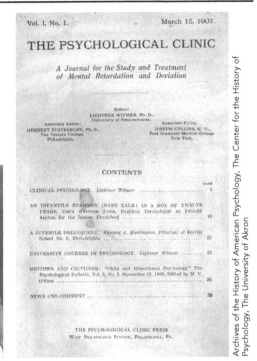

Figure 6.3   Lightner Witmer, the founder of school and clinical psychology and the first issue of his journal, *The Psychological Clinic* in 1907

and a social worker. The team was involved jointly in the testing of the patient, rendering the diagnosis, and designing and conducting the treatment. Historian John O'Donnell (1979) has described how Witmer used his clinical method:

> Children would be referred to the clinic through the school system. Following medical diagnosis, subjects would undergo an anthropometric, optometric, and psychometric examination. ... Witmer converted such experimental apparatus as the chronoscope, kymograph, ergograph, and plethysmograph into diagnostic devices merely by substituting the child for the trained introspectionist. Similarly, the Seguin form board – formerly used as a pedagogical tool – was transformed into an instrument for testing a child's powers of memory, visual discrimination, and muscular coordination. Complementing psychologist and physician, the social worker would prepare a case study of the child's background. Clinical records were compiled with the threefold purpose of correlating

case histories in order to produce generalizations, of standardizing tests, and of establishing new diagnostic techniques. Testing completed, a final diagnosis would be made, followed by attempts at remedial treatment. (pp. 6–7)

Thus, the physician was involved to rule out any kind of a medical problem. The optician used, of course, to make sure that vision was normal. Hearing would be checked if that appeared to be a problem. The assessment instruments included both apparatus and mental tests from psychology. The chronoscope was a device to measure time and was the instrument Wundt and Cattell had used to measure the speed of mental processes. The most expensive instrument, the Hipp chronoscope, was manufactured by Mathias Hipp, a Swiss instrument maker; it was capable of measuring time in thousandths of a second. The kymograph was a device with a rotating drum that recorded responses over time. The ergograph measured muscle contraction and was likely used in conjunction with the kymograph to look at muscle contraction over time as a measure of fatigue. These instruments would have been part of the psychometric testing along with mental tests of sensory and cognitive functions that Cattell used. Once a diagnosis had been made and the course of treatment agreed upon, it was most likely the social worker who carried out the treatment, which might involve consultation with teachers and/or parents.

In its first decade, the clinic handled approximately 400 cases. The majority of the children would have been diagnosed with some kind of educational handicap, including learning disabilities and intellectual disability (the label would have been "feeblemindedness" in 1896), and disorders of conduct. The University of Pennsylvania catalog of 1909 included the following statement of the psychological clinic: "The Psychological Laboratory undertook in March, 1896, the study and remedial treatment of mentally and morally retarded children and of children suffering from physical defects which result in slow development and prevent normal progress in school" (Fernberger, 1931, p. 25). Gradually the emphasis in the clinic shifted to children of average intelligence, intellectually gifted children, and adults. Indeed, in the 1920s, Witmer became especially interested in the intellectually superior child.

Specialty clinics were added over time. In 1914, one of Witmer's students, Edwin B. Twitmyer, was put in charge of a portion of the clinic directed at the diagnosis and correction of speech defects. In 1920, another recent Penn graduate, Morris Viteles, who would go on to be an influential figure in industrial psychology, headed a special clinic for vocational guidance. Several years later, another Penn graduate, Robert Brotemarkle was put in charge of a clinic that was, in essence, a counseling center for students at the university. The workload of the clinic grew enormously so that by 1931, case records numbered nearly 10,000 over the history of the various clinic departments. The journal continued its publication, somewhat as the research arm of the clinic, publishing normative data across case types, reporting on testing procedures and, especially, standardization of those procedures, and, as always, reporting on interesting cases and innovative treatments (Fernberger, 1931).

In today's histories of psychology, Witmer is usually named as the founder of clinical psychology in America. Yet he is also accorded the same honor for the field of school psychology (Baker, 1988; Fagan, 1992). Indeed, Witmer's work in the clinic, especially in the first decade, would be closer to modern school psychology than it would be to today's practice of clinical psychology. Beyond his role as founder of these two important applied specialties in psychology, he is important historically because of his willingness to use his science to 'shed light on the problems of humanity.' His goals as a practicing psychologist were both prevention and intervention (Fagan, 1992). As O'Donnell (1979) has written, "while others called for an applied psychology, Witmer enacted one" (p. 14).

A Psychology of Business

Through the work in child study and the work in Witmer's clinic, we have described the beginnings of the applied specialties known as educational psychology, clinical psychology, and school psychology. Interest in each of those fields was partly motivated by the social changes in America that reflected urbanization, the growth of factory jobs, passage of child labor laws and laws for compulsory education, and new waves of immigration that had led to the opening of Ellis Island as an immigration center in 1892. Because of immigration and the new compulsory schooling laws, school enrollments increased by 400% between 1890 and 1900.

There were also dramatic changes in the workplace occurring at the turn of the twentieth century:

> The shift from rural to urban was almost complete; cotton was yielding to steel. The industrial urban center was the embodiment of the modern. Technology thrived and modern conveniences amazed and seduced.

> Telephones, electricity, movies, radio, and automobiles offered the promise of the new, helping to create a culture of consumerism that kept hopes high and the economy moving. As expenditures for goods and services increased, so too did the demand for human labor. The influx of immigrants from overseas and the migration of rural Americans to the major cities of the Northeast and Midwest provided industry with labor, and individuals with hope for a better life. (Benjamin & Baker, 2004, p. 157)

Work is a defining part of human life. It is the means by which societies exist. It is of crucial importance to employers, stockholders, consumers, families, and particularly to the worker who may spend 50 to 60 years or more in the workforce. It is not surprising that in looking for places where the science of psychology might have some practical benefit, psychologists discovered the world of business.

The Psychology of Advertising

It was no accident that experimental psychology's initial venture into the business world was in the field of advertising. At the end of the nineteenth century, the telegraph, the proliferation of national magazines, and the railroads created vast new markets for goods. New technologies increased production outputs such that it was possible for businesses to create surpluses. There was a need to sell those extra goods, and a national market had become available. Advertising would be crucial.

Advertising had developed as a business after the American Civil War. By the 1880s, there were advertising journals that served this new trade. As competition rose and advertising prices escalated, businesses wanted proof that advertising was effective. Advertisers argued that their business should be less guesswork and more science, and they looked for expertise that might help them understand the motives, desires, and behavior of consumers (Benjamin, 2004). Enter psychologists.

The first foray into this field was in 1895 from Harlow Gale, a psychologist at the University of Minnesota who had studied with Wundt. Gale sent a questionnaire to 200 businesses asking about their advertising practices. It was an extensive questionnaire that would have required much effort to complete; consequently, he received only 20 forms in return. Perhaps because of the poor return rate, or maybe the confusion of the data, this was Gale's first and only venture into the psychology of business.

Walter D. Scott

The first psychologist who could be said to work in business was Walter Dill Scott (1869–1955) who earned his doctorate with Wundt in 1900. Scott is usually identified as the founder of industrial/organizational psychology in America because of a sustained and productive career in that area. He was a young assistant professor at Northwestern University when he was contacted by John Mahin, head of the leading advertising agency in Chicago. Mahin asked if he would write a series of 12 articles on the psychology of advertising for an advertising magazine that Mahin wanted to publish. Scott agreed and the articles began their appearance in *Mahin's Magazine* in 1902. The following year they were collected and published as Scott's first book, *The Theory of Advertising* (1903). Scott wrote another 21 articles for the magazine and those became his second book, *The Psychology of Advertising* (1908).

You might be asking yourself, what expertise did Scott have in advertising? Did he take courses on the subject when he was in college? Did he do research on the topic? The answer to those questions is essentially no. Although he did undertake a few studies in advertising, for example, one on various typefaces, he mostly had no real background in the field. But that didn't stop him from writing articles on suggestion, perception, illusions, mental imagery, and the value of the return coupon – just some of the topics he covered in his magazine articles. Scott reasoned that as a psychologist, he was trained in experimental methods and somewhat knowledgeable about perception, motivation, learning, emotion, attention, and memory – all topics that he believed should be important in advertising. In truth, then, many of his articles represented his arm-chair theorizing about advertising phenomena, based on his knowledge of psychological principles and phenomena. Yet Mahin seemed pleased with the products, and Scott became recognized as the leading psychological expert on advertising by the advertising community (Kuna, 1976).

Scott's theory of advertising emphasized that the consumer was "a nonrational, suggestible creature under the hypnotic influence of the advertising writer" (Kuna, 1976, p. 353). Scott emphasized suggestion in his advertising work. He wrote, "Man has been called the reasoning animal but he could with greater truthfulness be called the creature of suggestion. He is reasonable, but he is to a greater extent suggestible" (Scott, 1903, p. 59). In applying suggestion to advertising, Scott used two techniques in particular: the direct command and the return coupon. The direct command was often the headline of an ad: "Use Ipana Toothpaste" or "Get the Promotion You Deserve." Scott believed that such

WALTER DILL SCOTT   L B HOPKINS   JOSEPH W HAYES
ROBERT C CLOTHIER   BEARDSLEY RUML   STANLEY B MATHEWSON

ANNOUNCE

THE SCOTT COMPANY

ORGANIZED

TO OFFER TO INDUSTRY METHODS
LEADING TO THE SOLUTION OF PROBLEMS
IN THE FIELD OF INDUSTRIAL PERSONNEL

TO SHARE WITH INDUSTRY THE RE-
SULTS OF RESEARCH WHICH MAY PROVIDE
A BETTER UNDERSTANDING OF THE SOCIAL
ECONOMIC AND PSYCHOLOGICAL FACTORS IN
INDUSTRIAL ADJUSTMENT

TO OFFER TO INDUSTRY A CONSULTING
SERVICE WHICH COMBINES THE INDUSTRIAL
AND SCIENTIFIC POINTS OF VIEW

751 DREXEL BUILDING
PHILADELPHIA

Figure 6.4   A business advertisement for Walter Dill Scott's consulting firm founded at the end of World War I, and Harry L. Hollingworth at age 35

statements were effective because they suggested a particular action without arousing competing actions. Likewise, the return coupon suggested a direct action – cut out the coupon, fill it out, and mail it in. Both techniques were thought to stimulate compulsive obedience.

Scott also promoted the importance of mental imagery as a means of *suggestion*. He noted that advertisements for pianos should describe the instrument in such a way that the reader could hear it. Food ads should make the consumer taste them, and perfume ads should cause readers to experience the exotic smells.

Harry L. Hollingworth

Scott's popularity opened the doors for other psychologists to enter the advertising field, for example, Harry Hollingworth, mentioned at the beginning of this chapter for his caffeine studies. Hollingworth became active with the Advertising Men's League of New York City by offering a night course on the subject through Columbia University's extension service. The lectures from that course were published in his book, *Advertising and Selling* (1913). Furthermore, his course led to offers from businesses to get involved with advertising research. By 1913, the Zeitgeist in psychology was changing. Suggestion, a mentalistic concept that was difficult to measure, was giving way to more objective, observable behaviors. Hollingworth began to work with companies using return coupons so he could gauge the effectiveness of each ad by comparing the coupon to the sales that it generated. He would test the various coupon ads on his own without knowledge of the sales data, and then when his studies were complete, send his results to the company and ask for their sales data. They and he discovered that the correlation between the two sets of figures was a remarkable .82 (Hollingworth, 1913; Kuna, 1979). Hollingworth became much in demand for his ability to pretest advertisement effectiveness.

Hollingworth was interested in more than just the effectiveness of various ads. He wanted to understand the psychology of advertising. What were the components that led to buying behavior? His model of advertising research became the dominant paradigm in the work of other psychologists who joined him in the field. Although, Hollingworth and Scott remained in their academic positions, other psychologists would find work full time in the advertising world as a new applied psychological specialty was created.

Münsterberg and Industrial Efficiency

Recall from Chapter 4 that William James recruited Hugo Münsterberg (1863–1916) from the University of Freiberg in 1892 to take charge of the psychology laboratory at Harvard. Münsterberg didn't stay in the laboratory very long. Early in his time in America, he began to write articles for popular magazines, as many psychologists of his time did. Münsterberg seemed especially to enjoy the attention he received from such matters such that he increased his applied work, essentially abandoning the laboratory to more junior colleagues at Harvard. Before his death, he had written important books on industrial psychology, psychology and law, psychology and teaching, psychotherapy, and the psychology of motion pictures. He was, without a doubt, the major figure in America in applied psychology in his time.

Münsterberg published two books on the psychology of business, but it was his first one that proved to be such a significant contribution. The book was published in 1913, entitled *Psychology and Industrial Efficiency*. At the time of its publication, *efficiency* was a buzzword in American business. Efficiency experts were followers of the theories of Frederick Winslow Taylor (1856–1915), an engineer, whose program, known as *scientific management,* claimed that in business and industry, there was one right way to do any job. Münsterberg promoted psychology as the science of human efficiency. The key to business efficiency was matching the skills and the talents of the worker to the requirements of the job. A good match of job and worker meant a more satisfied worker and better job productivity. Moreover, Münsterberg believed that psychology had the assessment tools to discover the perfect match. Psychologists would analyze the job and determine what mental and physical traits were required to do the job well. Then workers could be tested to see where they fit best.

In 1911, the San Francisco and Portland Steamship Company hired Münsterberg to create a test that could be used to select competent ship captains, an action undertaken six months before the Titanic sank in the North Atlantic. After a series of fatal accidents involving pedestrians, the Boston Elevated Railway Company hired him to devise a method to select competent trolley car operators. These and other studies that Münsterberg undertook so convinced him that psychology held the keys to increased work production, happier workers, and safer work environments that he asked the federal government to establish extension stations around the country through the Department of Commerce and Labor that would provide psychological expertise to local businesses and industry (Münsterberg, 1913).

Münsterberg is sometimes labeled the founder of industrial psychology, largely because of the importance of his 1913 book. There is no denying that the book did much to sell the value of psychology to leaders in business and industry; Münsterberg was always a great promoter of psychology. However, Scott already had 10 years of sustained work in the field before that book appeared. Moreover, Hollingworth and several others were also active before 1913.

Lillian Gilbreth's Engineering Psychology

Lillian Moller Gilbreth (1878–1972) is unique as a psychologist. She had a movie made about her life entitled *Cheaper by the Dozen* (no, not the one with Steve Martin, the 1950 film with Myrna Loy). The movie title comes from the title of a book written by two of her 12 children. Moreover, she is the only American psychologist to appear on a United States postage stamp (unless you count John Dewey who was really a philosopher). A 40-cent stamp was issued of Gilbreth in 1984 and is shown in Figure 6.5.

Gilbreth earned her PhD in psychology at Brown University in 1915. The previous year she published her first book entitled, *The Psychology*

Figure 6.5   Two psychologists who made significant contributions to industrial psychology: Hugo Münsterberg and Lillian Gilbreth

of Management (1914). Gilbreth was part of the efficiency movement along with her husband, Frank Gilbreth. The couple worked together in a consulting business started by Frank. One of their techniques was to use film in what were called *time-motion studies* as a way to analyze the components of a job and thus make recommendations about adjustments or changes to increase efficiency. Frank died in 1924, but Lillian continued their consulting business, moving it more toward businesses that were marketing to homemakers. Gilbreth wrote *The Home-Maker and Her Job* in 1927 and *Management in the Home* in 1954 as an outgrowth of her research on homemaking. She worked especially in kitchen design, interviewing and studying thousands of homemakers to determine the appropriate height of kitchen counters and appliances, and designing details of other kitchen fixtures to be more efficiently used. Some of her patents included an electric food mixer and shelves inside refrigerator doors.

In later life, Gilbreth designed kitchen layouts and equipment that aided physically disabled persons in doing housework. For example, she invented the trashcan that could be opened by stepping on a pedal at the floor. Her work is often labeled engineering psychology, another label for human factors psychology that will be discussed in Chapter 9. Engineering psychology refers to the design of equipment to interface better with human operators and human needs.

Gilbreth was the first woman to be a member of the American Society of Mechanical Engineers and the first woman elected to the prestigious

National Academy of Engineering. In her lifetime, she won several national awards from engineering societies. It was the initiative of those societies that succeeded in getting a postage stamp in her honor. Although scientific management (also called "Taylorism") would decline in popularity, principally because of its neglect of worker input and a lack of recognition of individual differences, Lillian Gilbreth's more worker-oriented approach remained popular with workers and management throughout her long career.

Business Psychology outside the Academy

We have highlighted just a few of the contributors to the beginnings of a field that was called business psychology (or economic psychology) in its early years but is called industrial-organizational psychology today. Most of the individuals we have talked about held positions in universities, such as Scott, Hollingworth, and Münsterberg. Although Gilbreth held positions (mostly part time) at Purdue University and Rutgers University, she was largely self-employed for most of her life. One of the accomplishments of applied psychology was not just that it generated applied research for professors to undertake, often at the request of businesses, but it created a new job market for psychologists to work within business and industry or as independent consultants. Elsie Bregman (1896–1969), a doctoral student with Cattell, found a career with Macy's Department Store in New York City dealing with personnel issues, especially selection and training (Koppes, 1997). Marion Bills (1890–1970) used her doctorate in psychology in a life-long career with Aetna Life Insurance Company where she was eventually a vice president (Koppes & Bauer, 2006). After the First World War, Walter Dill Scott founded the Scott Company, one of the earliest psychological consulting firms to aid businesses. Daniel Starch (1883–1979) used his doctorate in psychology to carve out a career in advertising. In 1922, he invented a technique to measure the readership of advertisements called the Starch Recognition Procedure that is still in use today. We will discuss the further development of this field and other applied specialties in Chapter 9.

Vocational Guidance

With urbanization and the technological advancements at the beginning of the new century, job choices had expanded enormously. That, and growing concerns about school dropouts and juvenile delinquency, spurred a strong interest in helping people make choices about their life's work. Thus began the vocational guidance movement in America in the first decade of the twentieth century, a movement that brought vocational exploration and counseling to the schools. One of the early figures in this movement was a Boston attorney, Frank Parsons (1854–1908). Parsons (1909) wrote that there were three steps in choosing a career wisely: (a) knowledge of yourself, (b) knowledge of occupations, and (c) knowledge of the relationship between the two.

Many educators saw vocational guidance as a function of the schools, arguing that teachers and administrators could provide the needed counseling. However, psychologists, who were growing in confidence with their development of mental tests, argued that such guidance should be the domain of psychology. Both Münsterberg and Hollingworth noted that psychological tests were designed to measure individual differences in a number of intellectual and personality domains. To the extent that they could be matched to occupations, those tests would be especially useful in vocational guidance. These concerns eventually led psychologists, such as Edward K. Strong, Jr. and others, to design tests that would match the interests of individuals (not just their skills) with various jobs, thus adding to the kinds of tests available in vocational guidance.

Vocational guidance is seen as one of the important roots of modern counseling psychology to be discussed in Chapter 9. What is clear about its history in the early twentieth century is that psychologists believed that their science offered the best hope for guiding individuals in career decisions, and they were unwilling to leave the job in the hands of educators who they viewed as relying on personal impressions and ignoring the tools of science. Psychologists were well aware of the career-counseling role that had been played by phrenologists and physiognomists in the nineteenth century; they were ready to change the nature of vocational guidance, to make it a product of genuine science. They would find that the talk was easier than the task.

Intelligence Testing

Cattell's anthropometric tests had been found lacking as measures of intelligence when Clark Wissler discovered all those zero correlations. That failure didn't make psychologists abandon the task of developing a valid measure of intelligence; it just made them look elsewhere. One who was looking was Henry Herbert Goddard (1866–1957) who had received his doctorate from Hall at Clark University. In 1906, Goddard accepted a position as Director of Research at the New Jersey School for Feebleminded Boys and Girls, located in Vineland. Drawing on his training at Clark, he assembled various pieces of apparatus from the psychological laboratory to test the children at Vineland. His hope was to develop a measure that would differentiate children with an intellectual disability according to the degree of their disability with the ultimate purpose being the design of appropriate educational programs. Educators and psychologists already recognized that there were degrees of intellectual disability. Classificatory labels included "idiot" and "imbecile," to which Goddard added the label "moron," with idiot being the lowest level of functioning and moron being the highest. Of course, those labels aren't used anymore, unless one is referring to politicians.

Goddard's research wasn't going anywhere. In the summer of 1908, he traveled to Europe because he had heard about places more advanced in their understanding of intellectual disability. There he learned about a French psychologist who had developed a mental test in 1905 that was said to measure performance in schoolchildren, especially children who were mentally retarded. The test had been revised in 1908 and norms had been developed to indicate the capabilities of children at particular ages (that is, the concept of mental age). The psychologist was Alfred Binet (1857–1911), and his test would become the model for intelligence testing for virtually the rest of the twentieth century (Nicolas & Sanitioso, 2012).

On his return to America, Goddard translated the test for an English-speaking audience and published it in 1908 as the *Binet-Simon Measuring Scale for Intelligence*. Unlike Cattell's tests, this one correlated positively with performance in school subjects. Other psychologists became interested in the test and adapted their own versions. One of those was Lewis Terman (1877–1956), also a graduate of Clark University, who, as a psychologist at Stanford University in 1916, published a new version of the Binet scale that eventually became known as the *Stanford–Binet Intelligence Test*. That test became the leading instrument for intellectual assessment and was unrivaled for more than 30 years until David Wechsler (1896–1981), a student of Woodworth's, developed his tests in the 1940s to measure intelligence in children and adults.

Whereas Goddard used the Binet test mostly for children with below average intelligence, Terman researched children at the other end of the scale. He was the founding author of a series of books based on longitudinal studies of a group of gifted children, assessed from childhood to old age. The *Stanford–Binet Test* also made popular the ratio of mental age to chronological age, known as the intelligence quotient or IQ,

Figure 6.6   Henry Herbert Goddard and postcard of the women's building of the Vineland School for Feebleminded Boys and Girls in Vineland, New Jersey where Goddard conducted his studies on feeblemindedness

a concept invented by William Stern (Lamiell, 2012). In calculating IQ, Terman multiplied the ratio by 100, which got rid of the decimal point that was in Stern's formulation.

When the United States entered World War I in 1917, Terman, Goddard, and other psychologists were asked to develop intelligence tests that could be given to groups (most intelligence tests prior to that time were administered as individual tests). To begin the task, the psychologists met at Vineland in 1917. In just a few months, they had developed two tests known as the *Army Alpha* and *Army Beta* (the latter designed for non-English speakers or those who were illiterate). By the end of the war, the two tests had been given to nearly 2 million soldiers and potential recruits. After the war, intelligence testing became a major job activity for individuals who worked as clinical and school psychologists. We will treat this topic further in Chapter 9.

Münsterberg and the Psychology of Law

The first applied psychology book that Münsterberg wrote was in 1908 on psychology as applied to the law. It was entitled *On the Witness Stand*. Münsterberg began his work in forensic psychology by studying the accuracy of memory, especially the validity of the testimony of eyewitnesses. He also was interested in the problem of false confessions, crime prevention, lie detection, and the decision processes of jurors, and he published articles on all of those topics. His formal involvement in the psychology of law began in 1906, the result of a controversial murder trial in Chicago involving Richard Ivens as the accused. John Sanderson Christison, a Chicago physician and famous criminologist, sent a pamphlet he had written on the Ivens murder case to Münsterberg, William James, and others, asking for their opinions on the guilt or innocence of the convicted man, thought to be intellectually disabled, who was soon to be executed. Ivens was being tried for the brutal murder of a young woman, a crime to which he had confessed, although he later retracted his confession. Münsterberg believed that Ivens' confession was obtained under duress and deception, and that it represented a false confession (see Münsterberg, 1908, pp. 139–145). The court decided otherwise and Ivens was hanged, despite letters from William James and Münsterberg stating their belief in his innocence. Hale (1980) wrote that Münsterberg was especially upset by the execution: "The failure of his and James's intercession involved more than a personal rebuff; it amounted to an attack on psychology itself" (p. 112). Münsterberg's views were challenged by attorneys and the public who questioned what special expertise psychology had in decisions made in the courtroom. Yet he believed this was a medieval view that failed to recognize the validity of the tools of the new science. Münsterberg (1908) wrote, "The time will come when the methods of experimental psychology cannot longer be excluded from the court of law" (p. 108).

Münsterberg did not see psychology making much headway in the courts in his lifetime. He saw this as a continued failure of the courts to recognize the human error within the judicial system and how psychology might correct that error. He wrote:

> The lawyer and the judge and the juryman are sure that their legal instinct and their common sense supplies them with all that is needed and somewhat more; and if the time is ever to come when even the jurist is to show some concession to the spirit of modern psychology, public opinion will have to exert some pressure. (Münsterberg, 1908, pp. 10–11)

Convinced that he had done what he could in this field, Münsterberg moved on to other applied interests in business, education, medicine, and the movies. Were he alive today he would find a growing specialty area in which he pioneered known as forensic psychology.

The New Profession of Psychology

This section shares the same title as that for Chapter 9. In Chapter 1, you saw that there has always been an applied psychology, that in early nineteenth-century America there were phrenologists and others offering a variety of psychological services including forms of psychotherapy, vocational guidance, parenting advice, and business consulting. In this chapter we have focused on what might be called the beginnings of the new applied psychology, an applied psychology based on the new psychological science.

In truth, there were many actions taken by these new applied psychologists that were not derived from their science. Titchener (1910b) made that very point in his Clark Conference address: "So far is experimental psychology from any general readiness to furnish ideas for application, that applied psychology has been obliged to think out ideas for itself; and so far is applied psychology from reliance upon the parent discipline, that some of its most widely used and most strongly emphasized ideas contravene established scientific principles" (p. 408). In the first part of that quotation, he was accusing applied psychologists of making up their science, and in the second part of contradicting it, perhaps through ignorance. It is ironic that many scientists in psychology today make the same claims about the practical work of their colleagues.

The difficulty for the early twentieth-century applied psychologists was that their science hadn't been designed to address the problems that they were called to solve. But individuals from outside the university – from businesses, from schools, from the military – came to psychologists and said: 'we need your help and we are willing to pay for it.' Academic psychologists were not paid handsome wages by their universities, and many of them, especially the younger ones, looked for ways to supplement their university salaries. These psychologists reasoned that most of the questions were about the workings of the mind, thus if they didn't have the answers, who would? Moreover, as noted earlier, there was a strong belief in the possibilities of their science to make the world a better place, for example, the fervor Münsterberg expressed in his belief in the potential psychology had to aid the judicial system.

Today there are many applied specialties in psychology, such as the ones discussed in this chapter – clinical, counseling, school, industrial-organizational, and forensic psychology – and there are many others, such as health psychology, sport psychology, and media psychology that are of more recent origin. In Chapter 9 we will discuss the development of the new profession in psychology, tracing the further developments in the fields described in this chapter. It is a story of a long and difficult struggle, of battles with other disciplines, notably psychiatry, struggles with federal agencies and state legislatures, and ultimately battles between the science and profession of psychology. Before we do that, we will describe two other schools of psychology that exerted considerable influence on both the science and practice of psychology – psychoanalysis in the next chapter and behaviorism in the next.

7

Psychoanalysis

Vienna had been Sigmund Freud's home since the age of four. Now at 82, ill with throat and mouth cancer from too many years of too many cigars, and recovering from mouth surgery, approximately his 30th surgery since 1923, Freud watched with disbelief as his country, boiling with anti-Semitism in 1938, collapsed around him. Under pressures from Adolf Hitler, Austria's chancellor resigned on March 11, 1938. The next day, the new chancellor, a Nazi puppet, welcomed the German troops into Austria. Freud listened to his radio, hearing the stories of scattered resistance against a crushing force. However, the invasion was over before it began. Hitler arrived in Vienna on March 14 to cheering crowds lining the streets. Then what had been a bad dream for Austrian Jews turned into the most horrific of nightmares. Gay (1988) wrote, "Incidents in the streets of Austrian cities and villages right after the German invasion were more outrageous than those Hitler's Reich had yet witnessed" (p. 619). German playwright Carl Zuckmayer was in Vienna at the time and described its horror:

> The underworld had opened its gates and let loose its lowest, most revolting, most impure spirits. The city was transformed into a nightmare painting by Hieronymus Bosch ... [the] air filled with an incessant, savage, hysterical screeching from male and female throats.... [what was] unleashed here was the uprising of envy, of malevolence, of bitterness, of blind vicious lust for revenge. (as quoted in Gay, 1988, p. 619)

Vienna, indeed all of Austria, was zealous hatred run amuck. Many Jews had already abandoned Austria for places they thought might be safe from the Nazis – Hungary, Holland, England, Canada, and the United States. But Freud stayed. He was in poor health and hoped that he would be able to die in Austria, in the apartment where he had lived and worked for nearly 50 years.

On March 15, only three days after the Nazi troops had entered Austria, Nazis searched Freud's home and office. They detained his son as a prisoner for the day. Friends of Freud were clearly worried about his safety and began work on a plan to rescue him and his family. Even with friends trying to assist, Freud was reluctant to leave, saying he felt like he would be deserting the ship to leave Austria in such trying times. However, when his daughter Anna was arrested and held by the Nazis on March 22 for a full day of interrogation, his reluctance disappeared.

Freud, his wife, and Anna, were finally able to leave for England by train on June 4, 1938. The following day they crossed the English Channel and were in London. Freud tried to get his four sisters out of Austria as well, but was unable to. He left behind the sum of $20,000 to assist them, money that was likely confiscated by the Nazis. One sister died of starvation at the Theresienstadt camp, and the other three were murdered in another of the camps, probably Auschwitz (Gay, 1988).

Freud survived only 15 months in London. He was impressed by the reception he received in England, especially the recognition he received and how thoughtful people were toward him. His last months were spent in great pain as the cancer spread. Finally, in September 1939, he was enduring incredible pain. He talked with Anna about his situation and with his personal physician, Max Schur, who also had emigrated from Vienna. He reminded Schur of their agreement that when the end came, he would not be allowed to suffer needlessly. Schur gave him two injections of morphine on September 21 and a third the following day. Freud slipped into a coma and died on September 23 (Gay, 1988).

Freud's Early Training

As a 17-year-old medical student at the University of Vienna in 1873, Sigmund Freud (1856–1939) took a course entitled "General Biology and Darwinism." That course, especially the ideas of Darwin, would cement his resolve to pursue a career as a research scientist. He also took several courses from Franz Brentano. The person with whom Freud worked most closely was Ernst Brücke (1819–1892), one of the most famous physiologists of his day. Brücke convinced Freud not to pursue an academic career, but instead to work in clinical practice as a neurologist. While at the University of Vienna, Freud also met Josef Breuer (1842–1925), a physician and physiologist in Brücke's lab who would have a significant influence on Freud.

In 1885, Freud received a scholarship to study with the neurologist Jean-Martin Charcot (1825–1893) at the Salpêtrière Hospital in Paris,

Figure 7.1 The entrance to Freud's Vienna home at 19 Berggasse. The Freuds lived in two adjacent apartments on the second floor, comprised of 12 rooms. On the right is his home in London. Both are museums today, open to the public

a complex of some 45 buildings, storied in their history. At the time, Charcot was at the peak of his fame for his expertise in hypnosis, his treatment of hysteria, and for his studies demonstrating the induction of traumatic (or hysterical) paralysis. Freud was excited about this opportunity, and Charcot did not disappoint. In one of his notebooks, Freud wrote about Charcot's style in working with students on clinical cases:

> On Tuesdays Charcot held his 'consultation externe' at which his assistants brought before him for examination the typical or puzzling cases among the very large number attending the out-patient department. … [Some cases] gave him the opportunity of using them as a peg for the most instructive remarks on the greatest variety of topics in neuropathology. He seemed to be working with us, to be thinking aloud and to be expecting to have objections raised by his pupils. Anyone who ventured might put in a word in the discussion and no comment was left unnoticed by the great man. (as cited in Freud, Freud, & Grubrich-Simitis, 1978, p. 114)

From this description, it would seem that Charcot, despite his exalted reputation, involved his students in a genuine dialogue in trying to unravel the mysteries in their clinical cases. Charcot also influenced Freud by an off-hand remark at a party that Freud attended where he overheard Charcot talking about the hysterical symptoms in one of his female patients, saying that in such matters it "was always about the genitals." In his history of the psychoanalytic movement, Freud (1917) described that comment and several other episodes in Paris that helped him understand the overwhelming importance of the relationship between sexual issues and neuroses.

Freud wrote from Paris to his fiancée, Martha Bernays, describing the experience of attending one of Charcot's famous Friday morning lectures:

> Charcot, who is one of the greatest physicians and a man whose common sense borders on genius, is simply wrecking all my aims and opinions. I sometimes come out of his lectures as from out of Notre-Dame, with an entirely new idea about perfection. But he exhausts me; when I come away from him I no longer have any desire to work at my own silly things. My brain is sated as an evening in the theater. Whether the seed will ever bear fruit, I don't know; but what I do know is that no other human being has ever affected me in the same way. (letter dated Nov. 24, 1885, as cited in Freud, Freud, & Grubrich-Simitis, 1978, p. 114)

The seed did bear fruit, perhaps even beyond Freud's most ambitious dreams. Freud would open his neurological practice in 1886, and he married Martha Bernays in the same year. They would have six children in the first nine years of their marriage.

Josef Breuer and the Case of Anna O.

In 1880, Breuer began treating a young woman, given the case name of "Anna O.," who, after the death of her father, to whom she was greatly attached, experienced problems such as headaches, partial paralyses, periods of overexcitement, visual disturbances, and loss of sensation. Other symptoms appeared later including multiple personalities, speech difficulties, bizarre hallucinations, and an inability to drink. The latter problem was, of course, quite serious. In one of the sessions with Breuer, Anna O. told him about seeing a woman allow her dog to drink from a glass. She was extremely disgusted by the sight and now, in telling Breuer about the incident, the emotion seemed to subside and she could drink again. Breuer seized on this occurrence as a way to treat her other symptoms. Using hypnosis, he attempted to reach the causes of each of her physical or psychological symptoms, and when they were discovered and dealt with in the psychotherapy, the symptoms disappeared. Breuer called this the *catharsis method* or cathartic cure: symptoms were believed to be the result of pent-up emotions and if the emotion was released, then the symptoms should disappear. By 1882, Breuer had cured Anna O. of all her symptoms, or so he wrote. But work by Henri Ellenberger (1972) led to the discovery

Figure 7.2   Sigmund Freud, at left, as pictured on a 50 shilling Austrian note from 1986. The 1954 German stamp honoring Bertha Pappenheim

of a manuscript in Breuer's hand, written in 1882, that showed a relapse of many of the symptoms and the fact that he had placed her in a sanatorium in Switzerland for further cure. Anna O. would recover. When Ernest Jones published his biography of Freud in the 1950s, he revealed her name – Bertha Pappenheim. She was a pioneering social worker and feminist activist. In recognition of her accomplishments, the German government issued a postage stamp honoring her in 1954.

Freud first learned about Breuer's treatment of Anna O. in mid-November 1882 (Gay, 1988). Freud was fascinated by the account, and the two men talked further about it on other occasions. It would lead Freud to his theory of psychoanalysis, although he and Breuer would disagree over the interpretations of the case; Freud offered a much more sexual interpretation that made Breuer uneasy. It was the opening case in their collaborative book (Freud's first book), published in 1895 (see Breuer & Freud, 1957/1895), and it was Freud's starting point in the first lecture he gave at the Clark conference in America in 1909 (Freud, 1910). Anna O. has long been considered the cornerstone case for psychoanalysis and it set the stage for his use of case histories to develop his theories and methods (Sealey, 2011).

Although Breuer had an important role in the origins of psychoanalysis, a debt that Freud regularly acknowledged, the development of psychoanalysis was largely based on the work of Freud. Exactly what were his contributions? Historian Frank Sulloway (1979) has written that psychoanalysis can be defined "in terms of three interdependent achievements by Freud: (1) a method, (2) a theory of the neuroses, and (3) a theory of the normal mind" (p. 11). We will describe each of these in turn, beginning with psychoanalysis as a theory of the normal mind.

Psychoanalysis as a Theory of the Normal Mind

In describing mind, Freud (1949) wrote, "mental life is the function of an apparatus ... made up of several portions. ... To the oldest of these mental provinces or agencies we give the name of *id*" (p. 14). The id was part of the tripartite construction of the mind, the other two components being the ego and superego. The id is present at birth and "contains everything that is inherited" including the instincts (p. 14). The id includes the life instincts, which are sexual in nature and the death instincts, such as aggression, which are destructive in nature. The id is the most primitive part of the mind and the most inaccessible, both for its owner and for the psychoanalyst. The id operates wholly at an unconscious level, meaning that the individual has no direct access to it. The id has no morality; it does not know right from wrong, it only knows what it wants and provides the motivation to reach those wants as immediately as possible. It seeks pleasure and works to avoid pain. Its pleasure-seeking energy Freud called *libido*, and he viewed it as a sexually based energy. Thus, this part of the mind, if left unchecked, could create much trouble for the individual. Enter the ego.

The purpose of the *ego* is to help the id satisfy its demands. Whereas the id is said to operate according to the *pleasure principle*, the ego operates according to the *reality principle*. The ego functions to control the instincts, but not to inhibit them. The ego is the rational part of the mind; it serves as the mediator between the id and the external world. Freud (1949) wrote that it "has the task of self-preservation ... it performs that task by ... storing up experiences ... by avoiding excessive stimuli ... by dealing with moderate stimuli ... and, finally, by learning to bring about appropriate modifications in the external world to its own advantage" (p. 15). The ego might suppress certain actions or might just delay them until circumstances are more appropriate.

Whereas the id exists at birth, and the ego develops shortly thereafter, the superego develops in childhood through the child's experiences, parental teachings, cultural milieu, and so forth. The *superego* represents the individual's moral compass. Unlike the ego, which tries to achieve the id's desires, the superego may act in direct opposition to the id, attempting to thwart id desires. Across individuals, the id would be viewed as a common component of mind. But egos and superegos, because they develop out of experiences in the world, could differ considerably across individuals.

According to Freud, the ego operates partly at the conscious level and partly at the unconscious level. Its function requires that it take into account three separate factors: the desires of the id, the current situation, and the moral code of the superego. Because of that role, it is often described as the executive component of the mind. As is the case for many executives, the stress can sometimes be overwhelming.

Psychoanalysis as a Theory of the Neuroses

Freud developed his theory of neuroses largely from the clinical cases that he treated. Many of these patients were women and most of them were diagnosed with the label *hysteria*. We have mentioned this term earlier with regard to Charcot's work. It was a common diagnosis for a broad range of symptoms including those suffered by Anna O. In addition, symptoms of sexual dysfunction were quite common in individuals diagnosed with hysteria, or more broadly, neuroses. Central to Freud's theory of the etiology of neuroses were his views on anxiety, defense mechanisms, and childhood sexuality.

Anxiety and Defense Mechanisms

As we have noted, for the ego, like many executives, the pressures of the job can be enormous. When the demands from any of the three factors overwhelm the ego, *anxiety* develops. Concerns about the id demands give rise to *neurotic anxiety*. *Moral anxiety* is experienced from violations of the restrictions imposed by the superego, and *objective anxiety* is the term Freud used to describe what is experienced by threats from the external world.

To deal with these kinds of anxieties, the ego develops *defense mechanisms* as a way to cope. There are approximately a dozen defense mechanisms including repression, denial, projection, displacement, rationalization, and reaction formation. By definition, these defense mechanisms operate at an unconscious level. Thus in the case of *repression*, if the individual experiences some traumatic event that could lead to anxiety, one way to ward off that anxiety would be to repress any memory of the event. This is, in essence, unconscious forgetting, which means the traumatic event is no longer accessible in consciousness.

In *rationalization*, the individual may invent new ways to think about disappointing or tragic events. Consider, for example, a woman who interviews for a job that she really wants, but she performs poorly in the interview and doesn't get the job. To admit to herself that her poor performance was responsible for her failure would be anxiety producing. However, she can use rationalization to lessen the sting by saying that as she learned more about the job in the interview, she realized that it wasn't a position that she really wanted.

In using the defense mechanism *projection*, the individual attributes negative qualities to others that are part of the person making the attribution. A man might complain that his boss is passive aggressive, when in fact, that is not a trait of the boss but of the man himself. By projecting that trait onto someone else and not seeing it as part of one's own personality; it allows the individual to reduce anxiety.

Whereas the defense mechanisms that are part of the ego's arsenal can be used to help the individual avoid or reduce anxiety, they also can contribute to psychological problems, principally the creation of neuroses. For example, repression of anxiety can create problems because of the psychic energy needed to keep the anxiety repressed. Eventually the defense mechanisms can break down, and neuroses or psychoses can result. For Freud, various personality disorders and neurotic conditions existed because of failure of the three components of the mind to work effectively together. And much of what had to be worked out in childhood was the appropriate resolution of sexual issues.

Childhood Sexuality

At the end of the nineteenth century, infants and children were seen as innocent, and certainly so when it came to the issue of sexual desires. Such desires were presumed to emerge in adolescence. But Freud, because of self-analysis of his dreams and because of the commonalities of life events that he observed in his patients, offered a very different view, one that was considerably disturbing to many of his contemporaries. He argued that sexual desires and sexual pleasure existed in infancy and throughout the stages of child development.

In the mid-1890s, Freud presented data from more than 25 of his patients, both male and female, regarding the cause of their hysteria. He argued that in every case the cause was some sexual trauma in infancy or early childhood, often rape. These claims generated considerable controversy in the medical establishment as well as the rest of society because it called for recognition that sexual molestation of children was far more common than anyone had imagined. This theory of the etiology of hysteria has been called Freud's *seduction theory* (although he didn't use that label), meaning that the children were seduced by adults into sexual encounters. As scholars have noted, it was not about seduction, but about child abuse and rape (Triplett, 2004). By September 1897, however, Freud completely reversed his opinion, arguing that when patients recalled these events, they were not recalling actual sexual assaults but instead were reporting sexual fantasies as though they had really occurred (see Masson, 1985). It was difficult for ordinary citizens to know which was worse – believing that sexual assault on children was rampant or that infants and young children harbored secret sexual fantasies about their parents and other caretakers. (There is considerable controversy among psychologists, psychoanalysts, and historians on why Freud made such a radical reversal in what he believed. See Esterson, 1998, 2001; Israels & Schatzman, 1993; and Masson, 1984 for some of the principal arguments on this topic.)

With the reversal of the seduction theory Freud's view of child development took on an entirely different meaning. Freud described the development of personality in childhood as an orderly sequence of psychosexual stages, so named because each stage involved sexual issues to be dealt with appropriately. These were oral, anal, phallic, latency, and genital. In the oral stage, for example, pleasure is associated with sucking, at the breast or even sucking one's thumb. The anal stage begins in the second year of life and pleasure there is said to be associated with expulsion of the feces. The phallic stage begins around age four. Sexual pleasure is derived from the genitals and masturbation may begin in this stage. Freud described a major sexual conflict in this stage that he referred to as the *Oedipal complex*, in which the child has sexual desires for the opposite sex parent. (Note that the complex is named after Oedipus, a tragic figure in a 5th century play by Sophocles, who as king, kills his father and marries his mother.) Normal development requires that the child resolve the complex by identifying with the same sex parent and developing more appropriate feelings for the opposite sex parent. Freud believed that failure to resolve this complex would lead to serious neuroses. Its successful resolution, however, was largely responsible for the development of the superego.

Some of Freud's ideas can seem far-fetched in contemporary thinking (and we haven't even mentioned penis envy or castration anxiety yet). However, it must be remembered that Freud lived in a time when there was considerable repression of normal human sexuality, and, indeed, gross ignorance by many people on the subject of sex. In his practice, Freud found evidence of how this inability or unwillingness to deal with sexual matters (in married women, for example) created serious psychological problems of adjustment. Despite the controversy of his ideas, his work on this subject had two profound effects on subsequent beliefs in the field of psychology: an emphasis on the critical significance of experiences in infancy and childhood on the development of adult personality and a recognition that sexuality is a normal part of human behavior, a source of great pleasure and intimacy.

Psychoanalysis as Method

Psychoanalysis as method describes a method for treatment but also a method for research, not for experimental research but for use in exploring the mind – normal or abnormal. When Freud began treating his patients, he used a number of techniques, such as hypnosis, to try to uncover the problems that were producing their neurotic symptoms. Some methods seemed more successful than others did. The problem was, of course, that the information he needed to discover lay deep in the unconscious, protected by unconscious defense mechanisms and by conscious resistance and deceit. How would he get at such information? Eventually he discovered a technique that worked better than his other procedures. He simply asked his patients to say whatever came to mind, just to begin talking about anything they wanted to talk about. The method was called *free association*. The job of the therapist was to listen to what was being said and what wasn't being said. The therapist knew that this talking was in full consciousness when all the ego-controlled guards would be working, so the therapist had to look for hidden meanings in the freely associated material, things that the patient might not have meant to reveal.

In addition to this method, Freud also used *dream analysis*, a technique that he had discovered when he psychoanalyzed himself and found that free association would not work for that. In dream analysis, Freud would ask the patient to recall the dream in as much detail as possible. He would ask questions, at times, probing that recall. He differentiated between the *manifest content* of the dream, which was the dream as actually recalled, and the *latent content* of the dream, which was the hidden information of the dream and, Freud believed, the real meaning of the dream. Because patients would recall their dreams while conscious, defenses were in place, thus disguising the dream's real meaning. Therefore, the analyst had to go beneath the surface report and discover the true meaning of the dream. This technique, and its relation to Freud's theory of mind, was fully explored in what is regarded as his most important book, *The Interpretation of Dreams*, published in 1899 (Freud, 1913). In that book, Freud explored one of his great insights about dreams, the dream as *wish fulfillment*. He wrote:

> … the dream is not senseless, not absurd, does not presuppose that a part of our store of ideas is dormant while another part begins to awaken. It is a psychic phenomenon of full value, and indeed the fulfilment of a wish;

it takes its place in the concatenation of the waking psychic actions which are intelligible to us, and has been built up by a highly complicated intellectual activity. (Freud, 1913, p. 103)

For Freud, dreams were the royal road to the unconscious, the avenue by which the deepest secrets of the mind could be explored, secrets that were hidden even from the dreamer by the mechanism of *repression*.

Among the defense mechanisms, repression stands alone in importance for Freud. He wrote, "The theory of repression is the main pillar upon which rests the edifice of psychoanalysis" (Freud, 1917, p. 9). According to Freud, in the therapeutic situation, the patient's repression is aided by two processes: resistance and transference. *Resistance* occurred when a patient refused to reveal or perhaps even think about certain material in a therapy session, because the information was too traumatic or too embarrassing. Although initially frustrated by this phenomenon, Freud recognized it to be a normal occurrence in therapy and one that could be illuminating for the analyst in that it targeted avenues to be explored.

Transference occurred in therapy when the patient transferred feelings, such as, love, sexual desires, hate, anger, or envy, from the original object, for example, a husband or mother or wife, to the therapist (see Decker, 1998). Love represented a positive transference, whereas hate or anger signified negative transference. Positive transference was seen as an aid in therapy. In transferring positive feelings about a father to the therapist, the patient was endowing the therapist with considerable power, and therefore, would work harder to please the therapist, and would be more likely to follow the therapist's counsel. Negative transfer, on the other hand, could be destructive and required great skill from the therapist to convince the patient that these were feelings from the past and not from present events, to minimize their negative impact. Freud (1949) wrote:

> If we succeed, as we usually can, in persuading the patient of the true nature of the phenomena of transference, we have struck a powerful weapon out of the hand of his resistance and have converted dangers into gains. For the patient never forgets again what he has experienced in the form of transference; it has a greater force of conviction for him than anything that he can acquire in other ways. (p. 70)

For Freud, these two phenomena, resistance and transference, were key to his psychoanalytic method. They were the tools needed to trace back the neurotic symptoms through the patient's life history to their root cause.

Psychoanalysis in America

You will recall that Freud made his only visit to America in 1909 at the invitation of G. Stanley Hall. The conference was in celebration of the 20th anniversary of Clark University, a fact that no doubt amused Freud, that Americans would believe that something that was 20 years old was a cause for celebration. Europeans have a different sense of time and history, as was evident when Wundt declined Hall's invitation to speak at the same conference, explaining to Hall that he would be busy on those dates, speaking at the anniversary celebration of his own university – the 500th anniversary of the University of Leipzig, founded in 1409!

Freud was excited about his invitation. In 1909 at the age of 53, he was far from the household word he would become, thus the invitation to speak in America was important recognition for his work. He would also be receiving an honorary doctoral degree from Clark as part of the ceremonies. Freud sailed from Germany with two colleagues: Swiss psychoanalyst Carl Jung (who is discussed later in this chapter) and Sandor Ferenczi, a Hungarian. Freud and Jung would stay at Hall's home in Worcester. The conference took place in September over the span of several days. Jung gave three lectures at the conference, all on his work with his word-association method, and Freud – the star of the show – gave five lectures on psychoanalysis.

Freud began his first lecture describing a case study with which you are now quite familiar, the case of Anna O.:

> Ladies and Gentlemen: It is a novel and confusing experience for me to appear as lecturer before an eager audience in the New World. I assume that I owe this honor only to the connection of my name with the topic of psychoanalysis and, consequently, it is of psychoanalysis that I intend to speak. ... I was a student, occupied with preparations for my final examinations, when another Viennese physician, Dr. Josef Breuer, applied this method for the first time in the case of a hysterical girl ... We shall start by examining the history of this case and its treatment. (as cited in Rosenzweig, 1994, p. 397)

Although Freud had been eager to visit America, he was not sanguine about the understanding or treatment that his ideas would receive at the hands of the Americans. He and Jung had written several letters to each other in the months before their trip discussing this issue. In a letter to Jung in January 1909, Freud wrote, "I also think that once [the Americans] discover the sexual core of our psychological theories they will drop us. Their prudery and their material dependence on the public are too great" (as cited in McGuire, 1974, p. 196).

From the author's collection

Figure 7.3 The S.S. George Washington, a German-owned ocean liner built in 1908, was based in Bremen, Germany, and carried Freud, Jung, and Ferenczi to New York City where they arrived after a six-day voyage

No doubt the Americans were prudish with regard to sexual matters; nevertheless, Freud's ideas would enjoy a reception in America that Freud likely never imagined even in his best-case fantasies. Of course, it may not have been the reception that he wanted. Historian of psychology, Gail Hornstein (1992) has described the rather remarkable course of events that transpired after Freud's visit: "When psychoanalysis first arrived in the United States, most psychologists ignored it. By the 1920s, however, psychoanalysis had so captured the public imagination that it threatened to eclipse experimental psychology entirely" (p. 254). By then Freud had become a household word, and he made his first appearance on the cover of *Time* magazine in October 1924 (Fancher, 2000). The new experimental psychologists who had battled the phrenologists and the mesmerists and the spiritualists for the ownership of the science of psychology, now found themselves in a struggle with psychoanalysts for that turf. How did psychoanalytic ideas so rapidly infuse themselves into American culture? Hale (1995) has written:

> … in America rebellious intellectuals supplied an important sustaining agent in the spread of psychoanalysis – an enthusiastic clientele. The writers in the group were the first to publicize psychoanalysis. … The Great War [World War I] provoked a disillusioned turn to their rebellion against

Clark University Archives

Figure 7.4 Some of those in attendance at the 1909 Clark University Conference (*front row, left to right*): Titchener, James, William Stern (inventor of the intelligence quotient), Leo Burgerstein (an educational psychologist), Hall, Freud, and Jung; (*second row*) the first three individuals (*left to right*) are Carl Seashore (known for his work on the psychology of music), Joseph Jastrow, and Cattell. Henry Herbert Goddard is in the back row, far right

> traditional American culture … [they] launched attacks on the entrenched American faith in morality and the superiority of Anglo-Saxon race and culture … [and emphasized] the importance of the sexual instinct and the evils of "repression." (p. 57)

Although psychoanalysis did not have an immediate impact on American psychology, it did influence America's medical community. By 1911, the American Psychoanalytic Association had been formed, and two years later the first of several American psychoanalytic journals was established – the *Psychoanalytic Review*. Postdoctoral training programs in psychoanalysis were also being established to train American psychiatrists in Freud's method (Kurzweil, 1998).

American psychologists were aghast. Here was a theory of mind that postulated that the important processes in mental functioning were wholly unobservable and could only be discovered via methods that probed the unconscious, such as the interpretation of latent dream content. So psychology was not about the study of consciousness but about unconsciousness! For those psychologists who would soon be focused on behaviors and not mental processes, they were told that all behaviors were the result of unconscious motives and thus not directly observable. Therefore, it is no surprise that psychologists did not find much utility in Freud's theories or methods.

Eventually psychoanalysis had an important impact on the practice of psychology, particularly in clinical psychology, and it affected some of the assessment tools used by those practitioners, for example, the use of *projective tests* such as the *Rorschach Inkblot Test* and the *Thematic Apperception Test*. Those developments will be discussed in Chapter 9. Further, psychoanalysis would have a profound impact on American culture as expressed in art, literature, drama, films, and the language of everyday life (Burnham, 2012; Kaplan, 1998). The picture for mainstream experimental psychology is more difficult to assess. Many of Freud's ideas have been discarded, many of them unable to be put to scientific test. Freud's theories have been criticized as based in anecdote and limited case studies and not in science. He has been criticized for building a theory that could not be falsified, thus violating one of the requisites of a scientific theory. This criticism includes both the notion of hypotheses that cannot be tested and the creation of too many concepts that can be used to explain opposite outcomes, for example, if behavior X occurs, it is due to identification, but if behavior Y occurs, it is due to reaction formation.

Still, there is a great deal in American psychology that can be associated with Freud, much of which is in the field of clinical psychology: recognition of unconscious processes, importance of early experiences in shaping later behaviors, psychological disorders resulting from psychic rather than somatic causes, defense mechanisms in coping with anxiety, and greater attention to matters of sexual behavior. Moreover, Freud's work has greatly increased public interest in psychology, although in many cases it isn't the kind of public interest most psychologists would want.

Freud spent his entire life working on his psychoanalytic system. Over the years, he attracted a number of bright disciples who joined him in that work. Many of those disciples would have their own ideas and sought to modify, sometimes dramatically, Freud's theory. It was a rebellion that Freud could not tolerate; he was authoritarian and paternalistic. One by one, he cut off all contact with those he considered to have deserted the one true approach. He wrote:

I believe I have shown that the new theory which desires to substitute psychoanalysis signifies an abandonment of analysis and a secession from it. Some may be inclined to fear that this defection may be more unfortunate for the fate of psychoanalysis than any other because it emanates from persons who once played so great a part in the psychoanalytic movement and did so much to further it. I do not share this apprehension. Men are strong so long as they represent a strong idea. They become powerless when they oppose it. Psychoanalysis will be able to bear this loss and will gain new adherents for those lost. (Freud, 1917, p. 58)

Much of that statement was directed at Carl Jung who had ceased his contact with Freud three years earlier. These two men had been very close, almost like father and son. Yet in one of his last letters to Jung, a truly stinging farewell, Freud wrote, " ... I propose that we abandon our personal relations entirely. I shall lose nothing by it, for my own emotional tie with you has long been a thin thread – the lingering effects of past disappointments. ... " (McGuire, 1974, p. 539).

The Neo-Freudians

Although there are many individuals who could be discussed in a section treating the evolution of Freud's ideas, the brief coverage here will be limited to three who, it can be argued, had the greatest impact: Alfred Adler, Carl Jung, and Karen Horney. All three believed that Freud had overemphasized sexuality in his theory, and each sought to develop a theory of mind that offered a different interpretation of the life force.

Alfred Adler's Individual Psychology

Alfred Adler (1870–1937) was born in Vienna. He has been described as a sickly child who during a severe illness overheard the attending physician tell his father that he likely would not survive. Adler said that he made up his mind to prove the physician wrong. Adler earned his medical degree from the University of Vienna in 1895. He began his work in ophthalmology and then switched to general medicine. After reading Freud's *The Interpretation of Dreams*, he was drawn to a career in psychiatry, and he became part of a small discussion group that met regularly at Freud's home. He would become the first of Freud's disciples to break ranks with the master.

The split occurred in 1911, shortly after Freud had arranged for Adler to be elected president of the Vienna Psychoanalytic Society.

Adler had come to some major differences with Freud in his views on psychoanalysis. Like Freud, he viewed the libido as the id's energy force but he did not see it as principally sexual. For Adler, sexual pleasure was only one of the goals; libido was more generally a life force. He presented the ideas to the Society in February 1911. Freud was furious with Adler's reinterpretation of one of his basic concepts and there was fierce debate. The result was that Adler left the 35-member Society (either voluntarily or by being expelled) and took a number of members with him (Stagner, 1988).

Adler developed a rival school of psychoanalysis that he called *individual psychology*. Initially his group called itself the Society for Free Psychoanalysis, meaning they were free of Freud's dominance, but soon changed its name to the Society for Individual Psychology. Individual psychology emphasized *social*, not biological, motives as the primary determinants of behavior. Individuals sought superiority (clearly drawing on Adler's childhood), sought to gain mastery over their environment, and strived for perfection. These strivings were part of a goal of seeking a significant life, a life that mattered beyond the individual. Life was more directed to strivings for the future than being under the control of past events. Adler recognized humans as social creatures who sought a meaningful life through contributions to society. Much of his theory was described in his most important book, *The Practice and Theory of Individual Psychology* (1924).

Adler recognized the uniqueness of individuals, a reality embodied in his writings about style of life, later changed to *life style*, a collection of qualities unique to a particular individual. The individual's life style is responsible for self-consistency in attitudes and behaviors and for the unity of personality. Adler believed that a person's life style – the principal component of personality – developed in childhood. It operated at an unconscious level, and it defined the individual in terms of thoughts, feelings, and behaviors. Life styles were a combination of a number of behavioral and personality variables, especially embodied in activity level and social interest. Social interest was particularly important because it was the motivation to contribute positively to the larger human community. Adler developed a typology of life styles, for example, the *getting individual* who is always taking but never giving anything back, or the *ruling individual* who has high activity but little or no social interest. The best adjusted and most fulfilled of the life styles is the *socially useful individual* who is high in activity and high in social interest (Adler, 1924).

Adler was interested in several topics that would become part of psychology, such as the inferiority complex, power motivation, and birth order. He founded the first child guidance clinic in Vienna and encouraged the Austrian government to establish clinics elsewhere as well. He also wrote a number of popular books, such as *Understanding Human Nature* (1927) and *What Life Should Mean to You* (1931), intended for the public, explaining his individual psychology and how it could be used for a better life. He is often viewed as one of the important precursors to the development of humanistic psychology.

Carl Jung's Analytical Psychology

Although for a time, Freud considered Jung his heir apparent, the difficulties between the two men had begun before their trip to America. Gail Hornstein (1992) has written about a dinner conversation in 1909:

> Freud and Jung were having dinner in Bremen. It was the evening before they set sail for the Clark conference. ... Jung started talking about certain mummies in the lead cellars of the city. Freud became visibly disturbed. "Why are you so concerned with these corpses?" he asked several times. Jung went on talking. Suddenly, without warning, Freud fell to the floor in a faint. When he recovered, he accused Jung of harboring death wishes against him. (p. 254)

The incident was one of many that would drive a wedge between the two, leading to a very acrimonious parting.

Carl Gustav Jung (1875–1961) grew up in Switzerland, earning his medical degree in 1900 from the University of Basel in his hometown. His first job was in Zurich at the Burghölzli Hospital, which was a psychiatric facility and institution for the insane. He studied with Eugen Bleuler, the leading authority on *schizophrenia* in his time, who had coined the term. Jung worked there until 1909. Jung came to Freud's attention in 1906 when he wrote an article defending some of Freud's ideas on neuroses. He sent the article to Freud who was obviously pleased, writing a short letter of thanks to Jung. Their friendship would grow, but as it was with Freud, it was always that of master and pupil.

Jung's psychology is called *analytical psychology* to distinguish it from Freud's psychoanalysis. The break up came in 1913 when Jung published his *Psychology of the Unconscious*. He divided the unconscious into two parts. The *personal unconscious* contained the repressed wishes, experiences, motives of the individual, and the *collective unconscious* was a kind of racial ancestral memory in which the cumulative experiences of generations past were embedded deep in the psyche. The collective unconscious contained what Jung called *archetypes*, inherited behavioral tendencies of a mystical nature. These predisposed individuals to behave in certain ways. The most important of the archetypes was called the *self*. It served to integrate both conscious

Figure 7.5   (*Left to right*) Alfred Adler, Carl Jung, and Karen Horney

and unconscious personality components. The self developed by what Jung called the process of individuation, a process in which the person came to accept her or his archetypes into a unity of personality.

Like Adler, Jung saw libido as a generalized life energy and not just concerned with sexual pleasures. He believed that libido could be directed outward toward objects or other persons, or inward, toward the self. From this dichotomy, Jung derived the concepts of *extraversion* and *introversion*, arguably the single Jungian idea that has made its way into mainstream psychology, although one could also make a case for the *word association technique*, which was not invented by Jung but certainly popularized in America by him, based on articles he published in American psychology journals in 1906 and 1910, the latter representing his Clark conference lectures.

Jung's psychology has had impact in psychiatry and to a limited degree in clinical practice in psychology. Like Freud, many of his concepts, rooted in mysticism, religion, and spirituality, are untestable in the world of science. His work, however, has had influence in religion, art, and literature. Moreover, Jungian concepts of psychological types, in conjunction with his notions of extraversion and introversion, spawned a personality test developed in the 1940s known as the *Myers-Briggs Type Indicator*. That test is widely used today in industry and other settings despite convincing research that indicates it has little or no validity (Dawes, 1994; Pittenger, 1993).

Karen Horney: A Feminist View of Psychoanalysis

In 1922, Karen Horney (1885–1952) presented a paper at a psychoanalytic congress in Berlin on the castration complex in women, criticizing

Freud's views of women. It was the first salvo in her attack on Freud's demeaning views of women. Freud argued that the castration complex originates in girls when they realize they do not have a penis. According to Freud, they assume that they used to have a penis but it has been cut off. This results in penis envy, which manifests itself in the envy of males. Horney argued that the envy resided instead in males, in the form of *womb envy*. She tried to understand why males of her day seemed so adamant in denying opportunities to women – opportunities in education, in careers, in politics, in the arts, and so forth. She reasoned that unconsciously men felt inferior, and that they kept such sexual barriers in place so that they could maintain their illusory feelings of superiority over women. That unconscious inferiority, she said, resulted from womb envy. (Note: contemporary psychologist Carol Tavris has said that Freud was right about penis envy, but that he assigned it to the wrong gender.)

Horney never studied with Freud. She earned her medical degree in 1915 at the University of Freiberg. She was knowledgeable about psychoanalysis before her graduation and had undergone analysis with Karl Abraham, one of Freud's close disciples. Between 1922 and 1935, she published more than a dozen important articles taking issue with Freud's conception of woman and redefining men and women in the context of psychoanalysis (see these papers collected as Horney, 1967).

In 1932, seeing the signs of fascism, she fled Germany, immigrating to the United States. She settled first in Chicago, and then in 1934, in New York City where she was very much a part of the stimulating intellectual community there. She wrote all five of her books in the United States. There were a couple of other books published posthumously representing collections of her papers, unpublished or published elsewhere. One of her books, *The Neurotic Personality of Our Time* (1937) was somewhat autobiographical, speaking to her life-long search for love. It was a book that described the process of alienation and referred to life in the 1930s as "the age of anxiety" (Stagner, 1988, p. 352).

Contrary to Freud's ideas about anxiety as a product of psychic demands on the ego, Horney emphasized the social factors in life as the principal determinant. She wrote that anxiety "is an insidiously increasing, all-pervading feeling of being lonely and helpless in a hostile world" (Horney, 1937, p. 89). This was descriptive of her central concept, which she called *basic anxiety* or generalized anxiety. Another important concept was *basic hostility*, an outcome for individuals whose response to environmental factors was manifested in rage. According to Horney, individuals cope with anxiety and hostility by behaviors that take them toward others, take them away from others, or cause them to take action against others (Horney, 1937). These propensities were used to identify various personality types and their pursuit of what Horney identified as neurotic needs, for example, the need for personal admiration, the need for perfection, the need to exploit others, and the need for power.

Horney's work, published mostly in the 1920s and 1930s, has received new attention in recent years, beginning with the publication of her feminist essays in 1967, spurred by the women's movement. Her lasting contribution would appear to be her reinterpretation of Freud's views, providing a theory of psychoanalysis that did not view women as neurotic as a condition of birth. The most complete statement of her views on psychoanalysis can be found in her book, *New Ways in Psychoanalysis* (1939).

The Continued Popularity of Psychoanalysis

Our treatment in this chapter has focused on Freud with some minimal attention to several individuals who extended, revised, or (according to Freud) maligned his theory. Psychoanalytic ideas from Freud and other neo-Freudians beyond the three we discussed here, including Melanie Klein, Erik Erikson, Erich Fromm, Freda Fromm-Reichmann, Otto Rank, Harry Stack Sullivan, and others, continue to enjoy great popularity. Go into any bookstore and look at the titles that are on the shelves labeled "Psychology." The overwhelming majority are likely to be psychoanalytically based. Count the number of full-length biographies published on Freud (perhaps nearly 70, although not all are currently in print). Count the number on Wundt – there is one. When it comes to public access of psychology, psychoanalysis is still the stuff of talk shows, movies, magazine articles, and self-help programs.

In the 1920s, when psychoanalysis was gaining followers in the general public, American psychology was being overtaken by a new philosophy – *behaviorism* – that insisted that the object of study in psychological science was not consciousness but behavior. It is no surprise that psychoanalysis, a theory grounded in the study of the unconscious, would find it tough going within the university psychology community. The emergence and development of American behaviorism is the subject of the next chapter.

8

Behaviorism

With winter snows still a threat in February, workers in Brooklyn hurried to complete the new baseball park scheduled to open that spring. The year was 1913, and the Brooklyn Dodgers were looking forward to their first season at Ebbets Field. Across the East River in Harlem, construction continued on the Apollo Theater that would open the following year. The theater, which would launch the careers of so many black performers in its rich history, would not admit African American patrons until 1925. In February 1913, there were two other events taking place in New York City at opposite ends of Manhattan. Although, no one suspected it at the time, both of these events would shake the very foundations of their respective worlds. One event received an immense amount of publicity; the other went largely unnoticed.

At Lexington Avenue, between 24th and 25th streets, the 69th Regiment Armory Building was hosting an art show – not just any art show, but the first major public exhibition of modern art in America. "The idea was to give modern art a splashy debut before an ignorant New York public. It succeeded beyond its organizers' dreams" (Hughes, 1997, p. 353). It was called The International Exhibition of Modern Art but is usually referred to by historians as the Armory Show.

"No exhibition had ever had such a media blitz. For once, here was an art event that had the crunch of real news, the latest murder or the newest political scandal. It provoked a torrent of satires, cartoons, and hostile reviews. ... Madness was loose in the Armory, and New Yorkers, on reading the reviews, flocked to see it" (Hughes, 1997, p. 356).

There was Marcel Duchamp's *Nude Descending a Staircase, No. 2*, George Bellows' *Circus*, and Wassily Kandinsky's *Garden of Love*. There were works by Van Gogh, Manet, Picasso, Braque, Seurat, Matisse, and many others – nearly 1,300 works of art, art that most Americans had never seen. More than 70,000 visitors viewed the show, no doubt some in the same way they would flock to see a train wreck or a burning building. The mountain of negative reviews notwithstanding, when the show was over, the definition of art in America had been changed forever.

The other event certainly did not match the Armory Show in attendance or media attention. It was a lecture by psychologist John Watson on the campus of Columbia University. Watson was speaking at Columbia at the invitation of James McKeen Cattell. For years, Watson had been growing dissatisfied with progress in psychology; his complaints were both conceptual and methodological. He was disillusioned with the continued focus on mental states that seemed so elusive as objects of scientific study, and he was especially perturbed with the overwhelming reliance on the method of introspection (Watson, 1936). He had shared some of his dismay with colleagues at Johns Hopkins University and particularly with fellow animal researcher and Harvard University psychologist Robert Yerkes. But he had decided that he could no longer contain himself. He would take the gloves off and explain why the psychology of his teachers was nothing short of nonsense. Watson (1913) told his audience, "I do not wish unduly to criticize psychology. It has failed signally, I believe, during its fifty-odd years of existence as an experimental discipline to make its place in the world as an undisputed natural science" (p. 163). He continued, "The time seems to have come when psychology must discard all reference to consciousness; when it need no longer delude itself into thinking that it is making mental states the object of observation" (p. 164).

What must his audience have been thinking? Here was this 34-year-old psychologist, a youngster really, a graduate of the functional psychology program at the University of Chicago, an animal researcher, who was telling his elders that they had "failed signally" in producing a science of psychology, that their belief that it was possible to study mental states was nothing more than a delusion. Thus began what historians call the behaviorist revolution. As a revolution, it occurred ever so slowly as we will show. But behaviorism would prevail, banishing the structural and functional schools of psychology. It was a time when psychology lost its mind.

John Watson and the Founding of Behaviorism

John Broadus Watson (1878–1958) was born in poverty in rural Travelers Rest, South Carolina, to a religiously devout mother, who named him for a Baptist minister, and an alcoholic father who abandoned his family for long periods at a time. Watson attended Furman University, a Baptist college in nearby Greenville, where his mother hoped he would prepare to be a Baptist minister. He graduated with a master's degree in

1899 and served as a school principal for a brief time. His mother died that year, freeing Watson from the expectations she held for him. He was ambitious and eager to escape his life in South Carolina. He recognized that further education would give him other opportunities, and so he applied for admission to the University of Chicago. He was accepted, beginning his study there in 1900, taking courses with John Dewey and James Rowland Angell (Buckley, 1989). Watson (1936) wrote about how he supported his studies:

> I had to earn my living, which I did serving as a kind of assistant janitor. For two years I used to dust Mr. Angell's desk and clean the apparatus. I delivered books for an instructors' circulating library for $1.00 per Saturday. I waited on table for my board for two years at a $2.50 per week students' boarding house. One year later when I met Professor H. H. Donaldson, he asked me to keep his white rats for him, a job which helped me greatly on the financial side. (p. 273)

Initially Watson thought he would pursue study in philosophy rather than psychology, but he was turned off by his classes with Dewey. Instead, he chose to work with Angell and with the neurologist Henry Herbert Donaldson (1857–1938), both of whom supervised his doctoral research in which he used white rats to study the relationship between learning and changes in the nerve fibers in the rat's cortex. He received his doctoral degree in 1903 and, although he had offers elsewhere, he stayed on the faculty at Chicago as an instructor, working closely with Angell. He also married Mary Ickes, a young woman who had been a student in one of his classes.

As noted earlier, animal research was not an option in structuralism given the reliance on introspection. In a functional psychology that was concerned with learning as a means of adapting to changing environments, animals made excellent subjects. They could be bred and raised in conditions that allowed the researcher to control whatever stimulation they received, thus ensuring their behavioral naiveté. Most important, they proved to be excellent learners and problem solvers. Animal research would come to dominate functionalism and behaviorism. The origins of this work, of course, date from the work of Charles Darwin.

Beginnings of Comparative Psychology

Comparative psychology is a subfield of animal psychology. Whereas many animal psychologists study animal behavior for its own sake, comparative psychologists study the behavior of nonhuman animals in order to generalize their findings to human behavior. Comparative psychology is possible only if there is some tie between humans and these other animals, that is, some evidence that they share a common ancestry. Keeping human beings separate from the animal kingdom had been something that philosophers and theologians had been careful to do for centuries. But things would change.

In the early part of the sixteenth century, Copernicus had upset the world when he showed that the earth was not the center of the universe, and that it revolved around the sun. Suddenly our planet seemed a little less significant. Then, in the middle of the nineteenth century, Darwin demonstrated the morphological and behavioral ties between humans and the rest of the animal kingdom. Now humans seemed a little less significant. Several of Darwin's books were important for the birth of comparative psychology including *On the Origin of Species* (1859), *The Descent of Man* (1871), and especially *The Expression of the Emotions in Man and Animals* (1872). Darwin was interested in animal behavior but he also speculated about the relationship between animal and human behavior. That linkage would be more obvious in the work of his follower George John Romanes (1848–1894).

In his studies of animal behavior, Romanes used a method that he called *introspection by analogy* (recall that Romanes was mentioned briefly in Chapter 5 in the discussion of Washburn's book, *The Animal Mind*). Here is how Romanes (1883) described his method: "Starting from what I know subjectively of the operations of my own individual mind, and the activities which in my own organism they prompt, I proceed by analogy to infer from the observable activities of other organisms what are the mental operations that underlie them" (pp. 1–2). Romanes recognized that the mental processes in higher animals (e.g., mammals) should be closer to those of humans than would say the mental processes of insects. There was more danger in using the analogy in lower species. Still, he acknowledged that it was the only method he could use to try to understand the mental functioning of these animals. He wrote,

> ... if we observe an ant or a bee apparently exhibiting sympathy or rage, we must either conclude that some psychological state resembling that of sympathy or rage is present, or else refuse to think about the subject at all; from the observable facts there is no other inference open. Therefore, having full regard to the progressive weakening of the analogy from human to brute psychology as we recede through the animal kingdom downwards from man, still, as it is the only analogy available, I shall follow it throughout the animal series. (p. 9)

Although Romanes was an excellent biologist whose books were filled with insightful observations, his anecdotal method caused concern as the science of comparative psychology evolved.

C. Lloyd Morgan (1852–1936), also an English biologist influenced by Darwin, objected to the practices of Romanes and others attributing human mental processes, such as reasoning, to animals lower in the phylogenetic scale, when such attributions might not be warranted. He argued that in explaining animal behavior, a higher mental process should not be invoked if the behavior could be explained adequately by a lower mental process, a caution known as *Morgan's canon*. Morgan believed that his canon applied to human as well as animal behavior. Behaviorists, such as John Watson, would use the canon as a basis for rejecting psychological explanations that appealed to mental states, such as consciousness, instead of explanations wholly situated in behavioral terms.

Morgan did not rule out the use of introspection by analogy and, indeed, used the method himself, limiting its use primarily to mammals. Yet Morgan stressed the importance of empirical observations, ideally under controlled conditions. He also performed simple experiments with animals in their natural settings, by manipulating objects in their environment and observing how they reacted to these manipulations (Morgan, 1902). These developments moved comparative psychology closer to an experimental science. That status would be realized more fully in the work of the American psychologist Edward Thorndike and the Russian physiologist Ivan Pavlov.

Edward L. Thorndike (1874–1949) was a doctoral student with Cattell and joined the Columbia University faculty after graduation in 1899. Thorndike acknowledged the influence of Morgan in his own research. Thorndike began his animal research career testing baby chicks, first in his room, until his landlady objected, and then in the basement of William James's home. He continued his animal work at Columbia, testing the problem-solving ability of cats in escaping 15 puzzle boxes he had constructed. Each puzzle box required a different response for escape. Once the animal escaped the box, it was rewarded with food. Thorndike found that the animals learned to escape the boxes in a trial and error fashion, which led him to reject the idea that reasoning was involved (Dewsbury, 1984). He found that responses that led to escape were gradually learned, whereas responses that were not effective were gradually eliminated from the animal's behavior in the box. From these observations, he formulated the *law of effect*, which is today recognized as the forerunner of the *law of reinforcement*. Thorndike's (1905) law was stated as follows: "Any act which in a given situation produces satisfaction becomes associated with that situation, so that when the situation recurs the act is more likely than before to recur also" (p. 203). Thorndike's animal learning studies are usually described as instrumental learning. They are similar in some ways to the work of B. F. Skinner who will be discussed later.

Ivan Pavlov (1849–1936) won the Nobel Prize in Medicine or Physiology in 1904 and was arguably the most important scientist in Russia in his time. At about the time Thorndike was conducting his puzzle box studies, Pavlov was beginning to investigate an interesting phenomenon in his subjects (dogs), who were salivating before they were supposed to be doing that. Pavlov recognized the importance of this interesting phenomenon, and so he spent the last 34 years of his life working out the details of a kind of learning that is today called *classical* or *Pavlovian conditioning*. Pavlov discovered that dogs, which normally salivated in the presence of food, would start to salivate before the food was presented. This early salivation was elicited by the presence of stimuli that had been paired with the food previously so that the stimuli predicted the occurrence of food. Pavlov's extensive program of research eventually worked out the parameters of such conditioning phenomena as acquisition, extinction, spontaneous recovery, generalization, discrimination, conditioned inhibition, conditioned emotional reactions, and higher-order conditioning (Windholz, 1990). This work was recognized as exceptionally important in the 1920s when Pavlov was nominated four more times for what would have been a second Nobel Prize (Benjamin, 2003).

We have included this brief review of comparative psychology because this work was important for the beginnings of functionalism,

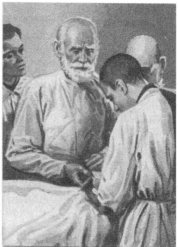

Archives of the History of American Psychology, The Center for the History of Psychology, The University of Akron

From the author's collection

Figure 8.1 Edward Thorndike (*left*), and Ivan Pavlov from a souvenir card in a 1935 pack of Max Cigarettes produced in South Africa

and because it was especially critical in shaping Watson's ideas about a behavioral psychology. In this section, it should be clear that the work in comparative psychology moved away from a concern with mental processes, as embodied particularly in the work of Romanes, to a concern with behavior and physiological processes, for example, escape from Thorndike's puzzle boxes and salivation in Pavlov's conditioning studies. Moreover, there was a growing realization that comparative psychology was an experimental science and not just an empirical one. Watson (1913) made these same points in his talk at Columbia University regarding his vision of a new science of psychology. He said, "I believe we can write a psychology, define it as [the science of behavior], and never go back upon our definition: never use the term consciousness, mental states, mind, content, introspectively verifiable, imagery, and the like" (p. 166).

Watson's Behaviorism

Watson (1913) began his Columbia address, "Psychology as the behaviorist views it is a purely objective experimental branch of natural science. Its theoretical goal is the prediction and control of behavior" (p. 158). He was concerned that psychology, which had expressed its intent decades earlier to join the natural sciences, had been unable to do so. He believed that two causes stood out above all others. One was the pursuit of consciousness as an object of study. The other was the use of introspection as a method. Introspection was, in Watson's view, a method that allowed so much personal bias into the observational process that it was rendered invalid as a scientific method. Thus, behaviorism called for a new object of study and a new methodology, virtually a total overhaul of the science of psychology. Only then, claimed Watson, would psychology be able to take its rightful place among the other sciences. To limit psychology to the study of behavior meant that some topics would disappear from the subject matter of psychology, topics such as dreaming, thinking, and imagery. Emotions could be studied in terms of their physical and physiological manifestations but not via introspective accounts detailing the perception of inner states.

Methods needed to change. Watson called for more objective forms of observation than what had preceded, with and without the use of scientific instruments. He approved of the reaction time methods in use by Wundt and Cattell, and the experimental studies of memory done by Ebbinghaus. He approved of some kinds of psychological tests so long as they were not mental tests. He approved of the puzzle box techniques of Thorndike and the delayed reaction method of Walter Hunter at Chicago, which was considered by some to be a method for assessing animal memory (Watson, 1914). Watson was especially in favor of the classical conditioning method and used it in his most famous study.

Conditioned Emotions: Little Albert

In 1919, when Watson was on the faculty of Johns Hopkins University, he wanted to see if he could condition an emotion in a human. Watson believed that humans were born with three innate emotions: fear, rage, and love. The task would be to take one of those emotions and condition it to a stimulus that previously did not elicit that emotion. The experiment was conducted with the assistance of one of Watson's graduate students, Rosalie Rayner, and performed on a human infant known as Albert B. or *little Albert*.

Watson demonstrated that at the beginning of the experiment, Albert had no fear of a white rat. During the experiment, Watson paired a loud noise with the presence of the white rat over several trials until Albert showed fear (crying, trying to crawl away) when the rat was placed near him. Watson found that the fear also generalized somewhat to other stimuli that shared a common quality such as fur, so that Albert exhibited some fear to a rabbit, a dog, and a fur coat, even though those stimuli had not been paired with the loud noise (Watson & Rayner, 1920). Little Albert was not deconditioned; his mother removed him from the hospital before that could happen. There is, however, no indication that Watson intended to reverse the conditioning. [The first deconditioning of a fear would be performed by Mary Cover Jones (1896–1987) four years later (Jones, 1924; Rutherford, 2006).]

The questions of Albert's identity and what happened to him after the study have been of interest to psychologists and students of psychology. After several years of detective work, including sophisticated analyses of photographic evidence, psychologist Hall Beck and his colleagues published an article in 2009 claiming that they had identified him, a boy whose real name was Douglas Merritte. Sadly, he died in 1925 at the age of six (Beck, Levinson, & Irons, 2009). Although the research by Beck and his colleagues is impressively thorough, their identification of Albert has been challenged by others who claim that Douglas is likely not little Albert and that "psychology's lost boy" is still missing (see Harris, 2011; Powell, 2010, 2011; Reese, 2010). In 2013, several Canadian psychologists reported that they have found him. They have identified another candidate who was a contemporary of Douglas Merritte and who was the son of a foster mother at Johns Hopkins Hospital. His name

(Left, Right): Archives of the History of American Psychology, The Center for the History of Psychology, The University of Akron

Figure 8.2 Rosalie Rayner (Watson) and John B. Watson

was Albert Barger, and they believe he was very likely the real Little Albert (Powell, Digdon, & Smithson, 2013).

The little Albert study had a number of methodological problems in its conduct that called the results into question, a fact that was recognized by Watson's contemporaries (Harris, 1979). Notwithstanding the methodological flaws, the study was used by Watson to promote the explanatory power of his behavioral psychology. Watson had demonstrated a rather remarkable outcome, the fact that it was possible to condition a fear to an object that previously had not been feared. The study quite dramatically illustrated the power of conditioning in the control of behavior. Not surprisingly, it became one of the most cited studies in the history of psychology.

Watson at Johns Hopkins University

When Watson delivered his address at Columbia in 1913, he was head of the Department of Psychology at Johns Hopkins University where he had joined the faculty in 1908. A month after his talk it was published in the journal *Psychological Review*, a journal that Watson edited. Cattell and James Mark Baldwin had founded that journal in 1894 as an alternative to Hall's journal, which increasingly had become a house organ, that is, a publication outlet largely for Hall's own students and faculty at Clark. Watson's article was entitled "Psychology As the Behaviorist Views It" and is often referred to as the *behaviorist manifesto*. It is the generally acknowledged starting point of behaviorism.

At Johns Hopkins, Watson continued his animal work, including summers spent on an island off the Florida Keys where he studied bird behavior. He also began a line of research on human infants, planning to extend his views on conditioning to humans. It was in his infant laboratory that the research occurred with little Albert. His career trajectory continued its meteoric rise. In 1915, he was elected president of the American Psychological Association. "He was thirty-six-years old and the wunderkind of American psychology" (Buckley, 1989, p. 86). How could Watson have been elected to this prestigious post when he had trashed the work of others so thoroughly two years earlier? His biographer Kerry Buckley (1989) has written, "Watson won the support of the majority of American psychologists because he articulated the hopes of many in the profession who struggled for the recognition of psychology as a full-fledged member of the scientific community. He was hailed by the younger members of the profession as a 'second Moses'" (p. 86), who would lead psychology out of the bondage of metaphysics and philosophy and into the promised land of scientific respectability.

As the fall semester began at Johns Hopkins in 1920, Watson was at the height of his career, a major figure in psychology, both nationally and internationally. He was one of the academic stars at Johns Hopkins and, to ward off offers from competing universities, the university's president gave Watson a sizeable increase in salary. Yet just a few months later, Watson was involved in a scandalous divorce, brought on by the discovery of his affair with his graduate student Rosalie Rayner. He was forced to resign from the university. Watson thought that he would get another academic position, but no offers were forthcoming (Benjamin, Whitaker, Ramsey, & Zeve, 2007).

Watson moved to New York City to seek work, believing that he could apply his behavioral theories to the world of business. [He had taught a course on the "psychology of advertising" at Johns Hopkins in 1917 (Buckley, 1982).] He landed a position at the J. Walter Thompson advertising agency where he eventually became vice president and a millionaire (Buckley, 1989). It is likely that the earlier work of Scott, Hollingworth, and others in advertising helped pave the way for Watson's being able to find work in that field. One of his letters of reference for that job was written by E. B. Titchener whose psychology Watson had so roundly condemned in his manifesto. Titchener did not agree with Watson's psychology, but he respected him as a scientist and felt that his banishment from Johns Hopkins was overly harsh.

Watson's divorce became final in December 1920, and Mary Ickes got custody of their two children. Watson would marry Rayner seven days later. They would have two children as well. In addition to his advertising work, Watson wrote regularly for the public, both magazine articles and popular books. One of his books on child rearing (Watson, 1928) was particularly controversial because it encouraged parents to raise their children by displaying very little affection toward them, which Watson believed would create a more independent and self-reliant child. It was a book he is said later to have regretted writing. Tragically, Rayner died in 1935 at the age of 36 from a rare form of dysentery. Watson remained in advertising work until his retirement in 1945, but Rayner's death had taken the joy from his life. He never recovered from that tragedy (Buckley, 1989).

Watson as Behaviorism's Founder

The intellectual roots of behaviorism predate Watson. There were contemporaries in psychology who shared some of Watson's ideas that psychology needed to move more toward the study of behavior. For example, University of Michigan psychologist Walter Pillsbury (1872–1960), a Titchener PhD student, had defined psychology as the science of behavior in his 1911 textbook on psychology. Max Meyer (1873–1967), a psychologist at the University of Missouri, attacked introspection and the study of consciousness in his 1911 book, *The Fundamental Laws of Human Behavior*. Moreover, these rumblings extended beyond the field of psychology, for example, in physiology where Maurice Parmalee published a book entitled *The Science of Human Behavior* in 1912. Yet even acknowledging the fact that the Zeitgeist was moving toward a behavioral psychology, the movement belonged to Watson. Watson's contribution was that he crystallized these scattered ideas into a systematic formulation that was *new*. In addition, he had the drive and the personality necessary to sell the idea. And for those reasons, most historians recognize him as the founder of behaviorism.

The Growth of Behaviorism

Although Watson's manifesto is said to have initiated a behavioral revolution in psychology, it was a slow revolution. Samelson (1981) has researched the literature following Watson's address showing that there was no immediate firestorm created by it, and that the rise of behaviorism was an event of the 1920s and not the 1910s. However, behaviorism would come to dominate American psychology like no school before or since for a period of nearly 50 years. Watson's call to arms for a science that would be capable of prediction and control was taken up by a number of psychologists who would become prominent in the twentieth century. We will close this chapter with a discussion of three of these: Edward Tolman, Clark Hull, and B. F. Skinner, individuals who are generally identified with the period of American psychology's history known as neobehaviorism.

Neobehaviorism

Neobehaviorism is generally described as the period in American psychology from 1930 through 1970. These psychologists were interested in theory, focused their research on learning and motivation, argued over the role of reinforcement in learning, and used animals, mostly rats, as their preferred objects of study. The three to be discussed here all developed and published their approaches to psychology in the 1930s. Each of them would have a substantial impact on psychology, although at different times. In the beginning, Hull and Tolman garnered most of the attention, proposing rival theories of behavior. Hull would gain the upper hand in that battle, enjoying immense popularity in the 1940s and 1950s. At that time, Skinner was a minor figure whose psychology seemed something of an outlier. However, in the 1960s Skinner's ideas would rise to prominence, as Hull would virtually disappear from the scene. Tolman would be rediscovered in the 1960s because of the relation of his work to the cognitive movement in psychology that was emerging in that decade.

Tolman's Cognitive Behaviorism

Edward Chace Tolman (1886–1959) earned his PhD at Harvard University under Hugo Münsterberg and Robert Yerkes, and spent almost his entire career at the University of California at Berkeley. He published his most important book in 1932, entitled *Purposive Behavior in Animals and Men*. For Tolman, behavior is, in a word, *purposive*; it is directed toward some goal. The purposiveness of behavior is determined by cognitions. How does a behaviorist justify such mentalistic terms? Tolman (1932) wrote, "Behavior as behavior, that is, as molar, *is* purposive and *is* cognitive. … it must nonetheless be emphasized that purposes and cognitions which are thus immediately, immanently, in behavior are wholly objective as to definition. They are defined by characters and relationships which we observe out there in behavior" (p. 5).

Tolman objected to Hull's theory, which allowed no place for cognitive processes in the explanatory accounts of behavior. Tolman could not understand how anyone could watch rats in a maze and not see that behavior was purposive, that rats had *cognitive maps* – spatial representations of their world – that allowed them to function effectively. Tolman argued that with experience, an animal builds up expectancies about the environment, and that these expectancies are one of the determinants of the animal's responding. In essence, the animal learns what leads to what.

Tolman objected to the approach of Watson that limited psychology to a strict stimulus–response framework. He called for a psychology that recognized the existence of *intervening variables* – processes within the organism that intervened between stimulus and response (recall the organismic variables in Woodworth's S-O-R formulation). Cognitions were examples of those intervening variables, and they were scientifically respectable so long as they could be tied to observable referents.

Tolman made a number of important contributions to psychology including the distinction between learning and performance, the demonstration of *latent learning*, the distinction between response and place learners, and cognitive maps. Most of Tolman's work was using rats to study learning. In the *learning–performance distinction*, he noted that learning could not be observed but could be inferred by measuring performance. Learning was said to set an upper limit on performance. Performance was behavior, learning an internal state. In measuring the learning, the goal of the experimenter was to establish the conditions so that performance would be maximized and thus be the best possible indicator of learning.

Tolman disagreed with both Hull and Skinner over the role of reinforcement in learning. He did not believe that reinforcement was necessary for learning to occur and his studies on latent learning supported that position. He showed that rats given time in a maze with no food reward present would nevertheless learn something about that maze (begin to construct a cognitive map) so that when the rat was placed in the maze with food in the goal box, the rat would require fewer trials to learn the maze than would a wholly naïve rat (Tolman, 1948).

In another demonstration of how rats construct cognitive maps, Tolman tested rats in a plus-shaped maze. One group always turned right at the intersection of the maze to get to the food, regardless of which arm of the maze they would be placed in to start. However, other rats were always fed in the same place regardless of where they started. Thus one group (response learners) had to learn to turn right to get food; the other group (place learners) had to learn to go to the same part of the maze on each trial. Tolman found that the place learners learned the maze faster than the response learners, indicating the development and use of cognitive maps that had aided learning (Tolman, 1951).

Tolman would win some battles with Hull but would eventually lose the war. Perhaps his cognitive concepts were just too much to accept in a behaviorism that was desperately trying to cut all ties to its mentalistic past. The alternative behaviorisms of Hull and Skinner would not admit such concepts as expectancies, cognitive maps, or purpose. Moreover, it was toward their way of thinking that American psychology was moving. However, all was not lost for Tolman; the importance of his ideas would be rediscovered and reclaimed in the 1960s and 1970s when psychologists found it possible once again to talk about consciousness and renew the study of mental events. That is the subject of the last chapter in this book, the history of cognitive psychology.

Hull's Hypothetico-Deductive Behaviorism

Clark Leonard Hull (1884–1952) earned his PhD in 1913 at the University of Wisconsin, where Joseph Jastrow, Daniel Starch, and V. A. C. Henmon served as mentors. Hull's major book describing his theory of psychology, *Principles of Behavior*, was not published until 1943, but most components of his system had been spelled out in a series of articles in the *Psychological Review* in the 1930s (see Amsel & Rashotte, 1984). Hull remained on the faculty at Wisconsin after his graduation, but in 1929 moved to Yale University where he spent the remainder of his career. His early work was on aptitude testing and hypnosis and he produced important books on both subjects. However, it was his theory of behavior, as expressed in his final three books that made him the most cited psychologist of his time. Here is how Hull (1952) conceptualized his theory:

> I came to the definite conclusion around 1930 that psychology is a true natural science; that its primary laws are expressible quantitatively by means of a moderate number of ordinary equations; that all the complex behavior of single individuals will ultimately be derivable as secondary laws from (1) these primary laws together with (2) the conditions under which the behavior occurs; and that all the behavior of groups as a whole, i.e., strictly social behavior as such, may similarly be derived as quantitative laws from the same primary equations. (p. 155)

That represented a great deal of faith in the lawfulness of human behavior, not to mention group behavior!

To establish his grand theory and to test its validity, Hull used what is called the *hypothetico-deductive method*. He began by stating a series of

Archives of the History of American Psychology, The Center for the History of Psychology, The University of Akron

Figure 8.3 (*Left to right*) Kurt Lewin (whose work will be discussed in Chapter 10), Edward Tolman, and Clark Hull at a psychology conference circa 1934. Hull and Tolman were theoretical rivals and often debated each other at the annual meetings of the American Psychological Association. Here they demonstrate that they can be less than serious at times. Note the cane that Hull is holding, the result of his contracting polio when he was an undergraduate student

postulates from which one could derive testable hypotheses. In other words, a hypothesis would be deduced from a postulate, then tested, and based on the results of the experiment, the hypothesis would be confirmed, giving support to the general postulate, or disconfirmed in which case the postulate might require modification, and then another hypothesis would be deduced from the revised postulate, and so on. Recall Thorndike's statement of the law of effect or law of reinforcement earlier in this chapter. Here is Hull's statement of that same law as one of the postulates of his theory.

Whenever a reaction (R) takes place in temporal contiguity with an afferent receptor impulse (s) resulting from the impact upon a receptor of a stimulus energy (S), and this conjunction is followed closely by the diminution in a need (and the associated diminution in the drive, D, and in the drive receptor discharge, s_d), there will result an increment, Δ (s→R), in the tendency for that stimulus on subsequent occasions to evoke that action. This is the "law" of primary reinforcement. (Hull, 1943, p. 71)

No doubt, you noticed that the law is a little more difficult to recognize in this form. In fact you may have to read Hull's version several times before you see that he is saying what Thorndike (1905) said, which was, "Any act which in a given situation produces satisfaction becomes associated with that situation, so that when the situation recurs the act is more likely than before to recur also" (p. 203). These kinds of labored, but precise, formulations were necessary to allow Hull to generate a quantitative behavioral theory as he described above, that is, that the primary laws of human behavior are "expressible quantitatively by means of a moderate number of ordinary equations."

Unlike Tolman, *reinforcement* was a key concept in Hull's system; without reinforcement, Hull stated that learning would not occur. Reinforcement was said to operate by means of *drive reduction*, or "diminution of the drive" as expressed in Hull's statement earlier. Drives represented bodily needs such as hunger, thirst, oxygen, avoiding pain, optimal body temperature, sleep, and sex (Hull, 1943). When the drives were activated due to bodily need, behaviors were instituted that led to the reduction of these drives. That reduction was reinforcing, meaning actions that led to drive reduction were likely to be repeated in subsequent situations.

Reinforcement was key to the strength of association between a particular stimulus and response, a concept that Hull called *habit strength*. According to Hull, habit strength grew as a direct result of the number of reinforcements experienced. Habit strength was in essence a measure of the strength of the S-R connection, that is, the strength of learning.

These are only a few of the many constructs in Hull's theory that are expressed in his numerous postulates and corollaries, but the intent has been to provide an indication of the nature of his method and what he intended to accomplish with his theory of behavior. What he created was a psychological theory that has no peer, before him or since. Because of the precision of his postulates, his theory did what good scientific theories are supposed to do – generate testable hypotheses. As a result, he created an industry in experimental psychology for almost two decades in which doctoral students did not have to look far for a testable question they could pursue in their dissertation research. Tests of Hullian theory were in abundance and the psychological literature filled with such studies. He was the most cited psychologist of his day:

"A frequently cited measure of his influence is that during the decade 1941–1950 approximately 40 percent of all experimental articles published in the *Journal of Experimental Psychology* and the *Journal of Comparative and Physiological Psychology* included references to his work" (Amsel & Rashotte, 1984, p. 2).

Hull's theory proved to be a two-edged sword for him, showing why there are advantages to being intentionally vague about your ideas – it is difficult for people to prove you wrong! But Hull made his theory explicit; it led to hundreds of tests of the adequacy of his postulates. It made him a very visible psychologist and, ultimately, a very invisible one when human behavior proved to be less lawful than he had hoped. Webster and Coleman (1992) have expressed this view, noting that "Hull's impact and subsequent decline [were] inevitable outcomes of the programmatic nature of [his] behavior theory" (p. 1063). Although Hull's views no longer hold sway in psychology, historians acknowledge his role in demanding a place for scientific theory in psychology. John Mills (1998) wrote that it is important to acknowledge Hull's "substantial intellectual achievement based on persistence in the face of many problems and the struggle to produce a theory that would be at once all-embracing and precise and that would meet his rather exacting standards of what it meant to be scientific" (p. 122).

Skinner's Radical Behaviorism

Burrhus Frederic Skinner (1904–1990) attained a fame that few scientists and fewer psychological scientists ever achieve, both within the scientific community and in the general public (Rutherford, 2003, 2004). A survey in 1975 showed him to be the best-known scientist in America among college students. After graduating from college, Skinner considered a career as a novelist. He even sent several short stories to poet Robert Frost who replied to Skinner that he thought he had the talent to be successful as a writer. However, Skinner opted for science instead, choosing psychology. He earned his doctorate from Harvard University in 1931, where he was most influenced by William Crozier, a physiologist. After faculty positions at the University of Minnesota and Indiana University, Skinner returned to Harvard in 1948 where he remained for the rest of his life. Although he officially retired from Harvard, he continued to write books and articles up to the time of his death from leukemia at age 86. His last article (Skinner, 1990) entitled, "Can Psychology Be a Science of Mind?" was completed the day he died. True to his life-long mission as the defender of a radical behaviorism, it was an attack on the mentalism of cognitive psychology and a reminder to psychology that it would never be a science dealing in the "explanatory fictions" that he saw in cognitive psychology.

Whereas Hull sought to found a behaviorism that used deductive methods to build a mathematical science of psychology, Skinner eschewed both theory and mathematics to build the most internally consistent system of psychology yet achieved, one that has carried Watson's goals of *prediction and control* to the highest levels psychology has seen. He called his psychology the *experimental analysis of behavior*. Skinner's behaviorism was first described in his 1938 book, *The Behavior of Organisms*. It emphasized the study of learning in animals, mostly rats and pigeons, and mostly in chambers that Hull called Skinner boxes, (the name stuck, although Skinner wasn't fond of it). Skinner proposed a form of conditioning that would be called *operant conditioning*, a form of instrumental learning akin to the learning exhibited in Thorndike's puzzle box studies. Whereas Pavlov studied S-R relationships in which a stimulus was said to elicit a response, Skinner cared little about the eliciting stimulus. Instead, he proposed an R-S psychology that focused on how *consequences* affected behavior. That is, he was interested in the stimulus events that *followed* a behavior.

Like Thorndike, Skinner recognized that some stimulus events led to increases in behavior (reinforcers), whereas others stimulus events led to decreases in behavior (punishers). Over the years, he plumbed the depths of those two concepts gaining understanding of the complexities of two of the most powerful shapers of behavior. At one level, his psychology is amazingly simple; at another, it is richly complex and nuanced. Most psychologists understand the former; few seem to master the latter.

When Skinner began his work in operant conditioning, it did not fit the dominant paradigm for psychological science at that time. True it made use of rats, and yes, it focused on learning and performance. However, the similarities stopped there. While many psychologists were adopting the multifactor experimental designs whose results could be teased apart using the new statistical method of analysis of variance, and while other psychologists were testing 20 and 30 rats in a series of maze tests to create aggregated learning curves, Skinner was conducting a number of studies using a single animal or only a few animals and no statistical analyses, other than perhaps some rate measures derived from the cumulative records of the animals responding over time. Skinner's studies were about "If I do this, then the rat does this, and then if I change to this, then the rat does that," and so on. It didn't seem to fit with psychology's striving for scientific respectability, for example, in the way that Hull was doing with his hypothetico-deductive method. Skinner's psychology was so far outside the mainstream that his students found it difficult to get their work published in psychology's journals or accepted for the programs at psychological conferences. Therefore, they founded their own journals and their own organizations. All of that would change though in the 1960s when the applied value of Skinner's work was realized, especially in education and clinical psychology. Suddenly Skinner's ideas and Skinner were popular.

Skinner identified a number of different patterns of reinforcement. *Continuous reinforcement* meant that every response that was supposed to be reinforced was reinforced. But in the real world that rarely happens. Instead, reinforcement occurs on an intermittent basis. Skinner referred to this more common pattern as *partial reinforcement*, and he showed that it produced behavior that was stronger (more resistant to extinction) than behaviors that had been continuously reinforced, a phenomenon referred to as the *partial reinforcement effect*. His research identified many partial reinforcement patterns that he called schedules of reinforcement. Some of these were based on the number of responses emitted by the subject, called *ratio schedules* and some were based on time intervals called *interval schedules*. The number of responses and time intervals could be either fixed or variable. Of greatest importance, he demonstrated how these various schedules could produce dramatically different patterns of responding.

Skinner's operant conditioning measures were aimed at changing behavior by strengthening it through reinforcers, suppressing it through punishers, and weakening it or eliminating it through extinction. He showed that there were a number of undesirable side effects when punishment was used, especially too frequently. He called for minimal use of punishment and, instead, emphasized the more positive outcomes of reinforcement whether in schools, the workplace, or parenting.

Skinner mined operant conditioning in the way that Pavlov had done with his form of conditioning. Skinner provided important findings on shaping, acquisition, extinction, discrimination, generalization, schedules of reinforcement, reinforcement delay, punishment, negative versus positive reinforcement, partial reinforcement effect, persistence, and too many other phenomena to list. He achieved a consistency of results that had not been seen before, demonstrating the explanatory power of his constructs.

Skinner was an inventor, always looking for ways to apply his behavioral technology to some public good. That work began during World War II when he developed a missile guidance system using pigeons (Capshew, 1993; Skinner, 1960). It continued in the 1940s with the design of a better crib for infants, called the baby tender or aircrib

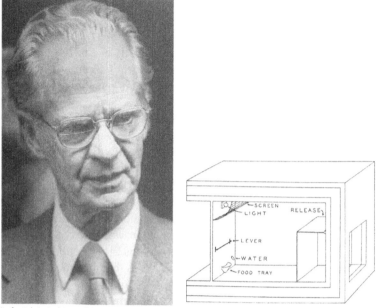

(Left, right): Archives of the History of American Psychology, The Center for the History of Psychology, The University of Akron

Figure 8.4 B. F. Skinner and a drawing of an early Skinner box

(Benjamin & Nielsen-Gammon, 1999; Skinner, 1945), and in the 1950s with Skinner's development of teaching machines and programmed learning (Benjamin, 1988; Skinner, 1958). Skinner's work proved to have important implications in designing classrooms, working with intellectually challenged children and adults, designing prison systems, improving parenting techniques, aiding teacher training, aiding military training, treating a variety of psychological disorders, creating better incentive systems for workers, and even designing cultures (Bjork, 1993; Rutherford, 2009; Skinner, 1948). Skinner's work was about using what he had learned about how good behaviors are promoted and bad behaviors are suppressed, which means that his work has relevance in virtually every setting. He often ranted about the rampant use of punishment in society – in schools, in homes, and in the workplace. He offered alternatives to punishment that promised a better outcome, and he had the data to support his claims.

In 1971, Skinner published his most famous book, *Beyond Freedom and Dignity*, a book that made the *New York Times* bestseller list and landed Skinner on the cover of *Time* magazine (September 20, 1971). In the book, he argued that much of people's lives were controlled by other forces not of their own choosing. He argued that freedom was largely an illusion. Skinner's views on freedom were much misunderstood, and certainly not well received. The misunderstanding started with a poor choice of title for his book, something Skinner later acknowledged. However, the principal message got lost in most reviews of the book. Skinner argued that people could not gain some control of their lives until they paid attention to the controls in place and decided what they wanted to do about them. For example, could schools be made more effective and more enjoyable for students and teachers if the nature of the controls were changed? Skinner never stopped working in his efforts to "save" the world (see Skinner, 1987).

Criticisms of Skinner have largely been directed at his unwillingness to look inside the animal, inside what is sometimes referred to as the "black box." Skinner has argued that he could build a scientific psychology without alluding to mental processes. Critics have found the system too narrow. Moreover, with the continued rise of cognitive psychology, critics of Skinner's ideas have multiplied. Likely many cognitive psychologists today would identify themselves as cognitive behaviorists, a label Tolman would have found comfortable. However, for Skinner, whose radical behaviorism is the successor to Watson's version, the label is an oxymoron. In his 1913 address, Watson called for psychology to come to the altar of behaviorism, to stop worshiping the false gods of mentalism and introspection. In B. F. Skinner, he found his high priest.

Behaviorism: A Final Note

What is the legacy of Watson's behaviorism in American psychology? Some would argue that his narrowing of the field limited the development of psychology and closed off important areas for research that only re-emerged in recent decades. Others would argue that psychology's progress as a science in the twentieth century was principally because of Watson, that he was the one figure who demanded a complete break with philosophy. Watsonian behaviorism strengthened the role of physiological processes in psychological explanations, expanded psychological methods, and made more evident the ties between animal and human behavior. And likely, cognitive psychology is a stronger scientific field because it adopted many of the tenets of behaviorism in establishing its science. We will look at that legacy in the final chapter of the book.

9

The New Profession of Psychology

In Chapter 4 we mentioned that G. Stanley Hall convened a meeting of psychologists in his home in Worcester, Massachusetts in the summer of 1892. Hall organized the meeting to discuss the need for a national organization for the new science of psychology, and what emerged was the founding of the American Psychological Association (APA), which held its first official meeting in Philadelphia in December of 1892 with Hall as its first president. At that summer meeting in Hall's home, the group talked about what kind of an organization they wanted. That dialogue continued over the next several years. Initially, membership was small but broad, including several philosophers and two psychiatrists. Women members were welcomed as well, a fact that was not common in scientific societies of that time, other than anthropology (Rossiter, 1982). It wasn't until 1895 that APA adopted its first constitution. That document began with a statement of the objectives of the Association. *There was only one* – the sole object of the Association would be the "advancement of psychology as a science" (Sokal, 1992, p. 115). Perhaps it never occurred to those pioneering psychologists that a profession of psychology would ever develop, or maybe they recognized that possibility, but didn't believe that an organization should serve both a science and a profession. For whatever reason, the APA members approved the one objective. Despite repeated protestations and pleas from their fellow members in the decades that followed, they stuck by that single objective for 50 years!

In Chapter 1 we described a variety of nineteenth-century psychological practitioners who were in business in America long before scientific psychology arrived. And in Chapter 6 we described the birth of a new applied psychology that grew out of the science of psychology as manifested in such areas as child study, clinical and school psychology, advertising, mental testing, and forensic psychology. It is the story of Chapter 6 that is continued here – the development of a *profession* of psychology. This profession was created by psychologists who by choice or by barriers did not obtain or seek employment in the universities but, instead, found work outside of the academy in schools, including those for intellectually challenged children; in insurance companies; in child guidance clinics; in department stores; in juvenile court facilities; in vocational guidance bureaus; in advertising agencies; and a host of other settings as the profession developed in the twentieth century. Although there are many specialty areas in contemporary psychology, and new ones evolving all the time, we will focus this chapter on the four primary specialties that the APA recognized in 1981. These specialties were in existence for much of the twentieth century and continue to be important today: clinical, school, counseling, and industrial-organizational (I-O) psychology (APA Committee on Professional Standards, 1981).

A Profession Defined

What is a profession? Most people would answer that question with an example, not a definition – medicine, law, teaching, for example. The word emerged in the twelfth century meaning "a business ... that one publicly avows," that is, one professes to be a doctor or a teacher (Simpson & Weiner, 1989, p. 572). But are all occupations professions? Is accounting a profession? What about welding? Or hair styling? What determines whether one's business is or is not a profession? The rules are not set in stone, but here is a good definition:

> a calling requiring specialized knowledge and often long and intensive preparation including instruction in skills and methods as well as in the scientific, historical, or scholarly principles underlying such skills and methods, maintaining by force of organization or concerted opinion high standards of achievement and conduct, and committing its members to continued study and to a kind of work which has for its prime purpose the rendering of a public service. (Gove, 1961, p. 1811)

This definition embodies many of the components that seem inherent in what gets defined as a profession: specialized knowledge involving intensive training; high standards of practice, usually supported by a code of ethics; continuing education so that practitioners stay current with the latest developments in the profession; and provision of a service to the public. Psychology would meet all of those criteria.

The American Psychological Association, the Canadian Psychological Association, and most state and provincial licensing boards have set the doctoral degree as the minimal standard for the independent practice of psychology. Such study requires a minimum of five years beyond the bachelor's degree, including a full year of internship work for fields such as clinical, counseling, and school psychology. Although these doctoral programs can be completed in five years, six to seven years is more the norm. Psychologists practice under a written code of ethics. The APA and CPA have such codes as do the licensing bodies for the states and provinces. Violation of the code can cause a psychologist's license to be revoked, meaning that the individual cannot offer services to the public as a psychologist. Continuing education is also typically required so that psychologists have to take additional courses or workshops, usually a fixed number of hours each year or every three years in order to maintain licensure. Certainly, psychologists provide a service to the public.

In addition to those characteristics, there are some other components of a profession. Most professions have a standardized curriculum, ensuring comparable training across programs. It is no doubt reassuring to know that regardless of the medical school, students will learn something about the heart, brain, and liver, although maybe nothing about bedside manner. A recommended curriculum exists in psychology as part of the APA and CPA accreditation processes. Furthermore, most professionals train in professional schools, and that is true now for many psychologists as well. Professionals have national and often regional and local organizations to which they belong that are important for the profession and the individual's professional development. Professionals have journals published in their field that typically address issues of concern to their professional practice. Finally, professionals are certified or licensed. If you want to practice medicine, you must be licensed to do so, otherwise you can be sent to jail. The same is true of psychologists who are licensed in every state and province in North America. A licensing law spells out the things a professional can do. It protects activities associated with the profession. Licensed physicians can give injections or engage in brain surgery. Lawyers and bank tellers cannot. Part of the story of this chapter is the professionalization of psychology in terms of these characteristics.

Experiences in World War I

We have noted that applied psychology was well underway before World War I. But the war placed psychologists in applied settings that they had not experienced before, and it did that for many psychologists who had shown no interest in doing applied work before the war. Recall that psychologists in that war were largely responsible for testing soldiers using the Army Alpha and Army Beta. That effort was headed by Robert Yerkes (1876–1956) who was president of APA

Archives of the History of American Psychology, The Center for the History of Psychology, The University of Akron

Figure 9.1 Those involved with the preparation of the Army Alpha and Army Beta tests for World War I are shown here in May 1917, on the steps of the "Training School for Feebleminded Boys and Girls" in Vineland, New Jersey. Henry Herbert Goddard, who was research director at the Vineland school, is in the middle of the front row. Robert Yerkes, who chaired the committee that produced the two tests, is in the middle of the back row. To the right of Yerkes is Walter Van Dyke Bingham, and next to him is Lewis Terman

in 1917 when the United States entered the war. Psychologists were also involved in another military testing effort, a personnel selection project headed by Walter Dill Scott, whose advertising work we discussed earlier. Scott was placed in charge of the Committee on the Classification of Personnel in the Army, whose primary task was to develop selection tests for officers. The Committee developed more than 100 selection instruments for 80 different Army jobs. Amazingly, given the short amount of time they had to prepare these tests, they tested 3.5 million soldiers using one or more of the tests. The tests were not developed from scratch; a number of them were modified from tests developed by psychologists (including Scott) before the war that had been designed to select salespersons and other business occupations. This effort was judged to be so successful that the military and Congress awarded Scott the Distinguished Service Medal in 1919.

He was the only psychologist to be so honored for his military service during that war (von Mayrhauser, 1989).

The other activity that involved psychologists occurred mostly at the end of World War I, and that was exposure to psychiatric cases in the Army hospitals. There were 40 Army hospitals, each of them employing at least one psychologist. Harry Hollingworth, who like Scott did research on advertising, was stationed at the Army hospital in Plattsburgh, New York, a hospital that contained a large number of cases that were labeled "shell shock" and would be diagnosed today as post-traumatic stress disorder (PTSD).

The term *shell shock* first appeared in a medical journal article in 1915 written by Charles S. Myers (1873–1946). Myers, a physician who had founded the first experimental psychology laboratory at Cambridge University in 1912, was assigned to the British medical corps during WWI. He was particularly interested in the psychiatric casualties of the war, men who exhibited symptoms similar to a diagnosis of hysteria. Because he believed the disorder was caused by close proximity to exploding gun shells, he labeled the condition "shell shock," a term he had heard the soldiers use. He recognized it as a genuine psychiatric condition and urged humane treatment for affected soldiers. However, military leadership typically viewed these soldiers as constitutionally weak and cowards. More than 300 British and commonwealth soldiers were executed during or shortly after WWI, based on charges of cowardice or desertion. Tragically, it is likely that many of these individuals suffered from PTSD (Jones & Wessely, 2005; Myers, 1915). In 2006, the British Parliament issued pardons for all of those executed soldiers.

Military attitudes toward shell-shocked soldiers in WWI in the U.S. and Canadian armies mirrored those of their British counterparts. In fact, the U.S. Army had hoped that psychologists could develop psychological tests that would screen these individuals during recruitment, and Robert Woodworth tried unsuccessfully to construct such a test. Like Myers, some psychologists and psychiatrists argued that these cases did not represent "weak" individuals as the Army believed, but that they were ordinary individuals whose mental disorder was the result of exposure to horrific conditions.

Hollingworth was like many of his experimental colleagues in WWI who were called on for expertise in clinical issues; he was largely unprepared to deal with his assignment, at least in terms of having any sort of clinical training in how to deal with psychiatric patients. In the Plattsburgh Army Hospital, as in the other Army hospitals, psychologists typically administered a test battery to the soldier upon admission that included an intelligence test, assessment of reasoning and decision making, vocational and aptitude tests, and a measure of morale. Once again, psychological testing proved to be what psychologists were asked to do in these jobs, rather than any clinical interventions such as psychotherapy (Holden, 1998; H. Hollingworth, 1920).

World War I impacted applied psychology in at least two ways. First, it exposed many psychologists to applied work who had not been involved in such activities before. Second, psychology's efforts, primarily in terms of the selection testing of Scott's committee and the intellectual assessment of Yerkes' committee, were viewed by the military and the public as successful. Historical research has suggested that both the Army and the WWI psychologists overestimated the quality of the job they did regarding the intellectual assessment (see Samelson, 1977). Nevertheless, the perception in 1919 was that they had succeeded, and that positive image opened many doors for the application of psychology after the war, especially for those interested in applying psychology to the problems of business and the treatment of psychological disorders. Research in applied psychology was expanding as well, so much so that G. Stanley Hall founded a new journal in 1917, the *Journal of Applied Psychology*.

Early Organizational Efforts in Professional Psychology

In today's psychology, psychologists identify themselves by their specialty area, labels like clinical psychologist or school psychologist or health psychologist and so forth. However, in the early decades of the twentieth century, there were no such divisions. Generally, psychologists who worked outside of the academy called themselves applied psychologists or consulting psychologists. The word clinical psychologist was also used, usually meaning someone who did intellectual assessments, but the label clinical psychologist had something of a generic quality to it, which would include the functions that today would be the purview of school and counseling psychologists. As mentioned in a previous chapter, many of these early applied psychologists were women, who found upon earning their doctorates, that most academic jobs were closed to them.

When these applied psychologists ventured into the public sector they found their competition was from the same pseudoscientific practitioners who had provided psychological services in the nineteenth century. The new psychologists were concerned that the public did not know how to tell the real psychologists from those with no training in psychology. (Of course, you might ask how much training the real psychologists had for the kinds of applied work they were doing.)

In 1917, a small group of applied psychologists formed an organization known as the American Association of Clinical Psychologists (AACP). It was led by J. E. Wallace Wallin (1876–1969) who worked in the public schools with intellectually challenged children and Leta S. Hollingworth (1886–1939) who was a member of the faculty at Teachers College, Columbia University, but had for a time worked in New York City for the Clearinghouse for Mental Defectives. (Leta Hollingworth was the wife of Harry Hollingworth and would become an eminent psychologist in several fields. Her work on the psychology of sex differences will be discussed in the next chapter.) The assumption in founding the AACP was that membership in the group would serve as a kind of credential for the public, identifying the person as a legitimate psychologist. The public did not really make such distinctions. Physicians and engineers, two recognized professions, were licensed and were thus protected, as was the public, from unscrupulous behavior. But no such licensure existed for psychologists. Anyone could, and many did, call themselves a psychologist without breaking any laws.

Leta Hollingworth called for APA to establish a committee to explore the possibility of certification in psychology; certification protects the label "psychologist," licensure protects the activities of what psychologists do. She suggested that APA publish a list of psychology departments that offered training in clinical psychology, and that there be some move toward standardizing a curriculum, which would include a year-long internship, to prepare psychologists to work in the applied fields. She also recommended that the doctoral degree be the minimal level of training for a clinical psychologist and that departments consider offering a new degree for clinical psychologists, a Doctor of Psychology (L. Hollingworth, 1918).

The APA worried that the AACP might divide psychologists and so considered making the group a part of APA. Many APA members objected, pointing to the constitution and reminding others that the one objective was to advance psychology as a science; advancing a profession was not what APA was supposed to be doing. However, in 1919, the group did become part of APA as the APA Section on Clinical Psychology. In 1921, the group persuaded APA to form a certification program to identify clinical psychologists. After several years, when fewer than 30 psychologists applied for certification, the program was abandoned.

The Section asked APA for other help. They called for the development of an ethics code for professional practice and consulting. They asked for more applied training opportunities in doctoral psychology programs. They asked psychology departments to hire more faculty who had significant practical experience. They asked for designated program time at the annual APA convention where the applied psychologists could discuss issues important to their work. The APA response to all of these requests was generally "no," and the Section members were given the mantra again and again that it would be unconstitutional for APA to get involved in advancing the profession of psychology (Benjamin, 1997).

Eventually the applied psychologists gave up on APA. The stock market crashed in the fall of 1929 and both the economy and morale in America turned ugly. Employment was even more of an issue now. In 1930, an independent group, the Association of Consulting Psychologists (ACP), was formed from the New York State Association of Consulting Psychologists. This group sought to improve job opportunities for applied psychologists, influence graduate psychology curricula, promote research in applied psychology, and establish a code of ethics. They published their code of ethics in 1933 and in 1937 started their own journal, the *Journal of Consulting Psychology*, the first psychology journal to treat professional issues. The ACP struggled to be a national organization but its membership and leadership was dominated by New York psychologists.

In an attempt to create a truly national group, members of the ACP and APA Section met and created a wholly new organization in 1938, the American Association for Applied Psychology (AAAP). The ACP and Clinical Section then dissolved, their members joining the AAAP, and the ACP journal became the journal of the new AAAP. The AAAP included four sections, each of which had its own officers and planned its own part of the annual meeting of the AAAP. Those sections were clinical, consulting, educational, and industrial. Total membership was about 410 in its first year. This organization proved very successful in meeting the needs of applied psychologists and grew in strength each year. But its existence would be short lived.

With World War II underway and the U.S. government recognizing it would have too many psychiatric casualties from that war to be handled by the woefully understaffed profession of psychiatry, it began to consider ways to increase the population of practitioners who could provide mental health services. In essence, the government told APA and AAAP to work together to organize psychology for the common good. Therefore, the two groups met, in conjunction with several smaller psychology groups to plan a new organization. What developed was a new APA, which incorporated AAAP into its new divisional structure. The new APA would have a headquarters office in Washington, DC, would work with the Veteran's Administration (VA) to train clinical psychologists, would form divisions to represent the specialty interests in psychology, and would have a new journal for professional psychology

Table 9.1 The Charter Divisions of the American Psychological Association: 1945

Division Number	Division Name
1	General Psychology
2	Teaching of Psychology
3	Theoretical and Experimental Psychology
4	The Psychometric Society*
5	Evaluation and Measurement
6	Physiological and Comparative Psychology
7	Childhood and Adolescence
8	Personality and Social Psychology
9	Society for the Psychological Study of Social Issues (SPSSI)
10	Esthetics
11	Abnormal Psychology and Psychotherapy**
12	Clinical Psychology
13	Consulting Psychology
14	Industrial and Business Psychology
15	Educational Psychology
16	School Psychologists
17	Personnel and Guidance Psychologists
18	Psychologists in Public Service
19	Military Psychology

*The Psychometric Society declined the invitation to become an APA division.
**Division 11 merged with Division 12 in 1946, leaving Number 11 vacant. Today APA has more than 50 divisions, but Numbers 4 and 11, by APA rules, remain unused.

(Benjamin, 1997). The new APA opened its offices in 1945 with a newly approved constitution whose objective statement read, "to advance psychology as a science [and] as a profession … " (Wolfle, 1946, p. 721). It had taken 50 years, but the practitioners finally had forced APA to recognize their existence.

The Role of Psychological Assessment

We have commented before that nothing defined twentieth-century American psychology like mental testing. It began with the mental tests of Cattell; then the intelligence tests of Binet and his translators in the United States, Goddard and Terman; then the assessment efforts of psychologists in the military in WWI, both intellectual and selection, which spawned a plethora of selection tests for use in industry after the war; then the personality assessment of the 1920s and 1930s which included the emergence of projective tests such as the *Rorschach Inkblot Test*. These were followed by the growth of assessments in the schools, some of which would be federally mandated; and a host of new psychological tests to measure everything from student attitudes toward learning to a checklist of student problems; and the development of interests and aptitude tests to aid vocational counseling (see Sokal, 1987).

Psychological testing is and has been a huge industry. It has made test publishing companies wealthy; given psychometricians job security as they try to ascertain the reliability and validity of these instruments; provided practitioners with some much-needed diagnostic tools; and provided aid and advice to millions of people who were in need of help. We will treat psychological assessment in the brief specialty histories that follow.

Clinical Psychology

The role of the early clinical psychologist was to administer and score psychological tests and, in some cases, to interpret the test results. They had acquired this role because psychologists developed the majority of tests, so it seemed natural that they give the tests and score them. However, it was important to the medical community that they knew their place in a field dominated by medical practitioners, that is MDs. Interpretation of the tests results, leading to diagnosis; a strategy for treatment; and treatment – those were in the job description of the physician, not the psychologist. But of course, things didn't stay that way. Despite the political efforts of the American Medical Association and the American Psychiatric Association to maintain their exclusive hold on their turf, psychologists' role in clinical matters would grow (Benjamin, 2005).

In the 1930s, clinical psychologists expanded their role from intellectual assessment to personality assessment, relying heavily on the *Rorschach Inkblot Test*. The Rorschach was a projective test based on Freudian ideas, the belief being that the individual would project unconscious thoughts and motives onto the ambiguous blots. Here was a test that allowed psychologists to do more than administer and score; on this test, they have to reveal the subtle interpretations of the responses. This test remained a prominent instrument in clinical psychology into the 1970s and is still in use today despite serious concerns about its validity (see Lilienfeld, Wood, & Garb, 2000). Other personality tests such as the *Thematic Apperception Test* (TAT), and the *Minnesota Multiphasic Personality Inventory* (MMPI) were added in the 1930s and 1940s. With each of these, the role of the psychologist expanded into interpretation and diagnosis.

World War II allowed the profession to take the next big step – providing psychotherapy. With a shortage of psychiatrists and a great need for mental health services, the United States Public Health Service (USPHS) and the VA worked with APA and university psychology departments to accelerate training in clinical psychology after the war. Psychologists had already been involved in doing psychotherapy during the war, pressed into that role because the need was so desperate. They had shown they could do the job and the government was eager to fill its needs as soon as possible. The APA established an accreditation program and in 1946, began evaluating doctoral programs in clinical psychology to assure minimal quality in their training. The VA became a major employer of clinical psychologists. The agency's projections for need had been accurate. In April 1946, of the 74,000 patients in VA hospitals, 44,000 (nearly 60%) were classified as neuropsychiatric patients (Miller, 1946)!

Psychology still had not reached agreement on a model for clinical training and the USPHS and VA were encouraging APA to make progress on that issue. With federal government funding, APA organized a conference of about 70 psychologists and a few individuals from related fields (psychiatry, social work, and nursing) who gathered in Boulder, Colorado in the summer of 1949 to hammer out recommendations for how clinical psychologists should be trained. They decided on a doctoral program that would provide strong training in science, but also provide the student with clinical skills, including a one-year predoctoral clinical internship. The chief architect of this plan was David Shakow (1901–1981), a distinguished clinical psychologist known for his clinical acumen as well as his pioneering research on schizophrenia (Cautin, 2006). Psychologist historian, Robin Cautin (2008) has written that Shakow's conceptualization of clinical psychology training came from his research on schizophrenia (which established many of the basic facts about the disorder that define it today), his experience of working with patients and physicians in the Worcester State Hospital (a mental asylum), and his training of psychological and medical interns in that setting. Shakow's model became known as the *scientist-practitioner model* (also called the *Boulder model*), and it continues to be a dominant training model today in many programs in clinical, counseling, and school psychology (Baker & Benjamin, 2000). What Leta Hollingworth had called for in 1918 had finally been achieved in 1949. Licensure was also finally underway in 1945 with laws passed in Connecticut and Virginia. It would take until 1977 for all states and provinces to pass psychology licensing laws.

The big change, of course, was that psychologists were now able to deliver psychotherapy. Clinical psychologists had been around psychotherapy in a variety of settings such as state hospitals and child guidance clinics, and they had been using psychotherapy in university counseling centers since the 1920s. The door was now open wide, thanks to the military, and psychologists were quick to join the ranks of the treatment givers. Their theory (and therapy) was dominated in the 1940s and 1950s by the psychodynamic ideas of Freud and the neo-Freudians, meaning that the goal of their therapy was to help their patients resolve interpersonal and intrapsychic conflicts. But their therapy techniques were more broad based. For example, group therapy methods, pioneered by psychiatrist Jacob Moreno, were in use after the war.

Behavior therapy techniques, often referred to as behavior modification, began to appear in the late 1950s (for example, Joseph Wolpe's systematic desensitization) and dominated the 1960s, including techniques based on Skinner's operant psychology. Essentially, these operant-based therapies involved the resourceful manipulation of reinforcers to increase the occurrence of desirable behaviors, and punishers or extinction techniques to decrease or eliminate undesirable behaviors.

With the social upheaval in America in the 1960s surrounding the war in Vietnam and civil rights, humanistic psychology added its therapeutic techniques to the practice of psychotherapy. *Humanistic therapies* encouraged self-exploration and self-determination. Humanistic psychologists emphasized the goodness of people and the potential for human growth that they believed was inherent in everyone as a life goal. People were seen as motivated toward self-actualization, that is achieving their ultimate potential and the sense of worth and satisfaction that accompanied that state. Humanistic therapies sought to help individuals discover their potential and to be able to pursue life as they wished.

Another major force in clinical psychology in the 1960s was the *cognitive therapies* that resulted from the re-emergence of cognitive psychology (which will be discussed in Chapter 11). Behavior therapies had been shown to be effective, but there was a growing recognition that the problem was often not behavioral, but the result of disordered or irrational thinking. The goal of these therapies was to restructure the individual's thought patterns and eliminate irrational thoughts. They focused more on mental states than behavioral states. Today these therapies are still very much in use because their validity has been substantiated by empirical studies. This group of therapies is labeled CBT or cognitive behavior therapy.

The 1970s became a golden age for psychologists who finally had become the major providers of psychotherapy in America, able to practice independently of psychiatry and reimbursable by health

(Left, right): Archives of the History of American Psychology, The Center for the History of Psychology, The University of Akron

Figure 9.2   Clinical psychologist David Shakow (*left*) and industrial psychologist Walter Van Dyke Bingham

insurance companies. But after a few decades, managed care and the rise of master's-level practitioner groups such as licensed professional counselors and marriage and family therapists changed the picture of psychotherapy once more and relegated clinical psychologists to a smaller role in that arena.

Industrial-Organizational Psychology

By the time of World War I, there were already a number of academic psychologists who were doing applied research in business, the most visible of whom were Scott, Hollingworth, Münsterberg, and Walter Van Dyke Bingham (1880–1952). Bingham established the first department of applied psychology at the Carnegie Institute of Technology (CIT) in 1915. CIT was a technical university and its president believed that psychology would be useful to its graduates. Bingham built an ambitious program at CIT, hiring Scott from Northwestern University and adding several other faculty who would become eminent applied psychologists. Working with local businesses in Pittsburgh, Bingham established the Bureau of Salesmanship Research in 1916 to develop selection instruments. Scott, who headed that bureau, would later modify some of those same selection tests for the Army during World

War I. A few years later Bingham founded the Research Bureau for Retail Training, a Division of Vocational Education, and a School of Life Insurance Salesmanship. No university had ever seen such an enterprise within a psychology department, and it likely could not have happened anywhere other than CIT. After the war, the program declined, mostly due to a decision from the university's administration to pour its resources into engineering programs. Scott left CIT to found a private consulting firm, the Scott Company. Other faculty dispersed to other university jobs and jobs within the business community, taking advantage of the applied experience of CIT and the exposure afforded by the publicity surrounding the war (Benjamin & Baker, 2003).

Much of the work after the war was in personnel psychology, partly stimulated by the continuing emphasis on efficiency and the belief that psychology could supply the tools for that work. Further, as businesses evolved, job specialization increased, making a good match between worker and job even more critical. Hall's *Journal of Applied Psychology* became the major outlet for this personnel work, publishing selection instruments for firefighters, police officers, pilots, telegraphers, mill workers, stenographers, and other occupations. Psychologists touted their wares in a rash of new books in the 1920s such as Kornhauser and Kingsbury's *Psychological Tests in Business* (1924), Griffith's *Fundamentals of Vocational Psychology* (1924), and Laird's *The Psychology of Selecting Men* (1925).

One of the forces in personnel psychology in the 1910s and 1920s was Katherine Blackford, a physician who promoted a program of physiognomy in selecting workers. Her methods were popular with businesses, and psychologists regularly attacked her in their books and articles. She recommended, for example, that businesses hire blonds for sales jobs because they were likely to have convex faces indicating traits of aggressiveness and persistence (Blackford & Newcomb, 1914, 1916). Eventually businesses abandoned her methods in favor of more scientific approaches.

The Great Depression of the 1930s, which resulted in a peak unemployment rate of 25%, would change the face of industrial psychology. Because hiring was often nonexistent, many companies laid off their personnel departments. Yet some businesses saw the unemployment lines as a pool to be tapped for better talent, making selection skills even more important. Industrial psychologists used this time to redefine their field. Up to this point, industrial psychology had emphasized job analysis, selection, and performance appraisal; that was the "I" side of the I-O designation. The 1930s, however, would add the "O" side, broadening the field to its current label of industrial-organizational, or I-O, psychology.

One of the emphases of the new organizational psychology was a focus on *human relations* in the workplace, an emphasis that had come out of the Hawthorne studies, a series of studies in the late 1920s and early 1930s at the Hawthorne Works of the Western Electric Company in Chicago. The studies focused on factors contributing to productivity, finding that management needed to pay much greater attention to assessing worker attitudes, interviewing workers, providing counseling programs in the workplace, allowing workers to have input into the establishment of workplace norms, and encouraging workers and supervisors to develop teams in a collaborative fashion (Mayo, 1933; Roethlisberger & Dickson, 1939). Moreover, personality tests began to be developed in the 1930s for industry use, tests that principally were designed to screen out employees who likely would be troublemakers in the workplace (Gibby & Zickar, 2008; McMurry, 1944). Finally, other studies in the 1930s and 1940s stimulated interest in the concept of *job satisfaction* as a principal component in productivity, and psychological tests and methods were developed to measure and improve worker satisfaction (Fisher & Hanna, 1931; Hoppock, 1935).

World War II brought another work outlet for I-O psychologists, the field of *human factors psychology*, sometimes called engineering psychology. This field was to aid in the design of equipment that involved a human interface so that operation of the equipment was more efficient and safer. Psychologists became involved in the design of airplane altimeters that were more easily read, radar images that could be more easily interpreted, bombsights that produced fewer visual errors, and control knob design and placement in aircraft that minimized negative transfer problems, thus reducing crashes when pilots flew different aircraft. After the war, human factors psychology continued to be part of the military work for psychology, but psychologists also found employment with IBM, General Motors, American Telephone and Telegraph, General Mills, and many other large companies. Working with engineers, psychologists helped design everything from clothes irons, arc welders, telephones, candy machines, and computers to automobiles, nuclear power plants, and space shuttles. It was a field that blended what psychologists knew about human behavior, perception, learning, memory, attention, fatigue, and motivation, with product design. Human factors psychology remains an important activity today, particularly in terms of the human–computer interface (Hoffman & Deffenbacher, 1992), but its practitioners are usually trained in departments of industrial engineering rather than psychology.

Organizational psychology has continued its growth into contemporary times. The field includes older topics such as worker motivation, job satisfaction, and leadership, and new areas, such as organizational communication, conflict management, organizational socialization, organizational climate, and organizational commitment. Many I-O psychologists came to believe that they could have greater impact in achieving their goals if they focused their efforts on changing organizations, rather than on changing workers or managers directly.

School Psychology

In previous chapters, we discussed the work of G. Stanley Hall in the child study movement and Lightner Witmer in founding and developing the first psychological clinic, largely involved in treating school-related problems in children and adolescents. Those programs represent the beginnings of school psychology (Fagan, 1992), a specialty field that, unlike the fields of clinical and counseling psychology, trains practitioners whose education typically stops at the master's degree level. School psychologists work for schools, in most cases for several schools within a school district, testing children and meeting with teachers and parents and other program specialists to see that children get the special services that they need to succeed academically. Whereas the nature of clinical and counseling psychology has changed much over the last century, the goals and functions of the school psychologist have remained much the same.

Although Witmer could rightly be called the first school psychologist, the first person to hold that title was Arnold L. Gesell (1880–1961), a student of G. Stanley Hall. Gesell earned a medical degree in addition to his PhD in psychology. He was hired by Yale University where he established a research laboratory and a clinic for child development. While at Yale, he worked part time as a school psychologist for the Connecticut Board of Education. Gesell's most important work was in developing a set of normative tables for physical and psychological development, a great boon to parents, educators, and pediatricians alike (Fagan, 1987a, 1987b).

The early psychology programs in the schools focused on identifying children who were "mentally defective" and moving them into special schools for the "feebleminded" such as the one in Vineland, New Jersey where Goddard worked. Furthermore, school psychologists were involved in assessing children at the other end of the intellectual spectrum. Stanford University's Lewis Terman was especially interested in intellectually gifted children. He worked to develop instruments, in addition to the Stanford-Binet, to identify these children and to recommend accelerated learning experiences for them. Leta Hollingworth was studying gifted children at about the same time. In fact, she wrote the first textbook on gifted education (L. Hollingworth, 1926) in which she recommended against acceleration and, instead, promoted enrichment opportunities for those children while keeping them with their same age mates.

The New York City schools, where Hollingworth had worked, were in the vanguard for school psychology. They established a certification program that required practitioners to have a master's degree in psychology, at least one year of experience in the schools, and pass an examination created by the city. Such actions stimulated the growth of training programs for school psychologists, first at New York University in 1929, and then at Teachers College of Columbia University the following year (Fagan, 1986). In 1935, New York was the first state to offer certification for school psychologists, followed by Pennsylvania (Benjamin & Baker, 2004). The first book on the topic of school psychology was written by Gertrude Hildreth, *Psychological Services for School Problems* (1930), and other books soon followed. By the end of the 1930s, the books, training programs, and recognition of the profession by certification, indicated that school psychology had come of age as a separate identity within the field of applied psychology.

As discussed earlier, intelligence testing had been the defining task of the clinical psychologists in their early years, but as the tools and responsibilities of that group expanded, such intellectual assessment shifted primarily to the work of school psychologists. All areas of psychological testing (e.g., personality, ability, achievement) have been challenged in terms of their validity; no tests have been attacked more often than intelligence tests. The principal reason for such attacks is that the stakes are so high in terms of the consequences of such assessment. It means, for example, that a child may or may not gain admission into selective programs. Intelligence tests have been challenged on a number of grounds, including the scope of the tests in measuring what contemporary psychologists see as only one kind of intelligence.

The greatest criticisms of these tests have been claims of cultural bias. That is, the fact that some ethnicities score lower on these tests is seen as a result of the inherent cultural bias of the tests, a fact generally acknowledged by many psychologists since the 1930s. A major voice on this issue in America in the 1930s was George I. Sanchez (1906–1972), the first Latino to earn a doctorate in psychology. His research showed the misuse of intelligence tests for placements of Mexican-American children, based on differences in language and culture (Sanchez, 1934). Sanchez was a tireless advocate for the elimination of barriers to education for Latino students, particularly the over-reliance of mental tests that were demonstrably prejudicial. A more in-depth discussion of this issue appears in the next chapter.

Archives of the History of American Psychology, The Center for the History of Psychology, The University of Akron

Figure 9.3 Arnold Gesell, pioneer practicing school psychologist and researcher in developmental psychology.

Although there were plenty of master's degree training programs, by 1953, there were only three doctoral programs in school psychology, a fact that worried school psychologists within the APA. The number of these doctoral programs grew slowly, and by 1971, APA extended its accreditation program to school psychology. Today, school psychology continues to be a blend of master's-level and doctoral-level personnel in the schools. Most of the former belong to a professional organization called the National Association of School Psychologists (NASP), founded in 1969. Many of those with doctorates in school psychology belong to NASP as well, but also hold membership in Division 16 of the APA, its division on school psychology. There are turf battles between the two, but they have cooperated on most important issues. Today in the United States, there are more than 200 institutions with training programs in school psychology and perhaps as many as 25,000 school psychologists (Benjamin & Baker, 2004).

Counseling Psychology

Counseling psychology emerged later than the other three specialty areas we have discussed to this point. Further, the roots for counseling psychology are not so easily identified. To some extent, it is a field that has a broader parentage, making its history more difficult to construct. Counseling psychology is a specialty that has always had something of a prolonged identity crisis. Its heritage is drawn both from the vocational guidance movement and the personnel work of industrial psychology. In fact, when the counseling psychology division (Division 17) was first established in APA in 1945, its initial name was the Division of Personnel and Guidance Psychologists. Over time, both of these functions have diminished, especially the personnel work, and counseling psychology has moved closer in practice to the role of clinical psychology.

Counseling psychologists existed in university counseling centers as early as the 1920s where they used the intellectual and personality assessments of the time to aid students, especially in the area of what had come to be called career counseling. They also developed many of those tests including tests that measured student interests and abilities, principally for vocational purposes. Counseling centers exist at virtually every college and university today, although the services have expanded considerably, including psychotherapy, alcohol and drug counseling, test anxiety counseling, learning skills programs, stress management programs, and crisis intervention (suicide prevention).

A major impetus for the transformation of counseling psychology away from its vocational counseling roots and toward a primary role of mental health counseling was the psychiatric realities of World War II. Mental health problems were plaguing the military: 17% of the new recruits were found to have psychiatric illnesses, most of the military discharges were due to psychiatric reasons, and psychiatric cases occupied over half of the beds in the VA hospitals. Such a high percentage of problems in the recruits alerted the government to the incidence of mental health problems in the general population. The outcome was passage of the National Mental Health Act of 1946 that established the National Institute of Mental Health (NIMH) and poured millions of dollars into research and training programs, including programs for clinical, school, and counseling psychologists (Pickren & Schneider, 2005).

Several counseling psychologists were involved in the Boulder Conference on clinical training, and the report of that conference addressed the hope that counseling and clinical psychologists might see an "eventual amalgamation" of their fields (Raimy, 1950, p. 113). Although there was no amalgamation, both fields drew closer together in that they eventually defined their specialties so that they treated all disorders in all kinds of clients in all kinds of settings. Although there were philosophical differences in training and in the approach of the field to the nature of intervention, in an effort to claim as much territory as possible, narrower definitions would not be the order of the day.

Conferences were organized at the University of Michigan in 1949–1950 and at Northwestern University in 1951 to define the field of counseling psychology and determine an agreed-upon program of doctoral training. The Northwestern Conference defined the goal of the counseling psychologist as:

> ... fostering the psychological development of the individual. This included all people on the adjustment continuum from those who function at tolerable levels of adequacy to those suffering from more severe psychological disturbances. Counseling psychologists will spend the bulk of their time with individuals within the normal range, but their training should qualify them to work in some degree with individuals at any level of psychological adjustment. (American Psychological Association. Division of Counseling and Guidance, 1952, p. 181)

Guidelines were also set in place for a suggested curriculum. As a result, the APA began accrediting counseling programs in 1952 and the VA created a job classification for them as well, primarily as vocational counselors. Because of the G.I. Bill, many veterans could afford a college education that would have been beyond their means without such government support. Counseling psychologists were supposed to help with those decisions. In addition, there were adjustment problems created by the combat service, and they dealt with those as well (Benjamin & Baker, 2004).

The identity crisis continued for counseling psychologists in the 1960s, as evidenced by at least two committees appointed by Division 17 to define counseling as separate from clinical. The first committee, composed of three leaders in the counseling psychology field, recommended that the field dissolve into clinical psychology. Its report was rejected and a second committee was appointed to produce a recommendation more palatable to the Division's leaders. The result was a reaffirmation of the Northwestern Conference language that counseling psychologists would function principally as mental health service providers for a range of settings, clients, and disorders. Students today who are trying to make a decision about applying to graduate school in one or the other often remain confused.

Like clinical psychologists, counseling psychologists developed psychotherapy skills as part of their treatment practices. They were especially influenced by the nondirective counseling program of Carl Rogers (1902–1987), first described in his 1942 book, *Counseling and Psychotherapy*. At first, it seemed like such a radical approach to the counseling community. Where was the counseling? There were no tests and no advice. However, the method gained credibility as therapists learned the active listening skills that allowed the therapist to reflect content and emotion, helping the client reach change through self-exploration and understanding. Counseling psychologists adopted other therapeutic styles as well, including psychodynamic, cognitive, and behavioral therapies. Rogers' ideas, part of the humanistic therapies, have continued to hold a prominent position of influence.

The Modern Profession

This abbreviated account cannot cover all that is important in the history of the profession of psychology. For example, we have yet to mention the Vail Conference in 1973 that offered an alternative training model to the Boulder model, one that called for a greater emphasis on the practitioner side of the scientist–practitioner training and also recommended a new degree in psychology called the Doctor of Psychology (PsyD) that would be specifically for practitioners (again, one of Leta Hollingworth's recommendations from 1918). This conference can be viewed as recognizing an alternative training model already in place in California that marked the start of the professional schools movement. That movement began in 1969 when Nicholas Cummings (1924–) founded the two campuses (San Francisco and Los Angeles) of the California School of Professional Psychology (CSPP), a school that was independent of any university and focused on the training of psychological practitioners. In less than a decade there were 20 professional schools, some associated with universities and some free standing such as CSPP. In order to facilitate the growth of these schools and to enhance the quality of professional training, Cummings also founded the National Council of Schools of Professional Psychology (NCSPP). Today, there are more than 85 professional schools that hold membership in NCSPP, many of which offer the PsyD degree. They graduate about twice as many psychologists each year as do the university-based programs in clinical and counseling psychology (Thomas, Cummings, & O'Donahue, 2002).

In this chapter, we have focused on the four professional specialties that are the oldest and the largest of psychological specialties. Three of them could be considered health-care specialties (clinical, counseling, and school), although some psychologists use that label only for the first two. Those two are undergoing a significant transformation at present in the nature of their practice. Managed care, a system of cost containment instituted by insurance companies that reimburse psychologists for their work, has greatly restricted the number of therapy sessions for which financial reimbursement can be obtained. That has caused a great deal of concern among these therapists who worry that the new brief therapies will not provide what the patient needs. Because of cost issues, many states and provinces have established licensure for several master's-level practitioner groups (such as Mental Health Counselor or Marriage and Family Therapist) that usually provide psychotherapy at a lower cost. Industrial–organizational psychologists have not been affected by these changes and continue to enjoy a field of stability and opportunity, although their turf has been invaded in recent years by clinical and counseling psychologists who offer *executive coaching* to corporate executives and managers (see Kilburg, 2006).

Of course, there are new professional specialties evolving all the time as well as some old ones that we have not treated in this chapter, such as *forensic psychology*, that was begun by Hugo Münsterberg whose work in that area was discussed in Chapter 6. Although psychologists have investigated performance in sports since the late nineteenth century (see Green & Benjamin, 2009), *sport psychology* is a new field in which psychologists work with individual athletes or teams, seeking to improve athletic performance. It is no surprise that psychological factors are extremely important in sport. In professional sports, where the competition is at such a high level and the economic stakes are so great, athletes will often use whatever edge they can get. Many psychologists have built successful careers in this new field, trying to give their clients that edge (Hays, 1995; LeUnes, 2008).

The largest of the new professional specialties, and the fastest growing, is called *health psychology*, a field that has enormous promise for the twenty-first century. It will be discussed in the epilogue of this book.

At the beginning of this chapter, we told you about the constitution of the American Psychological Association and how its objective statement was modified in 1945 – the first change in 50 years – to state that the Association would work "to advance psychology as a science [and] as a profession … " (Benjamin, 1997, p. 731). There was another important change in that statement, however, that hasn't been mentioned. That change is the subject of the next chapter.

10

A Psychology of Social Action and Social Change

The 1920s in America were called the "Roaring Twenties," "the Jazz Age," and, by politicians, "the New Era." The economy was soaring, industrial production was up 64% compared to 12% for the previous decade, automobiles were more affordable than ever, women had the right to vote, Babe Ruth was swatting home runs, Rudolph Valentino and Mary Pickford were starring on the big screen, and booze was still available in gin joints, speakeasies, and from moonshiners, despite the Eighteenth Amendment (Dumenil, 2001). There was a public euphoria that manifested itself in many ways. One of those was a greater-than-ever clamoring for psychological services.

The public seemed convinced that psychology held the keys to prosperity and happiness. Magazine articles and newspaper columns touted the services offered by the "new" psychologists. People were told that they shouldn't choose a marriage partner, raise their children, or choose a career without the help of a psychologist. Psychology clubs were formed in most metropolitan areas where people could gather to hear a speaker and discuss the latest notions of popular psychology, self-help books with titles such as "Calm Your Nerves" or "How to Be Happy" became commonplace. Popular psychology magazines appeared on newsstand shelves, including one whose sub-title promised "Health, Happiness, Success." It led Canadian humorist Stephen Leacock (1924) to conclude that America was suffering from an "outbreak of psychology."

One of the reasons that APA's Clinical Section had pressed APA for a certification program for applied psychologists in the 1920s was as a means to inform the public of the real psychologists. The public demand far exceeded the membership of APA, not to mention that fewer than 30 psychologists were certified. Americans wanted psychological services, and thousands of people were willing to meet that need under a variety of labels, including "psychologist."

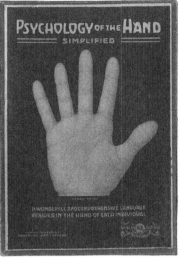

From the author's collection

From the author's collection

Figure 10.1   Two examples of popular psychology in the early decades of the twentieth century: *Psychology: Health, Happiness, Success* was the most visible of the more than 20 popular psychology magazines published in North America in the 1920s and 1930s. *Psychology of the Hand* was a game introduced in 1919, based on the notion of discerning ones personality from "reading" lines in the palm

The stock market crash in September 1929 ended the public euphoria and ushered in the decade of economic and psychological depression that we call the Great Depression. Unemployment reached unbelievable levels of nearly 25%. Millions of people suddenly found themselves out of work, homeless, and hungry. It was a time of soup kitchens, apple carts, and "Brother Can You Spare a Dime?" It was "riding the rails" for the homeless, living in the boxcars of trains, looking for a meal, or trying to escape from the police. It was the dustbowl, when drought and winds rendered the farmland in Oklahoma and other parts of the American Southwest useless and sent thousands of "Okies" west to California where they were exploited as part of migrant farm labor as depicted in John Steinbeck's novel *The Grapes of Wrath* (1939). It was a time of lawlessness and movie marquis criminals – John Dillinger, Bonnie Parker, and Clyde Barrow. It was a time of labor strikes and riots, escalating racial tensions and race riots in the North and South, and another potential world war brewing in Europe.

In the midst of the Great Depression and the escalating European conflict, a new psychological organization was formed. Its organizational meeting was held at the APA meeting in 1936 at Hanover, New Hampshire, led by a couple of young psychologists Ross Stagner (1909–1997) and David Krech (1909–1977), both around age 26, who had a rather radical idea. Given the social conflicts rampant in American society and in the world abroad, was it possible that the science of psychology had any bearing on those problems? That is, *was psychology applicable to curing the social ills of the world?* Given the prejudices among the purists toward applications of psychology in businesses or schools, you can imagine how they would react to a plan to apply the science of psychology to curing poverty, ending racism, and bringing peace to the world.

Nevertheless, the organization was formed. Its name was the Society for the Psychological Study of Social Issues (SPSSI), and it continues today as one of more than 50 divisions of the American Psychological Association. Its agenda is the other part of the new APA statement of objectives. In the 1945 constitution of the new APA, the objective statement read, "The American Psychological Association shall exist to advance psychology as a science, as a profession, *and as a means of promoting human welfare*" (italics added, Benjamin, 1997, p. 731). This is the story of psychology's social agenda.

This chapter is divided into three sections, each having to do with psychology's involvement in applications to social issues. The first deals with the pioneering research on the psychology of sex differences, featuring the work of Helen Thompson Woolley and Leta Hollingworth in the first two decades of the twentieth century. The second describes the research of Kurt Lewin, a Jewish émigré, who came to the United States in 1933 from Nazi Germany. Lewin pioneered modern experimental social psychology and applied social psychology in an imaginative and powerful program of work he labeled action research. The third section will treat psychology's conceptions of race as ideas evolved from the 1890s through the *Brown v. Board* Supreme Court decision of 1954, a decision in which SPSSI played a major role, particularly through the work of Kenneth and Mamie Clark.

The Psychology of Sex Differences

John Watson (1936) said that when he finished the final examination for his doctoral degree at the University of Chicago in 1903, he got his "first deep-seated inferiority." Here is how he described it: "I received my degree Magna Cum Laude and was told, almost immediately, by Dewey and Angell that my exam was much inferior to that of Miss

Helen Thompson who had graduated two years before with a Summa Cum Laude. I wondered then if anybody could equal her record" (p. 274). Thompson pioneered psychological research on sexual differences by actually conducting experiments. Most of the "research" on sex differences before and even after Thompson's work was little more than bias and conjecture. She summarized the field as follows: "There is perhaps no field aspiring to be scientific where flagrant personal bias, logic martyred in the cause of supporting a prejudice, unfounded assertions, and even sentimental rot and drivel, have run riot to such an extent as here" (Woolley, 1910, p. 340). So much for the "science" of sex differences!

Helen Bradford Thompson (Woolley)

When Helen Thompson (1874–1947) was a student at the University of Chicago in the late 1890s, she existed in a world that believed in male superiority on any number of physical and psychological traits. After all, the United States was 120 years old as a nation, and still half of its citizens were denied that most fundamental of rights – the right to vote. Why were women prohibited from voting? Some of the reasons given were that women were fickle, incapable of logical reasoning, of inferior intelligence, overly influenced by emotion, and hindered by their hormonal cycles. The dogmas that asserted the inferiority of women were plentiful and, as a budding psychologist, they interested Thompson.

Thompson was a student in the functional psychology extant at Chicago. According to Stephanie Shields (1975), "It was the functionalist movement in the United States that fostered academic psychology's study of sex differences. ... The incorporation of evolutionary theory into the practice of psychology made the study of the female legitimate, if not imperative" (p. 739). It was "known" that women were functionally different from men, and evolution offered the basis for the biological determinism supporting those differences. Research was not to be directed at discovering that there were differences per se, but instead to understand their nature and extent and to try to understand the causes of those differences.

With the encouragement of her advisor, James Rowland Angell, Thompson (1903) began a most ambitious study for her doctoral dissertation that marked "the first attempt to obtain a complete and systematic statement of the psychological likenesses and differences of the sexes by the experimental method" (p. 1). Using 25 males and 25 females, she put her subjects through a lengthy battery of sensory, motor, cognitive, and personality tests. She measured almost everything anyone knew to measure in her time, requiring approximately 20 hours of testing for each of her subjects.

Thompson's sensory measures included two-point thresholds, discrimination of lifted weights, taste thresholds, smell discrimination ability, absolute and difference thresholds for pitch, color discrimination, brightness perception, and color blindness. Motor tests included reaction time tests, tests of coordination, and rapidity of movement. Her cognitive tests measured memory, learning, creativity, and tests of knowledge in subject fields like history, english, physics, and math. Personality measures, tests of emotion, and questionnaires on intellectual interests were also administered. That is only a partial list!

Thompson (1903) found that men were better on most tests of motor ability, but not all; women did better on some of the coordination tasks. Men showed more creativity; women demonstrated senses that are more acute, better memory performance, and the ability to generate more word associations. "The assertion that the influence of emotion is greater in the life of women found no confirmation" (pp. 172–173). Thompson found more similarities than differences in performance, and she found the differences, when they did exist, to be rather small. What did it all mean? Here is how Thompson summarized her data:

> The point to be emphasized as the outcome of this study is that, according to our present light, the psychological differences of sex seem to be largely due, not to differences of average capacity, nor to difference in type of mental activity, but to differences in the social influences brought to bear on the developing individual from early infancy to adult years. The question of the future development of the intellectual life of women is one of social necessities and ideals, rather than of inborn psychological characteristics of sex. (p. 182)

Those who reviewed Thompson's studies did not always agree with her conclusions about social influences. G. Stanley Hall (1904) mentioned her studies in his magnum opus on adolescence, stating that "Miss Thompson…becomes feministic…in ascribing sexual difference of type of mental action to the differences of the influences that surround the sexes in early years" (v. 2, p. 565). E. L. Thorndike (1914), however, who in his many books had argued that greater variability among men accounted for their greater achievements, seemed impressed by the small differences Thompson found. He summarized the results of her studies as follows: "The most important characteristic of these differences is their small amount. The individual differences within one sex so enormously outweigh the differences between the sexes in these intellectual and semi-intellectual traits that for practical purposes the sex difference may be disregarded" (v. 3, p. 184).

(Left, right): Archives of the History of American Psychology, The Center for the History of Psychology, The University of Akron

Figure 10.2   Helen Thompson Woolley (*left*) and Leta Hollingworth used their research in the first two decades of the twentieth century to challenge existing dogmas that asserted the biological and psychological inferiority of women

It is important to understand that the dogmas asserting male superiority were just that, dogmas. Such assertions were not based on any data. Instead, they were based on centuries of prejudice and the assumption that sex differences were so blatantly obvious that they did not need to be tested. Therefore, if these assertions were not based on any data, Thompson's data were not going to cause most males to change their views. One of the great things about science is that it forces its adherents to pay attention to the data. Thompson was perhaps a little early; most psychologists were not ready to accept her conclusions.

Leta Stetter Hollingworth

Leta Stetter Hollingworth (1886–1939) had a first-hand knowledge of the societal barriers women faced. She had graduated valedictorian of her college class and had three years of teaching experience in Nebraska when she moved to New York City in 1908 to marry her classmate, Harry Hollingworth, who was about to finish his doctorate with Cattell. Leta Hollingworth tried to get a teaching job in New York City, but could not be hired because of a mandated disqualification – she was married, and married women were not allowed to teach. The reasoning was that they already had a full time job, which was, of course, to be a wife and eventually a mother.

With the money that the Hollingworths collected from the Coca Cola Company for their research on caffeine in 1911 (recall a discussion of that work in Chapter 6), Leta was able to pursue doctoral work in psychology at Columbia University. She finished her PhD at Teachers College in 1916, with Edward Thorndike as her mentor. Her dissertation tested a centuries-old belief that women, because of their hormonal changes, were impaired cognitively and emotionally for a portion of each monthly menstrual cycle. Her subjects consisted of 23 women (six of whom were tested daily) and two men (as control subjects), assessed over a three-month period on tests of learning, color perception, motor fatigue, color naming, speed of movement, arm steadiness, and naming opposites. She found that her data did "not reveal a periodic mental or motor inefficiency in normal women ... [that] no part of the period is affected ... the variability of performance is not affected by physiological periodicity ... [and] no regularly recurring period of maximum efficiency within each month is discernible" (L. Hollingworth, 1914a, p. 94).

Hollingworth studied other dogmas as well, including the *variability hypothesis*, which asserted that men were more variable than women, thus in any distribution there would be more men at the high and low ends, meaning that the highest achievements in any field would more often belong to men (Shields, 1982). With regard to intelligence, a higher proportion of males would be found to have achieved eminence in intellectual pursuits and a higher proportion, as well, would be found in institutions for the "feebleminded." This version of the hypothesis had been prominent since Darwin demonstrated the evolutionary advantage of variation. Initially, Hollingworth sought to test the variability hypothesis by taking advantage of her position at the New York Clearing House for Mental Defectives. She examined the data for individuals who were institutionalized for feeblemindedness and found that men *were* institutionalized in higher proportions. When she looked at age of admission, she discovered something very interesting: for those admitted after age 13, the overwhelming majority was female. She explained those differences, not in terms of biology, but with regard to the social roles of men and women that would allow intellectually challenged women to exist for a longer period outside the institution, that is, a longer period of usefulness (L. Hollingworth, 1913).

In another study, Hollingworth used the birth records of a New York hospital, for 1,000 consecutive male births and 1,000 consecutive female births. From the records, she was able to extract ten different physical measurements for each infant. In analyzing the results, she first reported on the size differences, "Male infants are on the average, without exception, slightly larger than female infants in all anatomical measurements. The difference is, however, much less than we had expected to find, and is in most cases so small as to be practically negligible" (Montague & Hollingworth, 1914, p. 364). In looking at the variability of the distributions for each of the ten measures, she used two different techniques. One showed six measures with no variability differences, three for greater female variability, and one for greater male variability. The other technique indicated that four measures showed no variability differences, whereas three favored females and three favored males. In essence, examining the physical measurements of males and females at birth did not support the variability hypothesis of greater male variability.

In a critique of the literature supporting the variability hypothesis, Hollingworth (1914b) found it flawed, confounded, and biased. The few studies that used proper controls and that were conducted systematically did not show variability differences. She concluded, as Thompson had a decade earlier, that:

> ... even if it were established that there *actually* is greater male variability in mental traits, it would only suggest, not prove, that there is greater *inherent* variability. For (a) the opportunity and exercise of the sexes has been dissimilar and unequal; (b) intellectual variability has had survival value for men, but for women it has had little or none – this by virtue of the different parts played by the sexes in the perpetuation of the species. (p. 529)

In an application of the principle of scientific parsimony, Hollingworth (1914b) wrote: "It is undesirable to seek for the cause of sex differences in eminence in ultimate and obscure affective and intellectual differences until we have exhausted as a cause the known, obvious, and inescapable fact that women bear and rear children, and this has had as an inevitable sequel the occupation of housekeeping, a field where eminence is not possible" (p. 529).

Both Helen Thompson, who became Helen Thompson Woolley in 1905, and Leta Hollingworth made important contributions to psychology outside of their work on sex differences. Thompson did important work in special education and other psychological, educational, and vocational services for children, and she was a national leader in the preschool movement of the 1920s (Milar, 1999, 2004). Hollingworth made important contributions in gifted education, clinical psychology, and educational psychology (Benjamin & Shields, 1990). However, it is for their sex differences work, which both used to begin their careers, that they are best known. Their work in the first two decades of the twentieth century perhaps contributed in some small way to the attitudinal changes that would finally lead to women having the right to vote in a nation that had too long denied them that right. Tragically, both women had their careers cut short. Leta Hollingworth died of cancer in 1939 at the age of 53. Helen Thompson Woolley was forced to resign from Columbia University because of mental illness at the age of 55. She lived another 17 years, much of that time with her daughter (Milar, 2004).

Kurt Lewin's Action Research

Kurt Lewin (1890–1947) was born and raised in Germany, fought for his country for four years as an artillery officer in World War I, was wounded in combat, and was decorated with the Iron Cross. He had almost finished the work on his doctorate in psychology at the University of Berlin with Carl Stumpf when the war broke out. His graduation was delayed until 1916, when he completed his work during a brief leave of absence from the military. After the war, he stayed on the faculty at the University of Berlin. With Hitler's rise to power in the early 1930s, Germany developed a most virulent anti-Semitism. Lewin, a Jew and sensing the dangers to come, left Germany in 1933 to come to the United States. His mother and sister fled to Holland where they were later captured by the Nazis and sent to the death camps where they were killed. Lewin served on the faculties at Cornell University, the University of Iowa, and the Massachusetts Institute of Technology (MIT). His years at Iowa, beginning in 1935, and at MIT, were arguably his most productive. At Iowa, he became one of the charter members of the Society for the Psychological Study of Social Issues (SPSSI) when it was formed in 1936, and he served as its president in 1941. Today, SPSSI's highest honor is the Kurt Lewin Memorial Award, given for outstanding research contributions for work having social implications.

There is no denying that Lewin's experiences as a Jew shaped much of his social psychological work. Some sense of that is contained in the following excerpt of a letter that he wrote to Wolfgang Köhler in 1933, a letter that was never mailed because to do so would have been too dangerous at that time in Germany. Lewin wrote:

> I think it is practically impossible for a non-Jew to gauge what being a
> Jew has meant for a person, even in the liberal era of the last 40 years.
> There have probably been very few Jewish children of any generation
> who have not been singled out from the natural group of their peers

between their 6th and 13th year. Quite suddenly and without any kind of predictable cause, they have been beaten up and treated with contempt. Whether instigated by teachers, by students, or simply by people on the street, these recurring experiences pull the ground out from under the feet of the young child, and cut off all possibility of objective discussion or unbiased evaluation. They throw the child totally back upon its own resources. They make all natural supports appear entirely deceptive and force the young person to exist in a conflicting world of appearance and reality right from the start. Very few children are capable of surviving such disrupting experiences without suffering serious damage to their natural growth. After all, these experiences are not just casual irritations, but instead involve the very foundations of life itself on which all important decisions are based. Thus the effects are ever present. (as cited in M. Lewin, 1986, p. 42)

It is difficult to imagine growing up under that kind of hatred, violence, and the unpredictability of such forces in daily life, but it has been the life of members of minority groups for centuries, including many African Americans for much of their history. Lewin's biographer, Alfred Marrow (1969) has stated that Lewin's first-hand knowledge of prejudice and discrimination and the contrast of his life in Germany and America led to his program of socially relevant research: " ... Lewin looked at American life using his European experience as a continual and inescapable point of reference. In his speculation and research, this led in the ensuing years to a deepening interest in problems of democratic leadership and of the conditions for effective individual and group growth; it gave rise to a widening concern about ways in which greater knowledge of human behavior could be used to deal with social problems" (p. 85).

Of all the European émigrés, Lewin was undoubtedly the most successful in attracting students to work with him (Ash, 1992). Consequently, his ideas spread more broadly in American psychology. Many of his students have written about the importance of his mentorship, and the various descriptions have much consensus. Lewin had a strong work ethic and contagious activity level. He was creative, friendly, and unpretentious. He was self-confident without being arrogant. He was brilliant, often difficult to comprehend in early interactions with students, but capable of bringing his students to a new plane of thinking. He was generous in sharing his ideas and giving credit to his students for their ideas. There were many personal qualities that attracted students to Lewin and bonded them to him with such loyalty; one of those was "his deep concern with social problems and his determination to do something about them" (Frank, 1978, p. 223). This was the embodiment of *social action research*. For Lewin, it was recognition that research on social problems was not enough; it was critical to discover ways to use that research to change situations, to make individuals better, to make groups better, and to make societies better.

In Lewin's time, the dominant theories in psychology, especially behaviorism and psychoanalysis, emphasized the role of personal history as determinants of behavior. For the former that was the history of reinforcers and punishers and the nature of associations. For the latter it was early life experiences and the unconscious conflicts they created. Lewin would place his emphasis in an entirely different place. He didn't deny the role of history, but he argued that there was a more powerful force in place that was often the principal cause of behavior, and that was the *situation*. He wrote that *behavior was a function of the interaction of the person and the environment* in which the person was operating. This notion of situational determinants would be a powerful influence on the work of many psychologists, particularly social psychologists such as Solomon Asch, Stanley Milgram, Philip Zimbardo, and Ellen Langer.

Lewin is often treated as one of the Gestalt psychologists (discussed in the next chapter). His use of field theory in explaining how situational forces operated and interacted, including how individuals were affected by members of a group, and in turn, affected the group, was consonant with the holistic views of Gestalt psychology. For Lewin, behavior was determined not by one factor, not by one cause, but by the interaction of the total forces within the individual's *life space*, a holistic characterization of causality that emphasized the interaction of environmental (situational) influences and personal factors of the individual.

Lewin was 57 years old when he died of a heart attack, yet his published work is incredibly impressive, both in terms of its quantity and quality. Partly, that is testimony to his work ethic, but also to the quality of students that he drew to his research group. Those names read like a *Who's Who* in the social psychology of the latter half of the twentieth century: Roger Barker, Alex Bavelas, Dorwin Cartwight, Tamara Dembo, Morton Deutsch, Sibylle Escalona, Leon Festinger, John R. P. French, Harold Kelley, Rensis Likert, Ronald Lippitt, Stanley Schachter, Pauline Sears, John Thibaut, Ralph White, and Alvin Zander. Lewin made important contributions to child psychology, personality, motivation, and industrial psychology, but the focus in this section is on the social psychological work. The contributions are too vast to discuss, but a partial listing provides a sense of the range of the work and the themes of its focus.

Lewin began his social psychology in 1935 with a discussion of prejudice and discrimination, applying those issues to minority groups in general but using Jews as his focus. The continued success of the fascist regimes in Germany and Italy led him into research that looked at autocratic versus democratic groups. He investigated aggression under conditions of different social situations. He studied the relationship of frustration and aggression. He investigated conflict and the ways in which conflicts were and were not resolved. In one of his most famous studies, he expanded his work on democracy versus autocracy, studying the effects of different leadership styles as they affected group behavior.

Group influence and group dynamics became a central focus of Lewin's work after 1939. The leadership studies were part of that work in understanding how an individual influenced the group. He was also interested in the interactions among group members – how those interactions affected individuals and how they changed the nature of the group. The dynamics of groups were very much a part of his Gestalt psychology views. This interest led to Lewin's move to MIT and the founding of the Research Center for Group Dynamics, an institute where much of the social action research took place (Lewin, 1945). That center is still active as part of the Institute for Social Research at the University of Michigan.

Lewin's action research was both personal and grand in its scope. For example, in his work on prejudice and discrimination "he recommended various kinds of action to the victims or potential victims of racial and religious prejudice, types of action which should enhance the strength and integrity of the individual victim, as well as alter discriminatory practices" (Heims, 1978, p. 238). Concerned about how German citizens might deal with the aftermath of a World War II defeat, and, no doubt, aware of the mistaken policies imposed on Germany after its defeat in the First World War, Lewin "considered the problem of how one might change a whole culture; in other words, how to alter the characteristic attitudes and patterns of action of either a small group or a whole society … [for example] to reform the character structure of the defeated Nazi-trained German population once the war was over" (p. 239). He thus envisioned psychology intervening on a grand scale to affect world history.

Lewin's conception of causality in human behavior represented a radical departure from his contemporaries. To believe that behavioral actions were the result of intrapsychic conflicts or early childhood experiences or that they were determined by the individual's past history of reinforcement and punishment meant that cause was seen to reside primarily in the person. Lewin did not deny that characteristics of the person were a part of the behavioral equation. But he argued that in most behavioral circumstances, it was characteristics of the situation that were far more powerful as causes. This belief in

(Left, right): Archives of the History of American Psychology, The Center for the History of Psychology, The University of Akron

Figure 10.3   Social psychologists Kurt Lewin (*left*) and Otto Klineberg made significant contributions to diverse areas of psychology, including research on prejudice and the psychology of racial differences

the ultimate *power of the situation* fostered, in his students, some of the most dramatic and revealing (and sometimes disturbing) studies in the history of psychology, for example, Asch's studies of conformity, Milgram's studies of obedience, and Zimbardo's prison studies.

Kurt Lewin was a psychologist who believed that he was obligated to use his science for public good, a belief that Skinner shared as well (as described in Chapter 8). In focusing on the importance of *situational variables* as determinants of behavior, he used his program of action research to discover how those variables functioned and how they could be altered or controlled in ways that ameliorated social ills. He was, without a doubt, one of the most influential psychologists of the twentieth century.

The Psychology of Race

Concerning the history of racism in America, psychology has been part of the problem and part of the solution (see Philogene, 2004; Winston, 2004). According to Robert Guthrie (1998), the word "race" did not appear in the scientific literature until 1750. It would become a topic of great interest among anthropologists in the nineteenth century, and psychologists would join in as well, in the tradition of individual differences research, in this case, the psychological differences that could be found between races. Francis Galton, certainly a principal promoter of individual differences, argued in his book *Hereditary Genius* (1869) that the black race was decidedly inferior to the white race in a number of ways, reflecting the general European prejudices regarding white superiority (Fancher, 2004). Many of the early American psychologists shared similar views, including G. Stanley Hall (1904) who labeled African Americans an inferior race in his book, *Adolescence*.

Race Differences in Intelligence

R. Meade Bache was a graduate student with Lightner Witmer at the University of Pennsylvania in 1895 when he published his comparative study of reaction time across three racial groups in the journal *Psychological Review*. Bache tested Native Americans, African Americans, and whites on both auditory and visual reaction time tasks. What he found likely surprised him: Native Americans had the fastest reaction times, followed by African Americans, whereas whites had the slowest times. Although those findings might appear to suggest white inferiority, Bache would not accept such an interpretation. Instead, he reasoned that a reaction time task involved behavior that was something akin to a reflex, and a reflex is a rather primitive response, likely mediated by the spinal column rather than the cerebral cortex. Bache reasoned that whites were disadvantaged in such a task because he believed that their brains were more contemplative and did not operate as quickly when the task was such a primitive one. Guthrie (1998) has referred to this as *scientific racism*, meaning those instances in which science is used to introduce or maintain beliefs about superiority of a particular race.

Frank Bruner took his doctorate with Robert Woodworth at Columbia University investigating auditory perception in black and white subjects. In a review of the "scientific" literature published in the *Psychological Bulletin* in 1912, he wrote:

> … the mental qualities of the Negro [may be summarized] as: lacking in filial affection, strong migratory instincts and tendencies; little sense of veneration, integrity, or honor; shiftless, indolent, untidy, improvident, extravagant, lazy, untruthful, lacking in persistence and initiative and unwilling to work continuously at details. Indeed, experience with the Negro in class rooms indicates that it is impossible to get the child to do anything with continued accuracy, and similarly in industrial pursuits, the Negro shows a woeful lack of power of sustained activity and constructive conduct. (pp. 387–388)

Another Columbia psychology graduate, George O. Ferguson (1916), used his dissertation research to investigate "The psychology of the Negro," finding that his black subjects were poor at abstract thought, but capable in terms of sensory and motor functioning. He indicated that his results suggested the type of educational effort that should be expended upon the several races. On the West Coast, Lewis Terman (1916) in his manual for the *Stanford-Binet Intelligence Test* cited studies on African Americans, Mexican Americans, and Native Americans indicating a much higher percentage of "morons" in those groups compared to rates found among whites. Terman called for investigations of IQ differences across races, predicting that "when this is done there will be discovered enormously significant racial differences in general intelligence, differences which cannot be wiped out by any scheme of mental culture" (p. 92).

By the 1920s, however, psychologists were beginning, ever so slightly, to question claims of racial differences, especially intellectual differences. Psychologists were not ready to say there were no differences, but they were willing to suggest that the differences were not as large as had been suspected, that they might be more qualitative than quantitative, and that factors other than heredity might be responsible for the differences. These changes in attitude were summed up by Floyd H. Allport (1890–1971) in his 1924 book, *Social Psychology*:

> [French sociologist Gustave] Le Bon mistakenly held that there is a gap between superior and inferior races amounting almost to a distinction of species. The vast differences in cultural adaptation between primitive and civilized races are to be ascribed as much to 'social inheritance' and environmental factors as to innate differences of capacity. It is fairly well established, however, that the intelligence of the white race is of a more versatile and complex order than that of the black race. It is probably superior also to that of the red or yellow races. (p. 386)

Robert Woodworth (1929) made no such claims of racial differences in intelligence in his introductory psychology textbook in which he pointed to confounds of environmental differences and different "cultural backgrounds." After reviewing the literature, he suggested that the best policy is to "suspend judgment and keep our eyes open from year to year for fresh and more conclusive evidence that will probably be discovered" (p. 58).

By the 1930s, there was at least one psychologist ready to take a bolder stand. Otto Klineberg (1899–1992), a Canadian psychologist, then at Columbia University, published two important books on the psychology of race in 1935. In the first book, *Negro Intelligence and*

Selective Migration (1935a), Klineberg addressed the finding that blacks in the North had higher IQ scores than blacks in the South, which was generally explained by the assumption that blacks who were of higher intelligence migrated from the South to the North, thus escaping some of the racial oppression of the South. However, Klineberg found that was not the case. He wrote, "As far as intelligence goes, the material reported in this study gives evidence to the effect that the Negro who leaves the South for the North is not on average superior to the Negro who remains behind, and that the present superiority of the northern over the southern Negro may be explained by the more favorable environment, rather than by selective migration" (p. 62). In the second book, *Race Differences* (1935b), he wrote, "The general conclusion of this book is that there is no scientific proof of racial differences in mentality. ... There is no reason, therefore, to treat two people differently because they differ in their physical type. There is not justification for denying a Negro a job or an education because he is a Negro. No one has been able to demonstrate that ability is correlated with skin color or head shape or any of the anatomical characteristics used to classify races" (p. 345). By the 1940s, Klineberg was not alone in such beliefs as many psychologists, particularly social psychologists, had come to believe that prejudice, discrimination, differing environmental opportunities, and cultural biases in tests were more likely explanations for the obtained intellectual differences among races. Just how did this change in attitude among psychologists come about? Was it based on new data on IQ differences? Was it just a few psychologists who had changed their minds or was this change more widespread in the field? These are questions that psychologist Franz Samelson (1978) raised in a historical study of this literature. He found that the attitudinal change was widespread, that very few studies in the 1940s looked at race differences in IQ except to talk about the sociological factors that would produce them. There were new data that questioned the earlier beliefs but Samelson argued that they were of little consequence in influencing this change in social paradigm. Instead, he argued that the shift from racism to studies of cultural bias was brought about by a change in the nature of the individuals who entered the field of psychology after 1920. He wrote:

American psychology up to 1920 was lily-white, consisting of native or imported Anglo-Saxons ... with an occasional Jew or half-Jew. ... From the twenties on, however, ethnics began to move into the profession in ever-increasing numbers, at first with recruits from Jewish backgrounds. ... In the subsequent shift from race psychology to concern with prejudice, one finds names like Klineberg, Herskovits, Feingold,

Hirsch, Viteles, Lasker, Katz, Lehman. ... It seems likely, however, that personal experience sensitized individuals to different aspects of the problem, and led some to question the assumptions taken as self-evident by others lacking such experience. (pp. 272–273)

Samelson (1978) mentions other factors that gave American psychologists "a powerful push toward the left" (p. 273), which included the revulsion felt toward Hitler's claims of a master race and the realities of dealing with a major economic depression. Even with this dramatic change in the way American psychologists have dealt with the subject of race and intelligence, there remains a die-hard group who insist that racial differences in IQ exist, that they are sizeable, and that they cannot be explained by environmental or cultural issues. See, for example, the June 2005 issue of the APA journal *Psychology, Public Policy, and Law* that features a lead article by J. Philippe Rushton and Arthur Jensen, accompanied by a series of articles commenting pro and con on their analysis. That this controversy continues does not surprise psychologist-historian Graham Richards (2004) who has argued that the continued concern with racial difference in intelligence is a "peculiarly American obsession" (p. 157).

Psychology and School Desegregation

Opportunities in higher education for African Americans were few in the beginning of the twentieth century. Although there were a number of black colleges in existence, graduate education was another matter entirely. For example, there were more than 10,000 PhDs awarded in the United States between 1876 and 1920. Only 11 of those went to African Americans (Guthrie, 1998). One of those was Francis Cecil Sumner (1895–1954) who earned his doctorate at Clark University with G. Stanley Hall as his mentor. Sumner's dissertation research was a comparison of the psychoanalytic ideas of Freud and Adler (Guthrie, 1998).

The first African American woman to get a PhD in psychology was Inez Beverly Prosser (ca. 1895–1934) who received her degree from the University of Cincinnati in 1933 where Louis Pechstein, a graduate of the functional psychology program at Chicago, was her mentor. Prosser's doctoral research examined personality differences in black children attending either voluntarily segregated or integrated schools. She found that in terms of favorable development of personality traits, black children fared better in voluntarily segregated schools (Benjamin, Henry, & McMahon, 2005).

Francis Sumner was chair of the psychology department at Howard University in Washington, DC from 1928 until his death in 1954. The

Figure 10.4 Mamie Phipps Clark and Kenneth Bancroft Clark. Their work on self-esteem and racial identity in African American children proved crucial in the NAACP's formulation of a strategy that would result in school desegregation being declared unconstitutional in the 1954 *Brown v. Board* Supreme Court decision

program that he established there inspired a number of African Americans to pursue careers in psychology, including Kenneth Clark and Mamie Phipps Clark. Mamie Phipps (1917–1983) was working on her master's degree at Howard when she met her husband to be, Kenneth Bancroft Clark (1914–2005) who was a doctoral student in New York. They worked together on several research projects in a subject that she had initiated as part of her master's degree research. They were interested in self-esteem in black children, wondering if it differed in black children who attended segregated versus integrated schools. Unlike Prosser's sample, their segregated children were from schools in the South where segregation was mandated by state law, upheld by the 1896 Supreme Court decision known as *Plessy v. Ferguson*, which established the "separate but equal" doctrine, which segregation states used to keep black students out of white schools. By federal law, these states were supposed to provide black schools that were "equal" in terms of their quality; but that was never enforced. On average, states where segregated schools were mandated spent ten times as much on white schools as they did on black schools.

The National Association for the Advancement of Colored People (NAACP) was searching for a way to end school desegregation in the 17 states and District of Columbia that practiced it under the "separate but equal" doctrine. To attack the inequalities of financial support of black schools versus white schools would be a long road of suing district by district, state by state. What was needed was something to overturn *Plessy v. Ferguson*, something that would declare that decision unconstitutional. If they could accomplish that, then the fights at the state and district levels would be unnecessary. The lead attorney for the NAACP was Thurgood Marshall (1908–1993), who would later be a distinguished Supreme Court justice (Williams, 1998). He wondered if there was a way to demonstrate that segregation was damaging to black children. He found his strategy in the psychological work of Kenneth and Mamie Clark.

The Clarks had both earned their doctorates at Columbia University. Kenneth earned his PhD in 1940, studying with Otto Klineberg. Mamie earned her degree in 1944 with Henry Garrett, who unlike Klineberg, believed that African Americans were intellectually inferior to whites. Mamie Clark chose him for an advisor to ensure that her graduate program would be as challenging as it could be. When the NAACP attorneys approached the Clarks, Kenneth was a faculty member at the City College of New York and Mamie was executive director of the Northside Center for Child Development in Harlem, a center she and Kenneth opened to provide social services to the people of that community (Markowitz & Rosner, 1996). Note that as a black woman; most academic jobs were closed to her.

Kenneth worked with the NAACP attorneys, testifying in the court cases in South Carolina, Delaware, and Virginia – three of the four cases that would be combined with one from Topeka, Kansas that would be known as *Brown vs. Board of Education, Topeka, Kansas*. In those lower court cases, Kenneth took the brown, black, and white dolls to court to demonstrate the kinds of tests that he and Mamie had used to measure self-esteem in black children. Their results, published in four separate articles, indicated that black children in segregated schools had lower self-esteem, and that "they passively and fatalistically accept their inferior status as practically an act of God" (K. Clark, 1952, Feb. 15).

Marshall found the Clarks through Otto Klineberg. Marshall knew of Klineberg's books on the psychology of race and approached him about helping with the lawsuits. Klineberg referred Marshall to Kenneth Clark. Clark supplied a recent article he had written for a White House conference; it was exactly the approach that Marshall had been seeking. Marshall wanted to get a summary of all the social science evidence that might bear on the damaging effects of segregation. That became a job for the Society for the Psychological Study of Social Issues. Kenneth Clark joined Isidor Chein and Stuart Cook, all three members of SPSSI, to write the original draft of what would be called the "Social Science

Statement" to be filed as an appendix to the NAACP brief. A version of that statement was published as an issue of SPSSI's journal, the *Journal of Social Issues*, and was edited by Clark (1953). The Social Science Statement filed with the Supreme Court was signed by 32 prominent social scientists including Floyd and Gordon Allport, Else Frenkel-Brunswik, Allison Davis, Nevitt Sanford, and Brewster Smith. Then they waited, and waited, for months.

Shortly after noon on May 17, 1954, the press corps at the Court was notified that a decision was about to be rendered in the *Brown* case. Chief Justice Earl Warren read the decision that, in part, stated:

> Segregation of White and colored children in public school has a detrimental effect upon the colored children. The impact is greater when it has the sanction of law, for the policy of separating the races is usually interpreted as denoting the inferiority of the Negro group. A sense of inferiority affects the motivation of the child to learn. Segregation with the sanction of the law, therefore, has a tendency to retard the educational and mental development of Negro children and to deprive them of some of the benefits they would receive in a racially integrated school system. Whatever may have been the extent of psychological knowledge at the time of *Plessy v. Ferguson*, this finding is amply supported by modern authority. ... We conclude that, in the field of public education, the doctrine of "separate but equal" has no place. (quoted in Kluger, 1975, p. 782)

The "modern authority" was, of course, the social science research in the appellant's brief. In fact, seven psychological and sociological studies were listed in a footnote of the Court's decision. The first study in that list of seven was by Kenneth Clark, his White House Conference report (Clark, 1950). It was the first time that psychological science had ever been used in a Supreme Court decision, arguably the most important court decision of the twentieth century, and certainly a watershed event for the science of psychology. The Clarks, Marshall, Klineberg, and everyone else associated with the case were ecstatic. An admirer wrote to Kenneth Clark asking him how it felt 'to set straight the course of American history' (Benjamin & Crouse, 2002).

May 17 would provide a flashbulb memory for many African Americans who could vividly remember where they were and what they were doing when they heard the news of the Court's decision. Francis Sumner, who had started Mamie and Kenneth Clark on their paths to psychology, would not know the outcome of the Court case. Sadly, he died from a heart attack a few months earlier, shoveling snow in front of his Washington, DC home.

A Final Note

The psychology of women and studies of sex differences re-emerged as hot topics in the 1970s as women's issues were debated in American society in the context of the failed Equal Rights Amendment to the U.S. Constitution. This new focus on women's issues led to the rediscovery of the work of Helen Thompson Woolley and Leta Hollingworth, work that had gone unrecognized for decades. Women, once rare as APA presidents, are now elected at about the same frequency as men. The Society for the Psychology of Women is one of the divisions of the American Psychological Association (No. 35), and there is now an APA Division for the Psychological Study of Men and Masculinity (No. 51).

SPSSI is Division 9 of APA, one of the 18 charter divisions when APA was reorganized in 1945. SPSSI, as a research society, and individual psychologists continue their socially relevant work today. Kurt Lewin's social action research is manifested in many areas of contemporary psychology. What seemed like such a radical idea in the 1930s, the notion that psychological science could be applied to the social ills of the world, doesn't seem so radical today.

11

Cognitive Psychology

The *Brown v. Board* Supreme Court decision in 1954 ushered in an era of social turmoil and change that continued through the civil rights movement of the 1960s and the Vietnam War. The assassination of a popular American president and then his brother who sought that office, the assassination of the leading civil rights voice of Martin Luther King, Jr., race riots, and violence on college campuses were defining events of the 1960s. There was Woodstock, the Peace Corps, Black Panthers, the Cuban Missile Crisis, Bob Dylan and Joan Baez, marijuana, and Students for a Democratic Society. The Beatles sang, *You say you want a revolution. Well we all want to change the world*. In the midst of this social change, there were rumblings within psychology as well. The once seemingly impenetrable edifice of behaviorism was crumbling, besieged by psychologists who could not find explanations for much of human behavior in the limited models of the time. This transformation in American psychology is often referred to as the cognitive revolution, when psychologists wanted to change their world.

In this final chapter, we describe the evolution of cognitive psychology in the second half of the twentieth century. In keeping with the chronology of our approach, this chapter tells the story of the emergence of modern cognitive psychology in the 1950s and 1960s when experimental psychologists, in increasing numbers, believed that they could not explain human behavior by continuing to ignore mental processes. Behaviorism had long dominated American psychology. For the new cognitive psychologists, it was the psychology of their professors, it was the psychology of their training, and it was the psychology of the jobs they hoped to obtain. If they had ideas about mind as opposed to behavior, they knew that it was probably best to be quiet about them. However, they would not be silent. The mentalistic psychology, those forbidden topics that John Watson had banished to some far off island, had found their way home. What followed was a radical, albeit gradual, change in the conceptualization and methodologies of psychology. What followed was the rebirth of cognitive psychology, a new psychology that would soon discover its historic ties with the psychologies of Wundt and Stumpf and Ebbinghaus and James and Titchener and the Gestalt psychologists.

One of the landmarks in the new cognitive psychology was the publication of Ulric Neisser's book, *Cognitive Psychology* (1967). Neisser defined cognition as:

> ... all the processes by which the sensory input is transformed, reduced, elaborated, stored, recovered, and used. It is concerned with these processes even when they operate in the absence of relevant stimulation, as in images and hallucinations. Such terms as sensation, perception, imagery, retention, recall, problem-solving, and thinking, among many others, refer to hypothetical stages or aspects of cognition. (p. 4)

This definition shows the influence of the computer metaphor. Indeed, the development of the computer, with its computer languages, models of information processing, storage, and information retrieval, played a key role in the conceptual models of cognitive psychology. Psychologists would recognize the related work in communications theory, artificial intelligence, and linguistics, as important for developing the new approach to the science of mind and behavior.

The terms listed in Neisser's definition would be found in the textbooks of late nineteenth-century psychology. They would be found, for example, in Wundt, James, and Titchener. In truth, these concepts never fully disappeared from American psychology, even at the peak of behaviorism's influence. Psychologist and historian Thomas Leahey (1992) has described the cognitive psychology that kept the flame alive from the time of James to the modern era:

> Certainly behaviorism brought an end to the lush excesses of Würzburg and late Titchenerian introspection, but it did not expunge the experimental psychology of consciousness. Practically speaking, what Wundt inaugurated was the scientific study of sensation and perception, including processes such as attention. Although after 1910 such studies no longer occupied center stage in psychology – being overshadowed by research on behavior, especially learning – they did not disappear ... The central work of mentalistic psychology continued, but it was no longer thought of as the study of consciousness. (p. 313)

Before we describe the new cognitive psychology of the 1950s and 1960s, it is necessary to back up in the chronology to treat some of this earlier work.

In Chapter 3, we described the various German psychologies that coexisted with Wundt's Leipzig laboratory. All of those psychologies could be labeled as cognitive, given the meaning of that term today: Wundt with his focus on sensation, perception, attention, and the speed of mental events; Ebbinghaus and Georg Müller on memory; Brentano on mental acts; Stumpf on the perception of tone; and Külpe on thinking, including his work on mental sets and imageless thought. In North America, Titchener continued the emphasis on sensation; Cattell on measurement of mental capacities; and James Mark Baldwin at the University of Toronto on speed of mental processes and memory.

With the rise of functional psychology, driven by the impact of Darwinian ideas of adaptation, the study of learning began to replace the study of sensation and perception (except at Cornell), and that emphasis on learning was maintained, even intensified, through the rise of behaviorism and the neo-behaviorists. Studies of sensation and perception continued, as Leahey observed, but they were no longer the product of introspective methods. Many were couched in a stimulus-response framework, similar to the more dominant studies of learning and motivation.

When psychoanalysis arrived in America in the 1910s, it was the first of two European imports that would challenge mainstream American psychology in the first half of the twentieth century. The other arrived from Germany, first appearing in the American psychology journals in the 1920s, and arriving in person in the 1920s and 1930s. This import was Gestalt psychology, a phenomenological and nativistic psychology that emphasized the study of perception, learning, thinking, and problem solving.

Gestalt Psychology

Gestalt psychology is perhaps best known for the phrase, 'the whole is different from the sum of its parts.' Although not a Gestalt psychologist, Wundt recognized the validity of that statement in his own system and would have been comfortable with it (see the discussion of apperception in Chapter 3). The statement reflects two important aspects of Gestalt psychology. First, Gestalt psychology is *holistic*; it opposes a reductionistic analysis of elemental parts because it recognizes that there are perceptual qualities in the wholes of experience that cannot be found in any study of the parts. Second, Gestalt psychology is *phenomenological*, meaning that it studies experience as it occurs, in meaningful units. Here is how Wertheimer (1938) defined his psychology:

> The fundamental "formula" of Gestalt theory might be expressed in this way: There are wholes, the behaviour of which is not determined by that of their individual elements, but where the part-processes are themselves determined by the intrinsic nature of the whole. It is the hope of Gestalt theory to determine the nature of such wholes. (p. 2)

Although Gestalt psychology has its roots in several philosophical systems in Germany and Austria, we begin with the work of Max Wertheimer (1880–1943), a German psychologist who is generally acknowledged to be the founder of Gestalt psychology. Wertheimer studied with Carl Stumpf at Berlin before earning his doctorate at Würzburg with Oswald Külpe. He was most influenced, however, by an Austrian philosopher/psychologist, Christian von Ehrenfels (1859–1932), whose ideas about form qualities (Gestaltqualitäten) eventually gave rise to Wertheimer's Gestalt psychology. The story goes that Wertheimer was traveling on a train on vacation in 1910 when he got an idea for an experiment. He got off the train in Frankfurt, purchased a toy stroboscope (a device that creates a series of successive pictures producing apparent motion), and tested his ideas in his hotel room. He continued that work at the Frankfurt Psychological Institute where he was joined by two recent graduates from the University of Berlin: Kurt Koffka (1886–1941) and Wolfgang Köhler (1887–1967), both of whom had earned their doctorates with Stumpf. Those three would become the triumvirate of Gestalt psychology, building a system of psychology in Germany that would dominate by the 1930s, displacing much of the influence that had been wielded in the psychology of Wundt's students. With Stumpf's retirement at Berlin, Köhler was given the chair in psychology there, arguably the most important psychology professorship in Germany.

Wertheimer's experiment with the stroboscope involved a form of apparent movement known as phi movement or the *phi phenomenon*. In Wertheimer's demonstration, two black lines, one vertical, the other horizontal, appeared against a white background, so that if they were seen simultaneously they would form a right angle. The lines were presented successively with a small interval between the offset of the first line and the onset of the second. When that interval was optimal (around 60 msec), the observer would see a form of apparent movement in which a single line appeared to be sweeping across the 90-degree angle from vertical to horizontal, back and forth. Lengthening or shortening the time interval caused the movement to disappear and the observer would see either both lines appearing simultaneously or the two lines appearing successively with no movement. Wertheimer labeled this apparent movement "phi movement."

Phi movement was not new to science, but Wertheimer's interpretation was. He saw the movement as an experience that was not reducible to its elements. That is, no amount of introspection could cause the apparent movement to be seen as its actual physical occurrence, which was two lines flashing on and off in succession. There was something more to the experience that was not evident in just the flashes of the lines. Motion pictures, like phi, are a form of stroboscopic movement. The movement that is seen in the movie theater is quite real, even though it is created by a series of still images projected on the screen, one at a time. This classic study by Wertheimer (1912) launched the Gestalt view, emphasizing their belief in studying experience as it occurred, rather than breaking it down into elements that they viewed as artificial (King & Wertheimer, 2005; O'Neil & Landauer, 1966). It would be another decade before most Americans would become very familiar with Gestalt ideas. In 1922, Kurt Koffka published an article in the American journal *Psychological Bulletin* entitled "Perception: An introduction to *Gestalt-theorie*." A more comprehensive treatment was provided in 1925 by a series of four articles on Gestalt psychology by Harry Helson in the *American Journal of Psychology*.

When Gestalt psychology arrived in America in the heyday of behaviorism, it was truly a clash of psychological cultures. Behaviorism argued that experience was not directly knowable. The Gestaltists argued that experience was the only thing worth knowing, and that it could be studied exactly as it occurred (Köhler, 1929). Behaviorism was a reductionistic, molecular psychology focused on S-R relationships, where responses were observable behaviors. Gestalt psychology was holistic and molar; it studied mental phenomena as they occurred.

(All): Archives of the History of American Psychology, The Center for the History of Psychology, The University of Akron

Figure 11.1 The Gestalt psychology triumvirate (*left to right*) Max Wertheimer, Kurt Koffka, and Wolfgang Köhler

Whereas behaviorism emphasized nurture in the nature-nurture arguments, the Gestalt theorists came down on the other side in the way
they viewed the mind. The Gestaltists did not argue for innate ideas,
but they did posit the existence of innate *organizing tendencies* in the
mind that were important for perception, learning, and memory. These
ideas were spelled out most clearly in descriptions of the organizing
principles for perception. According to the Gestaltists, these organizational processes help structure the perceptual world into meaningful
wholes. Thus, we are programmed to respond to qualities such as
similarity and proximity when we group items in a perceptual array
(*principles of grouping*). We tend to see incomplete figures as completed
(*closure*). We focus attention on a target stimulus that becomes the
figure against the rest of the perceptual field that is described as ground
(in *figure-ground perception*) (Koffka, 1935).

Behaviorists, adhering to their strict empiricism, were not accepting
of the idea of innate cognitive structures, and the nativist claims were
very much out of touch with the prevailing emphasis on environ-
mentalism. The Gestalt theorists argued that it was impossible to
make sense of how humans perceived their world without positing
the existence of such structures. Such ideas, which remained outside
the mainstream of American psychology in the 1930s, are very much
mainstream today. A more modern example would be linguist Noam
Chomsky's language acquisition device, a cognitive structure that
Chomsky argues is hard wired in all human brains that makes possible
the learning of language in a similar way across cultures and languages
(mentioned later in this chapter).

Edward Tolman might have seemed a sympathetic voice, but he was
not a cognitive psychologist in the sense of the Gestaltists. He was not
a nativist, and he did not study cognitive processes per se. Instead, he
studied learning in rat mazes, from which he posited the existence of
such intervening variables as cognitive maps and expectancies, because
those variables seemed necessary to explain the results of his studies. He
was, in today's vernacular, a cognitive behaviorist.

The organizing principles of the Gestaltists were extended to other
cognitive processes as well, for example, memory and problem solving.
Humans evidently seek closure in these areas as well. This recognition gave rise to the Zeigarnik effect. Research on this effect was initiated by an observation made by Kurt Lewin that waiters in restaurants
could recall the dishes that customers had ordered until the bill was
paid. However, once the bill was paid, the memory of those food orders
was erased. He proposed a motivational explanation saying that incom-
pleteness created a kind of psychological tension that kept the memory intact, but that once the tension was relieved (the bill was paid),

then the waiter would have little or no memory for the order. One of Lewin's students at Berlin (Lewin was considered part of the Gestalt group), Bluma Zeigarnik (1900–1988), tested this idea in 1927 by having subjects work on a series of problems. Some problems they were allowed to complete, but for other problems they were interrupted and not allowed to finish. When she tested the subjects later for their recall of the problems, they were twice as likely to remember the incompleted problems as the completed problems. This greater memory for incompleted tasks versus completed tasks is called the *Zeigarnik effect* (Zeigarnik, 1938). Of course, every student knows this effect, whether they ever heard of Bluma Zeigarnik or not. Just listen to students talking with one another after finishing an exam. The questions they can recall from the exams are the ones about which they were uncertain. The questions easily answered (thus completed) are rarely remembered.

The Gestalt psychologists made contributions in learning as well, particularly Wolfgang Köhler who conducted a series of classic studies on chimpanzees and chickens when he was stranded at a research station on the Canary Islands during World War I. In the chimp studies, the animals were to solve several problems in how to reach bananas that were hung out of reach at the top of the cage or placed out of reach outside the cage. Some solutions involved fitting sticks together to make a pole long enough to reach the bananas, or moving boxes underneath the hanging bananas. Most chimps solved the problems, but some did not. Köhler believed that successful problem solving meant seeing the problem as a whole, by linking all of the elements together in a unified whole, for example, correct placement of the boxes and jumping. Some animals seemed to realize that they needed to jump from the top of the box, but did not move the boxes underneath the bananas. Köhler argued that these chimps lacked the *insight* needed to solve the problem (Köhler, 1927).

Chickens are not the brightest animals, as Köhler discovered. One of Köhler's tasks required them to discriminate between two shades of gray, one light and one dark. Grain was available for a correct response, which was pecking on the dark gray card. It required around 500 trials for the chicken to learn such a discrimination! What had the animal learned? A behaviorist would argue that the chicken learned a connection between the dark card and the food and that association was stamped in by the reinforcement. But Köhler saw it differently. After the chicken had learned the discrimination, he presented the animal with two new gray cards. One was the same dark gray card that was reinforced in the earlier trials; the other card was an even darker gray. Most of the chickens pecked on the darker card and not on the one that had previously been paired with food reward. Köhler argued that such a result indicated that the chicken had learned the problem as a relationship, that is, as a whole – peck on the darker of the two cards. Studies such as these convinced the Gestalt psychologists of the impoverishment of a behavioral psychology, a notion that Köhler emphasized in the first chapter of his 1929 book, *Gestalt Psychology*.

One by one, the Gestalt psychologists came to America where they had to confront behaviorism head on. Koffka was the first to arrive in 1924. He held temporary teaching positions until he accepted a permanent position in 1927 at Smith College in Massachusetts. Wertheimer and Lewin arrived in 1933. Both were Jewish, and both left Nazi Germany and the escalating violence against Jews. Wertheimer joined the faculty of the New School for Social Research in New York City (we described Lewin's placements in the previous chapter). Köhler, who was not Jewish, held out the longest, hoping to help his young assistants at the University of Berlin, and believing that Gestalt psychology might be doomed in Germany if he left. However, by 1935, his situation was intolerable, and so he immigrated, joining the faculty of Swarthmore College in Pennsylvania.

With the exception of Lewin (at Iowa and MIT), the Gestalt psychologists in America were not in places to attract graduate students and thus spread their psychology. They were in a foreign land, learning to speak a foreign language, located in university positions less prestigious than they had held in Germany, and championing a psychology that opposed the dominant behaviorism on a number of grounds. Further, with the exception of Köhler, they were all dead by 1947, Koffka first in 1941, Wertheimer in 1943, and Lewin in 1947, thus, their period of direct influence was limited. Looking at psychology textbooks in the 1940s and 1950s as a way to gauge the influence of the Gestaltists shows that they were principally relegated to a description of their work on perceptual organization in the chapters on sensation and perception. Köhler's work on insight learning rarely appeared and virtually no attention was paid to the work on productive thinking of Max Wertheimer (1945). Eventually, however, that picture would begin to change.

Frederic Bartlett and the Constructive Mind

While American behaviorists were ignoring cognitive processes in the 1930s, the British were not. In 1932, Frederic C. Bartlett (1886–1969), head of the psychology department at Cambridge University, published *Remembering: A Study in Experimental and Social Psychology*, a book that introduced a new approach to the study of memory, one that fit nicely with the constructive approach the Gestalt psychologists were using in their studies of thinking and problem solving. Bartlett sought to study memory in a way quite different from Ebbinghaus. He believed that memory was greatly influenced by social and cultural factors, and that Ebbinghaus's associationistic procedures using non-meaningful materials (nonsense syllables) would not be able to reveal those aspects of memory. Bartlett's book described a series of studies, one of which asked subjects to listen to a story and then, from recall, tell the story to someone else. One of the stories Bartlett (1932) used was a Native American folktale known as *The War of the Ghosts*. Here is an excerpt from that story:

> One night two young men from Egulac went down to the river to hunt seals and while they were there it became foggy and calm. Then they heard war-cries, and they thought: "Maybe this is a war-party." They escaped to the shore, and hid behind a log. Now canoes came up, and they heard the noise of paddles, and saw one canoe coming up to them. There were five men in the canoe and they said ...
> "We wish to take you along. We are going up the river to make war on the people" ... So one of the young men went ... And the warriors went on up the river to a town on the other side of Kalama. The people came down to the water and they began to fight, and many were killed. But presently the young man heard one of the warriors say, "Quick, let us go home; that Indian has been hit." Now he thought: "Oh, they are ghosts." He did not feel sick, but they said he had been shot. So the canoes went back to Egulac and the young man went ashore to his house and made a fire. And he told everybody and said "Behold I accompanied the ghosts, and we went to fight ... They said I was hit, and I did not feel sick." He told it all, and then he became quiet. When the sun rose he fell down. Something black came out of his mouth. His face became contorted. The people jumped up and cried. He was dead. (p. 65)

Subjects had some difficulty retelling this story. It was long (just a little longer than the excerpt printed here), so that it exceeded what we would today call the capacity of working memory. In addition, it was "foreign," meaning it did not fit the cultural experiences of the British subjects being tested.

What Bartlett found was that subjects shortened the story, no doubt, because there was simply too much material to remember. However, of greater interest to him were the ways in which subjects constructed the story to have it make more sense in their own experiences. It was clear that there were parts of the story that subjects could not understand, and so they revised it, using their own experience in processing the meaning of the story, making the story fit better into Western culture, and adding information to the story that made sense in the context of the

Archives of the History of American Psychology, The Center for the History of Psychology, The University of Akron

Figure 11.2   Sir Frederic C. Bartlett (right)

individual's personal experiences. Thus for Bartlett, memory was not just about associations; it was about a mind that actively constructed incoming information. It was evidence that the mind was involved in *construction*, not just reconstruction.

In his important book, Bartlett introduced the concept of a *schema*, which is a cognitive framework that organizes past experiences related to particular concepts. According to Bartlett, experience gives rise to many schemata that any individual would hold. Individuals would have a schema for rudeness, which would be constructed from their experiences with rudeness in the past. This schema would operate in any ongoing cognitive activity where perceptions, judgments, or memories concerning rudeness would occur. The existence of schemata is evidence of the ways our culture and our own personal experiences influence the memories that we have. Schemata influence what information we choose to process from all that is available in our environment, how we will interpret that information, how we will recall that information, and how we will use the information.

Unlike Ebbinghaus, Bartlett was not chiefly interested in the product of the memory (that is, the actual recall), except for what that recall exhibited about the mental processing that went on between learning and remembering. He wrote, "In a ... constantly changing environment, literal recall is extraordinarily unimportant. ... Condensation, elaboration, and invention are common features of ordinary remembering, and these all very often involve the mingling of materials belonging originally to different schemata" (Bartlett, 1932, p. 204). Bartlett noted that what was constant about human memory was that it is "exceedingly subject to error," that remembering was "really a construction serving to justify whatever impression may have been left by the original" (pp. 175–176). In the same way that Ebbinghaus created a new approach to the study of memory in the associative tradition, Bartlett's simple, yet imaginative, approach to the study of memory created a new way to think, not only about memory but also about the other higher mental processes of consciousness.

Bartlett's ideas, which were most influential in British psychology, lay unrecognized in America through the heyday of behaviorism. For the most part, American psychologists would not discover his work until the 1960s, largely stimulated by rise of the concept of schema, especially in perceptual learning research, and by the success of Ulric Neisser's 1967 book. That book drew heavily on the work of Bartlett, particularly the notions of schema and processes of construction, and proved to be such an important stimulus for defining modern cognitive psychology (Bruce & Winograd, 1998; Roediger, 2000).

The Rise of Modern Cognitive Psychology in America

The evolution of modern cognitive psychology in America is not easily traced or summarized. This family tree has many branches. Historians and cognitive psychologists argue about which events are important for cognitive psychology's history, and even the order in which those events occurred. This final section of the chapter will describe influences that were both internal and external to psychology, focusing on the ideas of Karl Lashley, Allen Newell and Herbert Simon, Donald Broadbent, Jerome Bruner, Roger Brown, Noam Chomsky, George Miller, and Ulric Neisser.

Karl Lashley and the Hixon Symposium

In his history of cognitive science, Howard Gardner (1985) began his book with a discussion of the *Hixon Symposium on Cerebral Mechanisms in Behavior*, which took place in September 1948, at the California Institute of Technology with a lineup of very distinguished speakers across several scientific disciplines. The significance of the symposium, according to Gardner, was that it posed a direct challenge to the adequacy of behaviorism as an explanatory system for the complexities of human behavior. Gardner noted that several presenters with mathematical backgrounds were touting the new fangled computers, arguing that, as mechanisms of input, central processing, and output, they could be used to model brain functioning. However, the star of the show was physiological psychologist Karl Spencer Lashley (1890–1958), whose several mentors included John B. Watson. In his address on the problem of *serial order*, that is, how to explain linear sequences, such as the order of words in a sentence, Lashley " ... challenged the doctrine (or dogma) that had dominated psychological analysis for the past several decades and laid out a whole new agenda for research. ... [He] identified some of the major components needed for a cognitive science, even as he castigated those forces that had prevented its emergence before this time" (Gardner, 1985, p. 11). Lashley's (1951) address was relevant for a number of areas of cognitive psychology including learning, memory, perception, and especially language. Neither it, nor the Hixon Symposium, can be viewed as an impetus for the rebirth of cognitive psychology. Although the Lashley paper would eventually be cited frequently and widely among cognitive scientists in the 1960s as an important early article for their field, it was only after the fact that the article was discovered, as cognitive psychologist Darryl Bruce (1994) has shown. Still, it is important to recognize that Lashley not only offered prescient insights about where psychology needed to be headed, but also echoed the growing frustration among a number of psychologists trained in behaviorism, that as a philosophy of psychology it was far too limiting.

It is clear that the 1950s evidenced an impatience with the limitations of behaviorism and a desire to break out of that paradigm. Psychologists writing at the time were aware of the rumblings of the cognitive revolution. In a landmark book on thinking published in 1956, Harvard psychologist Jerome Bruner and his colleagues wrote:

> The past few years have witnessed a notable increase in and investigation of the cognitive processes. ... One need not look far for the origins of the revival. Partly, it resulted from a recognition of the complex processes that mediate between the classical "stimuli" and "responses" out of which stimulus-response learning theories hoped to fashion a psychology that would by-pass anything smacking of the "mental." The impeccable peripheralism of such theories could not last long. (Bruner, Goodnow, & Austin, 1956, p. vii)

In the midst of this rising dissatisfaction with behaviorism, other happenings spurred the interest in cognitive processes. One of the chief factors contributing to the rebirth of cognitive psychology was the computer, and it did not take psychologists long to recognize its worth for their field.

Computer Metaphors

Mathematician John von Neumann (1903–1957) was one of the speakers at the Hixon Symposium in 1948 who promoted a *computer metaphor* for the operation of the brain. He was a consultant on the first giant digital computer that had begun operation in 1945 at the University of Pennsylvania (later moved to the Aberdeen Proving Grounds in Maryland). It was dubbed ENIAC for Electrical Numerical Integrator and Computer. It weighed more than 60,000 pounds, it had no central memory, and its maximum storage capacity was 20 ten-digit decimal numbers. Amazingly, it stayed in operation for 10 years before its plug was finally pulled, replaced by a faster computer with greater memory storage. By the late 1950s when ENIAC's successors were in operation, the conceptualization of humans as information processors was commonplace.

Also in the 1950s, the field of *artificial intelligence* (AI) was developed jointly by Allen Newell (1927–1992), whose background was in physics, mathematics, and psychology, and Herbert Simon (1916–2001)

Photograph used courtesy of Carnegie Mellon University Archives

Figure 11.3   Herbert Simon

a polymath with expertise in political science, economics, and psychology. Both were faculty members at the Carnegie Institute of Technology (now Carnegie Mellon University) when they began to design a computer that could "think." Their first efforts were the Logic Theorist program, developed in 1955, and the General Problem Solver, developed in 1957. The latter was a computer program consisting of a core set of processes that could be used to solve different kinds of problems. In 1957, Simon, an avid chess player, predicted that in 10 years a computer would be capable of beating the best chess player in the world (Simon, 1991). He badly underestimated human capacity or overestimated the progress of computers. Either way, it would be 40 years before IBM's Deep Blue was able to defeat chess master Gary Kasparov in 1997. Simon, truly a genius despite his lack of talent as a prognosticator, contributed to many fields including work in economics for which he received the Nobel Prize in 1978.

Not all cognitive psychologists were ready to adopt the computer metaphor as a way of thinking about human cognition, but many did. It wasn't that they believed that the human mind worked like a computer but that various cognitive strategies could be tested with computer modeling. Moreover, the notion of the computer as an input-output device with processing systems intervening was very much the conceptualization of the human mind (Knapp, 1986). Computer engineers used *flow charts* to diagram the operational stages of information processing in the computer, and psychologists would borrow that strategy as a way to depict cognitive processing in the human.

Among the first, if not the first, to use a flow-chart model for human cognition was British psychologist Donald Broadbent (1926–1993), a student of Frederic Bartlett. He used a flow chart to describe the actions of his *model of selective attention*. Broadbent recognized that given the array of sensory information that humans encounter at any moment (William James's "great blooming, buzzing confusion") that there had to be a sensory filter early in the perceptual process that would remove much of the irrelevant information. Later research showed that such information was still being processed beyond that point, a finding that required the filter to be moved to a later spot in his information-processing model (Broadbent, 1958). This is a good example of how important the flow-chart models were for generating testable hypotheses.

A flow-chart model that is better known to most psychology students is the *information-processing model of memory* or multiple-store memory model, essentially a three-stage model positing a sensory memory store, short-term memory store, and long-term memory store. Most components of the model were proposed in 1968 by Richard Atkinson and Richard Schiffrin, and it has proved to be conceptually useful for decades although it has undergone modifications and has rivals today, alternative models that especially question its linear sequence.

Pioneers of the 1950s

In addition to the work on artificial intelligence and Broadbent's selective filter model of attention, there were other key contributors to cognitive psychology in the 1950s.

Jerome Bruner

We have already mentioned the book on thinking by Jerome Bruner (1915–) and colleagues. The book emerged from a number of studies of what was then called concept formation, and today would be referred to as categorization problems. Given a mixed array of stimuli, for example, shapes, paintings, or faces, how did individuals determine the categorizations used to form groups from subsets of these stimuli? The studies employed an old research method in psychology. Subjects were asked to think aloud as they worked on the various categorization tasks, that is, to verbalize what they were thinking about the materials they were sorting, in other words, to introspect. In the end, these verbal accounts proved especially useful in understanding what subjects were actually doing in these tasks.

Roger Brown

The Bruner, Goodnow, and Austin book had a fourth author, Roger Brown, a colleague of Bruner's at Harvard and one of the most creative psychologists of his generation. Brown added a 65-page appendix to the book entitled "Language and Categories" in which he extended the book's findings into an area that he knew well – the psychology of language. Roger Brown (1925–1997) made significant contributions to social psychology, child development, language, and memory. In language, he made his most important contributions, one of which was a delightful book entitled *Words and Things* (1958) that explored the degree to which language is limited by thought. The field of linguistics was expanding in importance in the 1950s, principally due to the work of MIT linguist, Noam Chomsky (1928–). In addition, Roger Brown's contributions were substantial in this field, especially his studies of how children learned language.

In the field of memory, Brown coined the term *flashbulb memory* and provided some of the earliest research on that topic. With his colleague, David McNeill, he invented a simple, but profound technique to study what seemed impossible to study, at least impossible to study in a laboratory, the elusive *tip of the tongue phenomenon*. Almost everyone recognizes what is meant by a tip-of-the-tongue (TOT) experience. Certainly, William James understood this phenomenon. Here is how he described it in his *Principles of Psychology*:

> Suppose we try to recall a forgotten name. The state of our consciousness is peculiar. There is a gap therein; but no mere gap. It is a gap that is intensely active. A sort of wraith of the name is in it, beckoning us in a given direction, making us at moments tingle with the sense of our closeness and then letting us sink back without the longed-for term. (1890, v. 1, p. 251)

These TOT experiences occur occasionally, but their appearance is both rare and unpredictable in terms of when they will happen. So if you want to learn about this fascinating aspect of memory failure how would you study it?

Brown and McNeill (1966) figured out a way. They read definitions of words to their subjects, words that were low frequency words, meaning that they were seldom used in everyday speech. However, they were words that many people would know nevertheless, words such as 'sextant,' meaning a navigational instrument that measures the altitudes of stars and planets. Subjects might have three experiences upon hearing a definition. First, they might have no idea of the target word. Second, they might know the word and say to themselves, 'sextant.' Neither of these experiences were of interest to the researchers. It was the third experience that was what they wanted to investigate. In this experience, the person would be sure that he/she knew the word, that saying it would be forthcoming soon, but was, in fact, unable to retrieve the word. That 'tingling sense of closeness' was the mental state that Brown and McNeill wanted to study. It was a tip-of-the-tongue experience and it had been produced in the laboratory where it could be studied. Subjects were told that when this third state occurred they were to begin filling out the questionnaire sheet in front of them. This sheet asked them to record the number of syllables that they thought the target word might have, to write what they believed to be the initial letter of the word, to list any words that seemed similar in sound and words that were similar in meaning, and finally, to list whatever word or words were coming to mind, even though they recognized that these words were not the target word.

In the course of six hours of testing, the study generated 233 TOTs that could be studied as the subjects were experiencing them. The results showed that subjects could often recall correctly the number of syllables and guess correctly the first letter of the target word. Many of the words retrieved, although not the target word, were similar in sound and/or meaning.

We have described this study in such detail for a reason. It is a quintessential example of what the new cognitive psychology was about, both methodologically and conceptually. The phenomenon had clearly been known about in the time of William James. But only anecdotal methods existed to study it. What Brown and McNeill were doing was studying the nature of a mental state, specifically what a person thinks about in this particularly exasperating state of memory failure. Moreover, in a single ingenious study they had been able to generate 233 of these cognitive states in their laboratory – mental states that could be systematically studied. Clearly, the target word has not been lost from memory. The problem is that the person cannot retrieve it. The behaviorists had given up on the study of such mental states because they seemed to be beyond the bounds of good science. What the cognitive psychologists recognized was that these mental states were important for not only understanding mental processes but for understanding behavior. They built their new science on a host of new methods, often using computers, which allowed them to study the cognitive processes in which they were interested and for which behavioristic explanations fell woefully short. The subject of language provides another example of behaviorism's failure.

Noam Chomsky

In 1957, B. F. Skinner published *Verbal Behavior*, in which he argued that language was like any other behavior: it was acquired as a result of reinforcement and punishment. Chomsky (1959) wrote a scathing 33-page review of the book that branded it naïve. Many psychologists who have found much value in many of Skinner's other books have never been especially fond of *Verbal Behavior*. Some characterize it as a case where Skinner got carried away with his theory and tried stretching it to account for behavior where it just didn't fit well. Indeed, Chomsky's review pointed out myriad problems with Skinner's ideas about language. Whether other psychologists liked his book or not, Skinner, late in his career, stated that he believed it was his most important book (Skinner, 1983). He also noted that he never read more than a half-dozen pages of Chomsky's critique (Skinner, 1967).

Chomsky is especially interested in issues of the structure of language, that is, its *syntax*, and argues that a behavioral account is simply not feasible given the number of possible sentences that could be uttered. In addition, the notion that those would be learned as correct or incorrect through some reinforcement/punishment contingency, not to mention the obvious fact that individuals produce many novel sentences for which they were never reinforced, seems absurd to Chomsky. Chomsky is interested in the meaning of language and has focused on grammar and the structure of sentences in conveying that meaning. He distinguished between the *surface structure* of a sentence and the *deep structure* of the sentence. The former refers to the sequence of words in the sentence, whereas the latter refers to the actual meaning of the sentence. Thus, two sentences may have different surface structures, meaning they are worded quite differently, but have the same deep structure, indicating that both sentences convey the same meaning. Chomsky developed a system known as *transformational grammar* to reveal how one sentence structure can be changed into another (Chomsky, 1965, 1972).

As noted earlier, Chomsky advocates a nativist view of language learning in positing a *language acquisition device* that is hard wired in the brain (another computer metaphor). He believes that such a device is necessary to account for the rapidity of first language learning, the difficulties of learning other languages later, and the universal elements that seem common across languages.

Chomsky's work in linguistics became well known to cognitive psychologists in the 1950s and 1960s. His ideas greatly stimulated work on verbal behavior and what was called verbal learning. As a result psycholinguistics became a viable field both within cognitive psychology and within linguistics.

Noam Chomsky has been honored in many ways including more than 25 honorary doctoral degrees from universities all over the world, election to membership in the prestigious National Academy of Sciences, and was a recipient of the Helmholtz Medal. However, his highest honor may have been bestowed on him by Herbert Terrace, a psychologist who had earned his doctorate with Skinner. In studying language in a chimpanzee, Terrace named his animal Nim Chimpsky.

George Miller

George A. Miller (1920–2012) is another of the pioneers in cognitive psychology who began his work in language. His start in the field came from some work he did as a student at Harvard University, investigating the intelligibility of speech in noisy aircraft, a problem that was

Figure 11.4   Roger Brown (*left*) and George A. Miller

stimulated by the Second World War. That work led to other studies and in 1951 to his first important book, *Language and Communication*. Miller's preface for this book shows that he was wrestling with treating essentially a cognitive subject from a philosophy of behaviorism, and he confesses to falling off the behaviorists' wagon now and again:

> The bias [in this book] is behavioristic – not fanatically behavioristic, but certainly tainted by a preference. There does not seem to be a more scientific kind of bias, or, if there is, it turns out to be behaviorism after all. The careful reader will discover occasional lapses. Undoubtedly in these instances, a scientific approach is possible, but the author was unable to find one or think of one. The argument nonetheless goes as far down the behavioristic path as one can clearly see the way. (p. v)

Miller's book was meant to pull together the scientific literature, from many fields, on the nature of language as human communication. And it did that admirably. It was, as he warned, decidedly behavioristic, especially so for one who a few decades later would be acknowledged as one of the founders of modern cognitive psychology. Miller would undergo a transformation of view, largely through the influence of Chomsky. Summarizing his cognitive views in 1965, Miller wrote that the psychology of language and communication required a "more cognitive approach to it." He believed that psychologists needed "to talk more about hypothesis testing instead of discrimination learning, about the evaluation of hypotheses instead of reinforcement of responses, about rules instead of habits, about productivity instead of generalization ... about sentences instead of words or vocal noises, about linguistic structure instead of chains of responses – in short, about language instead of learning theory" (p. 20). This passage captures well the opposing views of the new cognitive psychology and the old behaviorism, and makes clear Miller's movement to the cognitive camp.

Miller was involved with work other than language in the 1950s. In 1956, he published one of the most cited articles in the history of American psychology: "The magical number seven plus or minus two: Some limits on our *capacity for processing information.*" Here is a title that tells you most of what you need to know without ever reading the article, "Our processing of information is limited to around seven objects." In the studies described in this article, Miller defined what would become known as working memory capacity, about 5–9 items for auditory stimuli. In addition, he demonstrated that the capacity was fixed. More information could be processed, however, if information was formed into *chunks*, meaningful units of information. The bigger the chunks, the more information could be dealt with in working memory. Trying to recall the letters O-M-G-F-B-I-L-S-D-I-R-S exceeds working memory, but forming the 12 letters into four chunks such as OMG-FBI-LSD-IRS makes the recall quite easy because those chunks have meaning and thus hold together as one piece of information. Capacity issues for memory would become of even greater importance with the introduction of the Atkinson–Shiffrin model.

Naming the Field: Ulric Neisser

This new work on language, memory, attention, thinking, problem solving, and sensation-perception represented the efforts of a relatively small number of psychologists in the 1950s. Their numbers would grow in the following decade and their work would coalesce into a more coherent account of the processes of information processing and action. That account was provided by Ulric Neisser (1928–2012), whose 1967 book, *Cognitive Psychology*, is often credited with giving the field its name. Roediger (2000) has written, "Neisser's book became the rallying cry of the cognitive revolution in psychology" (p. 149). As noted earlier, Neisser's book was greatly influenced by the work of Frederic Bartlett, a debt acknowledged by Neisser. We used Neisser's definition of cognitive psychology at the start of this chapter. Contrast the following passage from this book with that quoted earlier from the preface of George Miller's *Language and Communication*:

> A generation ago, a book like this one would have needed at least a chapter of self defense against the behaviorist position. Today, happily, the climate of opinion has changed, and little or no defense is necessary. Indeed, stimulus-response theorists themselves are inventing hypothetical mechanisms with vigor and enthusiasm and only faint twinges of conscience. The basic reason for studying cognitive processes has become as clear as the reason for studying anything else: because they are there. ... Cognitive processes surely exist, so it can hardly be unscientific to study them. (Neisser, 1967, p. 5)

By the 1970s, cognitive psychology would exhibit those characteristics of a new discipline (in this case, a new-old discipline). New societies were formed to bring like-minded researchers together, new research journals were established, and new doctoral programs were founded. Today, cognitive psychology is the largest of the areas of experimental psychology. Some psychologists working in this field prefer the label cognitive science as opposed to cognitive psychology, reflecting their recognition that the field tends to be a multi-disciplinary one that has attracted scholars from engineering, philosophy, computer science, communications, brain imaging, education, and others, in addition to psychology.

The revolution that brought cognitive psychology to center stage in scientific psychology represents a gradual, but radical conceptual and methodological shift that incorporated much of the objective science of behaviorism and borrowed whatever else it needed, for example, computers, information theory, linguistics theory, communication networks, from other fields to try to understand the mysteries of human cognitive processes. Cognitive psychology continues today in that same vein, for example, using the field of neuroscience to reach a better understanding of the neurophysiological and biochemical processes that underlie cognition. Wundt, Ebbinghaus, James, Titchener, and many of the other pioneers in psychology would likely find much of interest in this field today.

Epilogue

When laboratory psychology arrived in North America in the 1880s, it was a time of great optimism for the new psychologists. William James, G. Stanley Hall, James McKeen Cattell, Harry Kirke Wolfe, and others wrote of their expectations for the new science, the science that several of them predicted would be the one in which the most progress would be made in the twentieth century. Although psychological science and practice have made great strides in the twentieth century as this book has shown, psychology's potential and promise may be even greater in the new century. One can argue convincingly that the problems that beset the world today are overwhelmingly behavioral in nature. *As behavioral problems, they will require behavioral solutions.*

In 1900, the leading causes of death in North America were influenza, pneumonia, and tuberculosis – bacterial and viral infections that still exist today but have been significantly reduced as health care threats by the development of modern drugs and vaccinations. A little more than a century later, the medical picture is quite different. Those early twentieth-century killers have been replaced by heart disease, cancer, and stroke. Whereas, drugs, radiation, and surgeries, the mainstays of modern medicine, play a vital role in the treatment of these disorders, they are only part of the solution. What is different about the killers of the twenty-first century is that they each are hugely affected by lifestyle variables. That translates into behavior, and that is the domain of psychology. This transformation in the causes of death and other health-related issues has fostered the development of *health psychology* as the fastest growing specialty area in psychology (Thacher & Haynes, 2000).

The healthcare budget continues to be one of the major expenditures in North America – for individuals, for businesses, and for governments. Canada provides health care for all of its citizens, whereas the United States has a program in place that masquerades as a "national plan." Parts of the new USA healthcare law have yet to take effect such that in 2012, 45 million Americans had no health insurance according to a study by the Centers for Disease Control and Prevention. These uninsured individuals exact a high toll on the healthcare system when they do receive services, largely because those services are received in an emergency care facility.

As this book goes to press there is confusion and exasperation with and considerable opposition to America's Affordable Healthcare Act.

Time will tell if the politicians, government officials, insurance companies, and healthcare sector can bring about a workable system that offers Americans what citizens of most Western nations already enjoy, a program of affordable healthcare.

Psychological factors are known to be responsible for many billions of dollars of that budget, and that doesn't mean in terms of psychiatric and psychological disorders, but for problems of physical health. For example, most cancer deaths in the United States are due to lung cancer, about 170,000 Americans each year, most of whom were cigarette smokers. Deaths due to smoking are the single largest preventable cause of death. All one has to do is to get smokers to stop smoking and prevent people who do not smoke from ever starting. That is a Herculean task. Addictions, including nicotine addiction, create strong psychological and physiological dependencies on the drug that make quitting difficult. Other cancer deaths are related to overexposure to the sun (skin cancers) and poor diets, especially avoiding foods (such as broccoli, cauliflower, and cabbage) that offer some protection against certain kinds of cancers, such as colon cancer. Stress is also a significant factor in cancer. It is believed to be responsible, in many cases, for the onset of cancer and for the acceleration of tumor growth.

Bernard Levin, a distinguished oncologist at Houston's famed M. D. Anderson Hospital, one of the leading cancer and research treatment centers in the United States, has written that lifestyle changes could prevent between 65% and 85% of all cancers. He cites such behavioral changes as eliminating tobacco use; reducing exposure to sun; exercising more; eating more fruits, vegetables, and whole grains; reducing fat consumption; limiting alcohol consumption; and being aware of one's family disease history and seeking proper medical screenings (Barth, 1998). None of these are medical issues per se. They are behavioral issues. They require that people change their behavior. Even if Levin's estimate is far too high and the figure is only 30% to 40%, *half of his estimate*, the potential for promoting better health and saving lives is still extraordinary. Whatever the accurate figure, psychology's role in cancer prevention and treatment is enormous. Of course, some of these same variables, smoking, overeating, poor diet, lack of exercise, stress, alcohol abuse, are significant factors in causing and exacerbating heart disease and stroke. The Centers for Disease Control and Prevention (CDC), headquartered in Atlanta, has recognized lifestyle as a key component in health, and consequently has added more psychologists and other behavioral scientists to its staff, and allocated significantly more of its research and prevention budget to behavioral factors in health and illness (Snider & Satcher, 1997).

It is evident that the medical profession also understands the importance of behavioral variables in twenty-first century medicine. For years the Medical College Admission Test (MCAT), required of all students applying to medical schools in the United States and Canada, has emphasized knowledge in the physical and biological sciences. Beginning in 2015 that exam will add a new section testing knowledge of the behavioral and social sciences. Such a change should ensure that practicing physicians and medical researchers will have had at least some exposure to psychological variables that play such a key role in the health of their patients.

Health psychologists, who often have training in clinical, cognitive, and social psychology, as well as behavioral neuroscience, may perform assessment work to increase the accuracy of clinical judgments, for example, distinguishing the symptoms due to physical illness from the symptoms that result from the person's psychological reaction to the illness. They work in stress management, with either groups or individuals, to help individuals reduce their reactions to stress, particularly stress that may be linked to jobs. They work in pain management, helping people cope with chronic pain when medications can offer only partial relief. The success of these interventions is evidenced by the fact that the fastest growing place of employment for psychologists in the beginning of the twenty-first century has been hospitals. Of course, health issues are not the only problems facing the world.

Divorce rates are still excessively high; child abuse is far too frequent; violence is prevalent in our society in our schools, in the workplace, and in our homes; quality of life is unnecessarily poor for the elderly; alcoholism and other addictions exact a terrible toll on individuals, families, and the broader society; racism and sexism continue to rip apart our social fabric; pollution and environmental waste are partly behavioral problems; reforming an educational system that does not seem to meet the needs of many students is mostly a psychological problem; and the job market is ever-changing, requiring new training strategies. The list could be made much longer. Psychology as the science of behavior and mental processes has the potential to enhance the quality of life today. For that goal to be realized, however, psychology's science and profession must work together in a true partnership that acknowledges the validity of each.

Throughout this book, we have described the evolution of the American Psychological Association (APA) that began in 1892. However, there is more to the story of this important psychological organization that needs to be told. Today APA is the largest psychology organization in the world, totaling more than 130,000 members including student members. You will recall that it began with a single objective, to promote psychology as a *science*, an objective that did not change until the reorganization of APA in 1945 that united the older scientific organization (APA) with a recently formed organization of psychology practitioners – the American Association for Applied Psychology (AAAP). That forced marriage of the old APA and the AAAP was essentially mandated by the U.S. government to address the impending problem of mental health casualties from WWII. AAAP had split off from APA because the practitioners had been largely unsuccessful in their efforts to get APA to address the professional issues that were important to them.

With the tremendous growth of clinical and counseling psychology in the decades following the Second World War, the strength of the professional group within APA grew much larger until the late 1970s, when their numbers were such that they had gained political and economic control of the organization. Psychological scientists found their needs often taking second place to the needs of practitioners. Just as the professionals had complained in the early decades of the twentieth century, the scientists now complained about how their needs were being ignored. Several commissions, consisting of practitioner and scientist members, were established to seek a solution, but the bottom line was that the practitioners finally had control of the organization after years of trying to get the scientists, then in control, to listen to their pleas, and they were not willing to give up any of that control. After failed efforts at a called-for reorganization of APA, a group of leading psychological scientists established a rival organization to address their needs. The American Psychological Society (APS) was founded in 1988 (the name was changed to the Association for Psychological Science in 2006) and currently has approximately 24,000 members (see Evans, Sexton, & Cadwallader, 1992; Cautin 2009a, 2009b).

Now more than 25 years after what could be characterized as an acrimonious divorce, the divide between the two organizations has grown wider. The APA has become largely a guild organization catering mostly to the concerns of practicing psychologists. APA continues to publish some of psychology's most prestigious scientific journals, but the quality of the scientific membership of APA has been seriously eroded by APS, which publishes its own stable of prestigious psychological journals. One of the most important claims made by professional psychologists throughout their history has been that their practice was grounded in psychological science and validated in its effectiveness. But today there are serious questions about the validity of that claim, raised by studies that cast doubt on the science base of contemporary psychological practice (see Baker, McFall, & Shoham, 2008; Foa, Gillihan, & Bryant, 2013). During World War II, the federal government realized that for an effective profession of psychology to exist, there needed to be close coordination between the universities that trained those professionals and the venues in which they practiced. It was because of that understanding that APA and AAAP were told to find a way to work toward common goals together. The need is still there if psychological practice hopes to maintain its effectiveness and psychological science wishes to maintain its relevancy. As of this writing, neither organization seems to want to work with the other in bringing about that kind of coordination.

This book began with a description of the academic and popular psychologies in place in America when the new laboratory psychology arrived from Europe at the end of the nineteenth century. There was an academic psychology in place in the 1880s called mental philosophy and a popular psychology in many forms, practiced by individuals who called themselves phrenologists, mesmerists, psychics, spiritualists, and even psychologists. Today mental philosophy has been replaced by an academic psychology that has developed full circle from the experimental study of consciousness (structuralism and functionalism) through the experimental study of behavior (behaviorism) to the experimental study of behavior and mental processes (behaviorism and cognitive psychology). Psychology has evolved from the age of schools of psychology to psychologists identifying themselves by their areas of research and/or practice, for example, social psychology, cognitive psychology, school psychology, clinical psychology, developmental psychology. There is a modern profession of psychology, born from the science of psychology, which employs the majority of psychologists in North America in roles as clinical psychologists, counseling psychologists, school psychologists, industrial-organizational psychologists, health psychologists, and several other practice specialties.

Finally, there is still a popular psychology, a psychology of the public, that is conveyed through self-help books, television and radio therapists, astrologers, psychic readers, and a host of self-proclaimed therapists, typically with no real training in psychology and no professional license in any of the mental healthcare professions. These individuals, many of whom could be characterized as charlatans, can practice their bogus therapies as long as they do not use one of the labels that is protected by licensure, such as psychologist, psychiatrist, or mental health counselor.

Although the public psychology often embarrasses and exasperates psychologists, there is little they can do about it, other than speaking out and trying to correct or denounce the most egregious examples of psychobabble and bogus therapy. Moreover, they can write about their own psychology for public consumption, both science and practice, seeking to educate the public about the potential of psychology for enhancing the quality of life. This potential is not new. Almost 40 years ago, then American Psychological Association president, George Miller, whose work we discussed in Chapter 11, wrote:

> The most urgent problems of our world today are the problems we have made for ourselves. They have not been caused by some heedless or malicious inanimate Nature, nor have they been imposed on us as punishment by the will of God. They are human problems whose solutions will require us to change our behavior and our social institutions. (Miller, 1969, p. 1063)

Psychological scientists and practitioners stand on the threshold of new opportunities in the application of their work, applications that can have a profound impact on this planet and the peoples who inhabit it. History will tell if they are up to the task.

References

Adler, A. (1924). *The practice and theory of individual psychology.* New York: Harcourt, Brace.

Adler, A. (1927). *Understanding human nature.* Garden City, NY: Garden City Publishing Co.

Adler, A. (1931). *What life should mean to you.* Boston: Little, Brown, and Co.

Allport, F. H. (1924). *Social psychology.* Boston: Houghton Mifflin.

American Psychological Association. Division of Counseling and Guidance, Committee on Counselor Training. (1952). Recommended standards for training counselors at the doctoral level. *American Psychologist, 7,* 175181.

Amsel, A., & Rashotte, M. E. (1984). *Mechanisms of adaptive behavior: Clark L. Hull's theoretical papers, with commentary.* New York: Columbia University Press.

Anderson, C. A. (1993). *Healing hypotheses: Horatio W. Dresser and the philosophy of new thought.* New York: Garland Publishing.

Angell, J. R. (1906). The province of functional psychology. *Psychological Review, 14,* 61–91.

APA Committee on Professional Standards. (1981). Specialty guidelines for the delivery of services. *American Psychologist, 36,* 639–681.

Arnett, J. J., & Cravens, H. (2006). G. Stanley Hall's *Adolescence*: A centennial reappraisal introduction. *History of Psychology, 9,* 165–171.

Ash, M. G. (1992). Cultural contexts and scientific change in psychology: Kurt Lewin in Iowa. *American Psychologist, 47,* 198–207.

Atkinson, R. C., & Shiffrin, R. M. (1968). Human memory: A proposed system and its control processes. In K. W. Spence & J. T. Spence (Eds.), *The psychology of learning and motivation: Advances in research and theory* (v. 2, pp. 89–195). New York: Academic Press.

Bache, R. M. (1895). Reaction time with reference to race. *Psychological review, 2,* 475–486.

Baker, D. B. (1988). The psychology of Lightner Witmer. *Professional School Psychology, 3,* 109–121.

Baker, D. B., & Benjamin, L. T., Jr. (2000). The affirmation of the scientist-practitioner: A look back at Boulder. *American Psychologist, 55,* 241–247.

Baker, T. B., McFall, R. M., & Shoham, V. (2008). Current status and future prospects of clinical psychology: Toward a scientifically principled approach to mental and behavioral health care. *Psychological Science in the Public Interest, 9,* 67–103.

Baldwin, J. M. (1892). The psychological laboratory in the University of Toronto. *Science, 19,* 143–144.

Barth, L. (1998, August). Leading the charge. *Continental Magazine,* 35–38.

Bartlett, F. C. (1932). *Remembering: A study in experimental and social psychology.* Cambridge: Cambridge University Press.

Bartholow, R. (1874). Experimental investigations into the functions of the human brain. *American Journal of the Medical Sciences, 134,* 305–313.

Beck, H. P., Levinson, S., & Irons, G. (2009). Finding Little Albert: A journey to John B. Watson's infant laboratory. *American Psychologist, 64,* 605–614.

Behrens, P. J. (1997). G. E. Müller: The third pillar of experimental psychology. In W. G. Bringmann, H. E. Lück, R. Miller, & C. E. Early (Eds.), *A pictorial history of psychology* (pp. 171–176). Chicago: Quintessence Publishing Co.

Behrens, P. J. (2009). War, sanity, and the Nazi mind: The last passion of Joseph Jastrow. *History of Psychology, 12*, 266–284.

Benjamin, L. T., Jr. (1988). A history of teaching machines. *American Psychologist, 43,* 703–712.

Benjamin, L. T., Jr. (1997). The origin of psychological species: History of the beginnings of the American Psychological Association divisions. *American Psychologist, 52,* 725–732.

Benjamin, L. T., Jr. (2000). The psychology laboratory at the turn of the 20th century. *American Psychologist, 55,* 318–321.

Benjamin, L. T., Jr. (2003). Behavioral science and the Nobel Prize: A history. *American Psychologist, 58,* 731–741.

Benjamin, L. T., Jr. (2004). Science for sale: Psychology's earliest adventures in American advertising. In J. D. Williams, W. N. Lee, & C. P. Haugtvedt (Eds.), *Diversity in advertising: Broadening the scope of research directions* (pp. 21–39). Mahwah, NJ: Lawrence Erlbaum.

Benjamin, L. T., Jr. (2005). A history of clinical psychology as a profession in America (and a glimpse at its future). *Annual Review of Clinical Psychology, 1,* 1–30.

Benjamin, L. T., Jr., & Baker, D. B. (2003). Walter Van Dyke Bingham: Portrait of an industrial psychologist. In G. A. Kimble & M. Wertheimer (Eds.), *Portraits of pioneers in psychology* (v. 5, pp. 141–157). Washington, DC & Mahwah, NJ: American Psychological Association and Lawrence Erlbaum.

Benjamin, L. T., Jr., & Baker, D. B. (2004). *From séance to science: A history of the profession of psychology in America.* Belmont, CA: Wadsworth.

Benjamin, L. T., Jr., & Crouse, E. M. (2002). The American Psychological Association's response to *Brown v. Board of Education*: The case of Kenneth B. Clark. *American Psychologist, 57,* 38–50.

Benjamin, L. T., Jr., Durkin, M., Link, M., Vestal, M., & Acord, J. (1992). Wundt's American doctoral students. *American Psychologist, 47,* 123–131.

Benjamin, L. T., Jr., Henry, K. D., & McMahon, L. R. (2005). Inez Beverly Prosser and the education of African Americans. *Journal of the History of the Behavioral Sciences, 41,* 43–62.

Benjamin, L. T., Jr., & Nielsen-Gammon, E. (1999). B. F. Skinner and psychotechnology: The case of the heir conditioner. *Review of General Psychology, 3,* 155–167.

Benjamin, L. T., Jr., Rogers, A. M., & Rosenbaum, A. (1991). Coca-Cola, caffeine, and mental deficiency: Harry Hollingworth and the Chattanooga trial of 1911. *Journal of the History of the Behavioral Sciences, 27,* 42–55.

Benjamin, L. T., Jr., & Shields, S. A. (1990). Leta Stetter Hollingworth (1886–1939). In A. N. O'Connell & N. F. Russo (Eds.), *Women in psychology: A bio-bibliographic sourcebook* (pp. 173–183). New York: Greenwood Press.

Benjamin, L. T., Jr., Whitaker, J. L., Ramsey, R. M., & Zeve, D. R. (2007). John B. Watson's alleged sex research: An appraisal of the evidence. *American Psychologist, 62,* 131–139.

Bjork, D. W. (1983). *The compromised scientist: William James in the development of American psychology.* New York: Columbia University Press.

Bjork, D. W. (1993). *B. F. Skinner: A life.* New York: Basic Books.

Blackford, K. M. H., & Newcomb, A. (1914). *The job, the man, the boss.* New York: Doubleday & Page.

Blackford, K. M. H., & Newcomb, A. (1916). *Analyzing character: The new science of judging men, misfits in business, the home, and social life* (2nd ed.). New York: Review of Reviews Co.

Blumenthal, A. L. (1975). A reappraisal of Wilhelm Wundt. *American Psychologist, 30,* 1081–1088.

Boring, E. G. (1929). *A history of experimental psychology.* New York: The Century Co.

Boring, E. G. (1942). *Sensation and perception in the history of experimental psychology.* New York: Appleton-Century-Crofts.

Brazier, M. A. N. (1961). *A history of the electrical activity of the brain*. London: Pitman.

Brentano, F. (1874). *Psychologie von empirischen Standpunkte*. Leipzig: Duncker & Humblot.

Breuer, J., & Freud, S. (1957). *Studies on hysteria* (trans. James Strachey). New York: Basis Books. (Originally published in 1895.)

Bringmann, W. G. (1975). Wundt in Heidelberg, 1845–1874. *Canadian Psychological Review, 16*, 116–121.

Broadbent, D. E. (1958). *Perception and communication*. London: Pergamon Press.

Brooks-Gunn, J., & Johnson, A. D. (2006). G. Stanley Hall's contribution to science, practice, and policy: The Child Study, Parent Education, and Child Welfare Movements. *History of Psychology, 9*, 247–258.

Brown, R. (1958). *Words and things*. Glencoe, IL: The Free Press.

Brown, R., & McNeill, D. (1966). The "tip of the tongue" phenomenon. *Journal of Verbal Learning and Verbal Behavior, 5*, 325–337.

Browne, J. (1995). *Charles Darwin: Voyaging, a biography*. New York: Alfred A. Knopf.

Browne, J. (2002). *Charles Darwin: The power of place*. New York: Alfred A. Knopf.

Bruce, D. (1994). Lashley and the problem of serial order. *American Psychologist, 49*, 93–103.

Bruce, D., & Winograd, E. (1998). Remembering Deese's 1959 articles: The Zeitgeist, the sociology of science, and false memories. *Psychonomic Bulletin & Review, 5*, 615–624.

Bruce, R. V. (1987). *The launching of modern American science, 1846–1876*. Ithaca, NY: Cornell University Press.

Bruner, J. S., Goodnow, J. J., & Austin, G. A. (1956). *A study of thinking*. New York: John Wiley & Sons.

Buckley, K. W. (1982). The selling of a psychologist: John Broadus Watson and the application of behavioral techniques to advertising. *Journal of the History of the Behavioral Sciences, 18*, 207–221.

Buckley, K. W. (1989). *Mechanical man: John Broadus Watson and the beginnings of behaviorism*. New York: Guilford Press.

Burnham, J. (Ed.) (2012). *After Freud left: A century of psychoanalysis in America*. Chicago: University of Chicago Press.

Cahan, D. (Ed.) (1993). *Hermann von Helmholtz and the foundations of nineteenth-century science*. Berkeley: University of California Press.

Cahan, E. D., & White, S. H. (1992). Proposals for a second psychology. *American Psychologist, 47*, 224–235.

Calkins, M. W. (1894). Association I. *Psychological Review, 1*, 476–483.

Calkins, M. W. (1896). Association II. *Psychological Review, 3*, 32–49.

Calkins, M. W. (1900). Psychology as a science of selves. *Philosophical Review, 9*, 490–501.

Caplan, E. (1998). *Mind games: American culture and the birth of psychotherapy*. Berkeley: University of California Press.

Capshew, J. H. (1992). Psychologists on site: A reconnaissance of the historiography of the laboratory. *American Psychologist, 47*, 132–142.

Capshew, J. H. (1993). Engineering behavior: Project Pigeon, World War II, and the conditioning of B. F. Skinner. *Technology and Culture, 34*, 835–857.

Cattell, J. McK. (1890). Mental tests and measurements. *Mind, 15*, 373–381.

Cattell, J. McK. (1893). Tests of the senses and faculties. *Educational Review, 5*, 257–265.

Cautin, R. L. (2006). David Shakow: Architect of modern clinical psychology. In D. A. Dewsbury, L. T. Benjamin, Jr., & M. Wertheimer (Eds.), *Portraits of pioneers in psychology* (v. 6, pp. 206–221). Washington, DC & Mahwah, NJ: American Psychological Association and Lawrence Erlbaum.

Cautin, R. L. (2008). David Shakow and schizophrenia research at the Worcester State Hospital: The roots of the scientist-practitioner model. *Journal of the History of the Behavioral Sciences, 44*, 219–237.

Cautin, R. L. (2009a). The founding of the Association for Psychological Science: Part 1. Dialectical tensions within organized psychology. *Perspectives on Psychological Science, 4,* 211–223.

Cautin, R. L. (2009b). The founding of the Association for Psychological Science: Part 2. The tipping point and early years. *Perspectives on Psychological Science, 4,* 224–235.

Chomsky, N. (1959). Review of Skinner's *Verbal Behavior. Language, 35,* 26–58.

Chomsky, N. (1965). *Aspects of the theory of syntax.* Cambridge, MA: MIT Press.

Chomsky, N. (1972). *Language and mind* (2nd ed.). New York: Harcourt Brace Jovanovich.

Clark, K. B. (1950). *The effects of prejudice and discrimination on personality development (Midcentury White House Conference on Children and Youth).* Washington, DC: Federal Security Agency, Children's Bureau.

Clark, K. B. (1952, Feb. 19). *Letter to William Delano.* In Kenneth B. Clark Papers, Rare Books and Manuscripts Collection, Library of Congress, Washington, DC.

Clark, K. B. (1953). Desegregation: An appraisal of the evidence. *Journal of Social Issues, 9(4),* 1–77.

Cole, T. R. (1984). The prophecy of *Senescence*: G. Stanley Hall and the reconstruction of old age in America. *The Gerontologist, 24,* 360–366.

Combe, G. (1825). *System of phrenology.* Edinburgh: Anderson.

Combe, G. (1835). *The constitution of man considered in relation to external objects.* Boston: Marsh, Capen, & Lyon.

Commager, H. S. (1965). *The nature and the study of history.* Columbus, OH: Charles Merrill.

Coon, D. J. (1992). Testing the limits of sense and science: American experimental psychologists combat spiritualism, 1880–1920. *American Psychologist, 47,* 143–151.

Cushman, P. (1995). *Constructing the self, constructing America: A cultural history of psychotherapy.* Reading, MA: Addison-Wesley.

Danziger, K. (1980). Wund's psychological experiment in the light of his philosophy of science. *Psychological Research, 42,* 109–122.

Danziger, K. (1983). Origins and basic principles of Wundt's Völkerpsychologie. *British Journal of Social Psychology, 22,* 303–313.

Darwin, C. R. (1859). *On the origin of species.* London: John Murray.

Darwin, C. R. (1871). *The descent of man.* London: John Murray.

Darwin, C. R. (1872). *The expression of the emotions in man and animals.* London: John Murray.

Davidson, E. S., & Benjamin, L. T., Jr. (1987). A history of the child study movement in America. In J. A. Glover & R. R. Ronning (Eds.), *Historical foundations of educational psychology* (pp. 41–60). New York: Plenum Press.

Dawes, R. M. (1994). *House of cards: Psychology and psychotherapy built on myth.* New York: Free Press.

Decker, H. (1998). Freud's "Dora" case: The crucible of the psychoanalytic concept of transference. In M. S. Roth (Ed.), *Freud: Conflict and culture* (pp. 105–114). New York: Alfred A. Knopf.

Dewey, J. (1896). The reflex arc concept in psychology. *Psychological Review, 3,* 357–370.

Dewsbury, D. A. (1984). *Comparative psychology in the twentieth century.* Stroudsburg, PA: Hutchinson Ross Publishing Co.

Dewsbury, D. A. (1992). Triumph and tribulation in the history of comparative psychology. *Journal of Comparative Psychology, 106,* 3–19.

Dewsbury, D. A. (2003). James Rowland Angell: Born administrator. In G. A. Kimble & M. Wertheimer (Eds.), *Portraits of pioneers in psychology* (v. 5, pp. 57–71). Washington, DC & Mahwah, NJ: American Psychological Association and Lawrence Erlbaum.

Domanski, C. W. (2013). Mysterious "Monsieur Leborgne": The mystery of the famous patient in the history of neuropsychology is explained. *Journal of the History of the Neurosciences, 22,* 47–52.

Dowbiggin, I. R. (1997). *Keeping America sane: Psychiatry and eugenics in the United States and Canada, 1880–1940*. Ithaca, NY: Cornell University Press.

Dumenil, L. (2001). The twenties. In P. S. Boyer (Ed.), *The Oxford companion to United States history* (pp. 788–789). New York: Oxford University Press.

Ebbinghaus, H. (1913). *Memory: A contribution to experimental psychology* (trans. H. A. Ruger). New York: Teachers College Press. (Originally published in 1885.)

Ellenberger, H. F. (1972). The story of "Anna O": A critical review with new data. *Journal of the History of the Behavioral Sciences, 8*, 267–279.

Esterson, A. (1998). Jeffrey Masson and Freud's seduction theory: A new fable based on old myths. *History of the Human Science, 11(1)*, 1–21.

Esterson, A. (2001). The mythologizing of psychoanalytic history: Deception and self-deception in Freud's accounts of the seduction theory episode. *History of Psychiatry, 12*, 329–352.

Evans, R. S. (1972). E. B. Titchener and his lost system. *Journal of the History of the Behavioral Sciences, 8*, 168–180.

Evans, R. B. (1984). The origins of American academic psychology. In. J. Brozek (Ed.), *Explorations in the history of psychology in the United States* (pp. 17–60). Lewisburg, PA: Bucknell University Press.

Evans, R. B. (1985). E. B. Titchener and American experimental psychology. In H. Carpintero & J. M. Peiro (Eds.), *Psychology in its historical context* (pp. 117–125). Valencia, Spain: Universidad de Valencia.

Evans, R. B. (1991). E. B. Titchener on scientific psychology and technology. In G. A. Kimble, M. Wertheimer, & C. L. White (Eds.), *Portraits of pioneers in psychology* (v. 1, pp. 89–103). Washington, DC & Hillsdale, NJ: American Psychological Association & Lawrence Erlbaum.

Evans, R. B., Sexton, V. S., & Cadwallader, T. C. (Eds.) (1992). *The American Psychological Association: A historical perspective*. Washington, DC: American Psychological Association.

Fagan, T. K. (1986). The historical origins and growth of programs to prepare school psychologists in the United States. *Journal of School Psychology, 24*, 9–22.

Fagan, T. K. (1987a). Gesell: The first school psychologist. Part I. The road to Connecticut. *School Psychology Review, 16*, 103–107.

Fagan, T. K. (1987b). Gesell: The first school psychologist. Part II. Practice and significance. *School Psychology Review, 16*, 399–409.

Fagan, T. K. (1992). Compulsory schooling, child study, clinical psychology, and special education: Origins of school psychology. *American Psychologist, 47*, 236–243.

Fancher, R. E. (2000). Snapshots of Freud in America, 1899–1999. *American Psychologist, 55*, 1025–1028.

Fancher, R. E. (2004). The concept of race in the life and thought of Francis Galton. In A. Winston (Ed.), *Defining difference: Race and racism in the history of psychology* (pp. 49–75). Washington, DC: American Psychological Association.

Fancher, R. E., & Rutherford, A. (2012). *Pioneers of psychology* (4th ed.). New York: W. W. Norton.

Fechner, G. T. (1966). *Elements of psychophysics* (trans. H. E. Adler). New York: Holt, Rinehart and Winston. (Originally published in 1860.)

Ferguson, G. O. (1916). The psychology of the Negro: An experimental study. *Archives of Psychology, 25(10)*, 138.

Fernald, D. (1984). *The Hans legacy: A story of science*. Hillsdale, NJ: Erlbaum.

Fernberger, S. W. (1931). History of the Psychological Clinic. In R. A. Brotemarkle (Ed.), *Clinical psychology: Studies in honor of Lightner Witmer* (pp. 10–36). Philadelphia: University of Pennsylvania Press.

Ferrier, D. (1876). *The functions of the brain*. London: Smith, Elder.

Finger, S. (1994). *Origins of neuroscience: A history of explorations into brain function*. New York: Oxford University Press.

Finger, S. (2000). *Minds behind the brain: A history of the pioneers and their discoveries*. New York: Oxford University Press.

Finger, S., & Wade, N. J. (2002a). The neuroscience of Helmholtz and the theories of Johannes Müller. Part 1: Nerve cell structure, vitalism, and the nerve impulse. *Journal of the History of the Neurosciences, 11,* 136–155.

Finger, S., & Wade, N. J. (2002b). The neuroscience of Helmholtz and the theories of Johannes Müller. Part 2: Sensation and perception. *Journal of the History of the Neurosciences, 11,* 234–254.

Fisher, V. E., & Hanna, J. V. (1931). *The dissatisfied worker.* New York: Macmillan.

Foa, E. B., Gillihan, S. J., & Bryant, R. A. (2013). Challenges and successes in dissemination of evidenced-based treatments for posttraumatic stress: Lessons learned from prolonged exposure therapy for PTSD. *Psychological Science in the Public Interest, 14,* 65–111.

Fowler, O. S., & Fowler, L. N. (1859). *Illustrated self instructor in phrenology and physiology.* New York: Fowler and Wells.

Frank, J. D. (1978). Kurt Lewin in retrospect – a psychiatrist's view. *Journal of the History of the Behavioral Sciences, 14,* 223–227.

Freud, E., Freud, L., & Grubrich-Simitis, I. (1978). *Sigmund Freud: His life in pictures and words.* New York: W. W. Norton.

Freud, S. (1910). The origin and development of psychoanalysis. *American Journal of Psychology, 21,* 181–218.

Freud, S. (1913). *The interpretation of dreams* (trans. A. A. Brill). London: George Allen & Unwin. (Originally published in Germany in 1899 with a 1900 copyright.)

Freud, S. (1917). *The history of the psychoanalytic movement* (trans. A. A. Brill). New York: The Nervous and Mental Disease Publishing Co.

Freud, S. (1949). *An outline of psychoanalysis* (trans. James Strachey). New York: W.W. Norton. (Originally published in 1940.)

Fuchs, A. H. (1997). Ebbinghaus's contributions to psychology after 1885. *American Journal of Psychology, 110,* 621–633.

Fuchs, A. H. (2000). Contributions of American mental philosophers to psychology in the United States. *History of Psychology, 3,* 1–18.

Furumoto, L. (1988). Shared knowledge: The Experimentalists, 1904–1929. In J. G. Morawski (Ed.), *The rise of experimentation in American psychology* (pp. 94–113). New Haven, CT: Yale University Press.

Furumoto, L. (1991). From "paired associates" to a psychology of self: The intellectual odyssey of Mary Whiton Calkins. In G. A. Kimble, M. Wertheimer, & C. L. White (Eds.), *Portraits of pioneers in psychology* (v. 1, pp. 56–72). Washington, DC: American Psychological Association.

Furumoto, L. (1992). Joining separate spheres – Christine Ladd–Franklin, woman – scientist (1847–1930). *American Psychologist, 47,* 175–182.

Galton. F. (1869). *Hereditary genius: An inquiry into its laws and consequences.* London: Macmillan.

Gardner, H. (1985). *The mind's new science: A history of the cognitive revolution.* New York: Basic Books.

Gay, P. (1988). *Freud: A life for our time.* New York: W. W. Norton.

Gibby, R. E., & Zickar, M. J. (2008). A history of the early days of personality testing in American industry: An obsession with adjustment. *History of Psychology, 11,* 164–184.

Gifford, S. (1997). *The Emmanuel movement: The origins of group treatment and the assault on lay psychotherapy.* Cambridge: Harvard University Press.

Gilbreth, L. M. (1914). *The psychology of management.* New York: Sturgis & Walton Co.

Gilbreth, L. M. (1927). *The home-maker and her job.* New York: D. Appleton.

Gilbreth, L. M. (1954). *Management in the home.* New York: Dodd, Mead, & Co.

Goodwin, C. J. (1985). On the origins of Titchener's Experimentalists. *Journal of the History of the Behavioral Sciences, 21,* 383–389.

Goodwin, C. J. (2006). Edmund Clark Sanford and the consequences of loyalty. In D. A. Dewsbury, L. T. Benjamin, Jr., & M. Wertheimer (Eds.), *Portraits of pioneers in psychology* (v. 6, pp. 2–17). Washington, DC & Mahwah, NJ: American Psychological Association and Lawrence Erlbaum Associates.

Gove, P. B. (Ed.) (1961). *Webster's new third international dictionary of the English language unabridged*. Springfield, MA: G. & C. Merriam Co.

Green, C. D. (2009). Darwinian theory, functionalism, and the first American psychological revolution. *American Psychologist, 64*, 75–83.

Green, C. D. (2010). Scientific objectivity and E. B. Titchener's psychology. *Isis, 101*, 697–721.

Green, C. D., & Benjamin, L. T., Jr. (Eds.) (2009). *Psychology gets in the game: Sport, mind, and behavior, 1880–1960*. Lincoln: University of Nebraska Press.

Griffiths, C. H. (1924). *Fundamentals of vocational psychology*. New York: Macmillan.

Grob, G. N. (1994). *The mad among us: A history of the care of America's mentally ill*. Cambridge: Harvard University Press.

Gruber, C. S. (1972). Academic freedom at Columbia University, 1917–1918: The case of James McKeen Cattell. *AAUP Bulletin, 58*, 297–305.

Guthrie, R. V. (1998). *Even the rat was white: A historical view of psychology* (2nd ed.). Boston: Allyn and Bacon.

Hale, M., Jr. (1980). *Human science and social order: Hugo Münsterberg and the origins of applied psychology*. Philadelphia: Temple University Press.

Hale, N. G., Jr. (1995). *The rise and crisis of psychoanalysis in the United States: Freud and the Americans, 1917–1985*. New York: Oxford University Press.

Hall, G. S. (1882). The contents of children's minds. *Princeton Review, 11*, 249–272.

Hall, G. S. (1893). Child study: The basis of exact education. *Forum, 16*, 429–441.

Hall, G. S. (1904). *Adolescence: Its psychology and its relations to physiology, anthropology, sociology, sex, crime, and religion* (2 vols.). New York: D. Appleton and Co.

Hall, G. S. (1906). *Youth: Its education, regimen, and hygiene*. New York: D. Appleton and Co.

Hall, G. S. (1917). *Jesus the Christ in the light of psychology* (2 vols.). New York: Doubleday, Page.

Hall, G. S. (1922). *Senescence: The last half of light*. New York: D. Appleton and Co.

Harper, R. S. (1950). The first psychological laboratory. *Isis, 41*, 158–161.

Harris, B. (1979). Whatever happened to little Albert? *American Psychologist, 34*, 151–160.

Harris, B. (2011). Letting go of Little Albert: Disciplinary memory, history, and the uses of myth. *Journal of the History of the Behavioral Sciences, 47*, 1–17.

Harris, L. J., & Almerigi, J. B. (2009). Probing the human brain with stimulating electrodes: The story of Roberts Bartholow's (1874) experiment on Mary Rafferty. *Brain and Cognition, 70*, 92–115.

Hays, K. F. (1995). Putting sports psychology into (your) practice. *Professional Psychology: Research and Practice, 26*, 33–40.

Heidelberger, M. (2004). *Nature from within: Gustav Theodore Fechner and his psychophysical worldview*. Pittsburgh: University of Pittsburgh Press.

Heims, S. (1978). Kurt Lewin and social change. *Journal of the History of the Behavioral Sciences, 14*, 238–241.

Helson, H. (1925). The psychology of Gestalt, Parts I and II. *American Journal of Psychology, 36*, 342–370, 494–526.

Helson, H. (1926). The psychology of Gestalt, Parts III and IV. *American Journal of Psychology, 37*, 25–62, 189–223.

Hildreth, G. (1930). *Psychological services for school problems*. Yonkers-on-Hastings, NY: World Book.

Hoffman, R. R., & Deffenbacher, K. A. (1992). A brief history of applied cognitive psychology. *Applied Cognitive Psychology, 6*, 1–48.

Holden, W. (1998). *Shell shock*. London: Channel 4 Books.

Hollingworth, H. L. (1913). *Advertising and selling: Principles of appeal and response*. New York: Appleton.

Hollingworth, H. L. (1920). *The psychology of functional neuroses*. New York: D. Appleton.

Hollingworth, L. S. (1913). The frequency of amentia as related to sex. *Medical Record, 84*, 753–756.

Hollingworth, L. S. (1914a). *Functional periodicity: An experimental study of the mental and motor abilities of women during menstruation.* New York: Teachers College, Columbia University.

Hollingworth, L. S. (1914b). Variability as related to sex differences in achievement: A critique. *American Journal of Sociology, 19,* 510–530.

Hollingworth, L. S. (1918). Tentative suggestions for the certification of practicing psychologists. *Journal of Applied Psychology, 2,* 280–284.

Hollingworth, L. S. (1926). *Gifted children: Their nature and nurture.* New York: Macmillan.

Hoppock, R. (1935). *Job satisfaction.* New York: Harper & Brothers.

Horney, K. (1937). *The neurotic personality of our time.* New York: W. W. Norton.

Horney, K. (1939). *New ways in psychoanalysis.* New York: W. W. Norton.

Horney, K. (1967). *Feminine psychology.* New York: W. W. Norton.

Hornstein, G. A. (1992). The return of the repressed: Psychology's problematic relations with psychoanalysis, 1909–1960. *American Psychologist, 47,* 254–263.

Hughes, R. (1997). *American visions: The epic history of art in America.* New York: Alfred A. Knopf.

Hull, C. L. (1943). *Principles of behavior.* New York: Appleton-Century-Crofts.

Hull, C. L. (1952). Clark L. Hull. In E. G. Boring, H. Werner, H. S. Langfeld, & R. M. Yerkes (Eds.), *A history of psychology in autobiography* (v. 4, pp. 143–162). Worcester, MA: Clark University Press.

Israels, H., & Schatzman, M. (1993). The seduction theory. *History of Psychiatry, 4,* 23–59.

James, H. (Ed.). (1920). *The letters of William James* (2 vols.). Boston: The Atlantic Monthly.

James, W. (1885). Experiments in memory. *Science, 6,* 198–199.

James, W. (1890). *The principles of psychology* (2 volumes). New York: Henry Holt.

James, W. (1902). *The varieties of religious experience.* New York: Longmans, Green.

James, W. (1907). *Pragmatism: A new name for some old ways of thinking.* New York: Longmans, Green, and Co.

James, W. (1909). The confidences of a "psychical researcher." *American Magazine, 68,* 580–589.

Jones, E., & Wessely, S. (2005). *Shell shock to PTSD: Military psychiatry from 1900 to the Gulf War.* New York: Psychology Press.

Jones, M. C. (1924). The elimination of children's fears. *Journal of Experimental Psychology, 7,* 383–390.

Jung, C. G. (1907). On psychophysical relations of the association experiment. *Journal of Abnormal Psychology, 1,* 249–257.

Jung, C. G. (1910). The association method. *American Journal of Psychology, 31,* 219–269.

Jung, C. G. (1916). *Psychology of the unconscious* (trans. by B. Hinkle). London: Moffat, Yard. (German edition published originally in 1913.)

Kaplan, E. A. (1998). Freud, film, and culture. In M. S. Roth (Ed.), *Freud: Conflict and culture* (pp. 152–164). New York: Alfred A. Knopf.

Kilburg, R. R. (2006). *Executive wisdom: Coaching and the emergence of virtuous leaders.* Washington, DC: American Psychological Association.

King, D. B., & Wertheimer, M. (2005). *Max Wertheimer & Gestalt theory.* New Brunswick, NJ: Transaction Publishers.

Klineberg, O. (1935a). *Negro intelligence and selective migration.* New York: Columbia University Press.

Klineberg, O. (1935b). *Race differences.* New York: Harper and Brothers.

Kluger, R. (1975). *Simple justice: The history of Brown v. Board of Education and Black America's struggle for equality.* New York: Random House.

Knapp, T. J. (1986). The emergence of cognitive psychology in the latter half of the twentieth century. In T. J. Knapp & L. C. Robertson (Eds.), *Approaches to cognition: Contrasts and controversies* (pp. 13–35). Hillsdale, NJ: Lawrence Erlbaum.

Koffka, K. (1922). Perception: An introduction to Gestalt-theorie. *Psychological Bulletin, 19,* 531–585.

Koffka, K. (1935). *Principles of Gestalt psychology.* New York: Harcourt, Brace.

Köhler, W. (1927). *The mentality of apes* (revised ed.). London: Kegan Paul, Trench, Trubner.

Köhler, W. (1929). *Gestalt psychology.* New York: Horace Liveright.

Koppes, L. L. (1997). American female pioneers of industrial and organizational psychology during the early years. *Journal of Applied Psychology, 84,* 500–515.

Koppes, L. L., & Bauer, A. L. (2006). Marion Almira Bills: Industrial psychology pioneer bridging science and practice. In D. A. Dewsbury, L. T. Benjamin, Jr., & M. Wertheimer (Eds.), *Portraits of pioneers in psychology* (v. 6, pp. 102–116). Washington, DC & Mahwah, NJ: American Psychological Association and Lawrence Erlbaum Associates.

Kornhauser, A. W., & Kingsbury, F. A. (1924). *Psychological tests in business.* Chicago: University of Chicago Press.

Krohn, W. O. (1893). The laboratory of the Psychological Institute at the University of Göttingen. *American Journal of Psychology, 5,* 282–284.

Kuna, D. P. (1976). The concept of suggestion in the early history of advertising psychology. *Journal of the History of the Behavioral Sciences, 12,* 347–353.

Kuna, D. P. (1979). Early advertising applications of the Gale-Cattell order-of-merit method. *Journal of the History of the Behavioral Sciences, 15,* 38–46.

Kurzweil, E. (1998). Freud's reception in the United States. In M. S. Roth (Ed.), *Freud: Conflict and culture* (pp. 127–139). New York: Alfred A. Knopf.

Ladd, G. T. (1887). *Elements of physiological psychology.* New York: Charles Scribner's Sons.

Laird, D. A. (1925). *The psychology of selecting men.* New York: McGraw-Hill.

Lamiell, J. T. (2012). Introducing William Stern (1871–1938). *History of Psychology, 15,* 379–384.

Lamont, P. (2013). *Extraordinary beliefs: A historical approach to a psychological problem.* New York: Cambridge University Press.

Langfeld, H. S. (1937). Carl Stumpf: 1848–1936. *American Journal of Psychology, 49,* 316–320.

Lashley, K. S. (1951). The problem of serial order. In L. A. Jeffress (Ed.), *Cerebral mechanisms in behavior: The Hixon symposium* (pp. 112–136). New York: John Wiley.

Lavater, J. (1775). *Essays on physiognomy.* As cited in Wells, S. (1866). New physiognomy or signs of character as manifested through temperament and external forms and especially in the human face divine. New York: Fowler and Wells.

Leacock, S. (1924, March). A manual for the new mentality. *Harpers,* 471–480.

Leahey, T. H. (1991). *A history of modern psychology.* Englewood Cliffs, NJ: Prentice Hall.

Leahey, T. H. (1992). The mythical revolutions of American psychology. *American Psychologist, 47,* 308–318.

Leahey, T. H., & Leahey, G. E. (1983). *Psychology's occult doubles: Psychology and the problem of pseudoscience.* Chicago: Nelson Hall.

Leary, D. E. (1987). Telling likely stories: The rhetoric of the new psychology, 1880–1920. *Journal of the History of the Behavioral Sciences, 23,* 315–331.

Leary, D. E. (1992). William James and the art of human understanding. *American Psychologist, 47,* 152–160.

LeUnes, A. (2008). *Sport psychology: An introduction* (4th ed.). New York: Psychology Press.

Lewin, K. (1945). The research center for group dynamics at M. I. T. *Sociometry, 2,* 126–136.

Lewin, K. (1986). "Everything within me rebels": A letter from Kurt Lewin to Wolfgang Köhler, 1933. *Journal of Social Issues, 42(4),* 39–47.

Lilienfeld, S. O., Wood, J. M., & Garb, H. N. (2000). The scientific status of projective techniques. *Psychological Science in the Public Interest, 1,* 27–66.

Lindenfeld, D. (1978). Oswald Külpe and the Würzburg school. *Journal of the History of the Behavioral Sciences, 14,* 132–141.

Locke, J. (1849). *An essay concerning human understanding.* Philadelphia: Kay and Troutman. (Originally published in 1690.)

Lombroso, C. (1911). *Criminal man.* New York: G. Putnam's Sons.

Lombroso, C., & Ferrero, W. (1899). *The female offender.* New York: D. Appleton.

Lyall, W. (1855). *Intellect, the emotions, and the moral nature.* Edinburgh: Thomas Constable.

Lycett, A. (2008). *Conan Doyle: The man who created Sherlock Holmes.* New York: Free Press.

Markowitz, G., & Rosner, D. (1996). *Children, race, and power: Kenneth and Mamie Clark's Northside Center.* Charlottesville: University of Virginia Press.

Marrow, A. J. (1969). *The practical theorist: The life and work of Kurt Lewin.* New York: Basic Books.

Masson, J. M. (1984). *The assault on truth: Freud's suppression of the seduction theory.* London: Farrar, Straus, & Giroux.

Masson, J. M. (Ed.) (1985). *The complete letters of Sigmund Freud to Wilhelm Fliess, 1887–1904.* Cambridge, MA: Harvard University Press.

Mayo, E. (1933). *The human problems of industrial civilization.* New York: Macmillan.

McCosh, J. (1886). *Psychology: The cognitive powers.* New York: Charles Scribner's Sons.

McGuire, W. (Ed.) (1974). *The Freud-Jung letters: The correspondence between Sigmund Freud and C. G. Jung.* Princeton: Princeton University Press.

McMurry, R. N. (1944). *Handling personality adjustment in industry.* New York: Harper & Brothers.

Meyer, M. F. (1911). *The fundamental laws of human behavior.* Boston: Badger.

Milar, K. S. (1999). "A coarse and clumsy tool": Helen Thompson Woolley and the Cincinnati Vocation Bureau. *History of Psychology, 2,* 219–235.

Milar, K. S. (2004). Breaking the silence: Helen Bradford Thompson Woolley. In T. C. Dalton & R. B. Evans (Eds.), *The life cycle of psychological ideas: Understanding prominence and the dynamics of intellectual change* (pp. 301–328). New York: Kluwer Academic/Plenum Publishers.

Mill, J. S. (1843). *A system of logic, racioinative and inductive, being a connected view of the principles of evidence, and the methods of scientific investigation.* London: John W. Parker.

Miller, G. A. (1951). *Language and communication.* New York: McGraw-Hill.

Miller, G. A. (1956). The magical number seven plus or minus two: Some limits on our capacity for processing information. *Psychological Review, 63,* 81–97.

Miller, G. A. (1965). Some preliminaries to psycholinguistics. *American Psychologist, 20,* 15–20.

Miller, G. A. (1969). Psychology as a means of promoting human welfare. *American Psychologist, 24,* 1063–1075.

Miller, J. G. (1946). Clinical psychology in the Veterans Administration. *American Psychologist, 1,* 181–189.

Mills, J. A. (1998). *Control: A history of behavioral psychology.* New York: New York University Press.

Montague, H., & Hollingworth, L. S. (1914). The comparative variability of the sexes at birth. *American Journal of Sociology, 20,* 335–370.

Morgan, C. L. (1902). *Introduction to comparative psychology.* New York: Charles Scribner's Sons.

Müller, J. (1948). *The physiology of the senses, voice, and muscular motion, with the mental faculties* (trans. William Baly), Vol. 2. London: Taylor and Walton. (Originally published in 1838.)

Münsterberg, H. (1908). *On the witness stand.* New York: Doubleday, Page & Co.

Münsterberg, H. (1913). *Psychology and industrial efficiency.* Boston: Houghton Mifflin.

Murphy, G., & Ballou, R. O. (Eds.) (1961). *William James on psychical research.* London: Chatto and Windus.

Myers, C. S. (1915, Feb. 13). A contribution to the study of shell shock. *Lancet,* 316–320.

Neisser, U. (1967). *Cognitive psychology.* New York: Appleton-Century-Crofts.

Nicolas, S., & Sanitioso, R. B. (2012). Alfred Binet and experimental psychology at the Sorbonne laboratory. *History of Psychology, 15,* 328–363.

O'Donnell, J. M. (1979). The clinical psychology of Lightner Witmer: A case study of institutional innovation and intellectual change. *Journal of the History of the Behavioral Sciences, 15*, 3–17.

O'Donnell, J. M. (1985). *The origins of behaviorism: American psychology, 1870–1920.* New York: New York University Press.

O'Neil, W. M., & Landauer, A. A. (1966). The phi–phenomenon: Turning point or rallying point. *Journal of the History of the Behavioral Sciences, 2*, 335–340.

Page, F. H., & Clark, J. W. (1982). Psychology at Dalhousie. In M. J. Wright & C. R. Myers (Eds.), *History of academic psychology in Canada.* Toronto: C. J. Hogrefe.

Parkyn, H. A. (1900). *Suggestive therapeutics and hypnotism.* Chicago: Suggestion Publishing Co.

Parmelee, M. (1912). *The science of human behavior: Biological and psychological foundations.* New York: Macmillan.

Parsons, F. (1909). *Choosing a vocation.* Boston: Houghton Mifflin.

Pfungst, O. (1965). *Clever Hans (the horse of Mr. von Osten).* New York: Henry Holt. (Originally published 1907.)

Philogene, G. (Ed.) (2004). *Racial identity in context: The legacy of Kenneth B. Clark.* Washington, DC: American Psychological Association.

Pickren, W. E., & Schneider, S. F. (Eds.) (2005). *Psychology and the National Institute of Mental Health: A historical analysis of science, practice, and policy.* Washington, DC: American Psychological Association.

Pillsbury, W. B. (1911). *The essentials of psychology.* New York: Macmillan.

Pittenger, D. J. (1993). The utility of the Myers-Briggs Type Indicator. *Review of Educational Research, 63*, 467–488.

Popplestone, J. A., & McPherson, M. W. (1984). Pioneer psychology laboratories in clinical settings. In J. Brozek (Ed.), *Explorations in the history of psychology in the United States* (pp. 196–272). Lewisburg, PA: Bucknell University Press.

Powell, R. A. (2010). Little Albert is still missing. *American Psychologist, 65*, 299–300.

Powell, R. A. (2011). Little Albert lost or found: Further difficulties with the Douglas Merritte hypothesis. *History of Psychology, 14*, 106–107.

Powell, R. A., Digdon, N. L., & Smithson, C. T. (2013, June 20). Searching for Little Albert: Evidence of a second candidate for "psychology's lost boy." Paper presented at the annual meeting of the Cheiron Society, Irving, TX.

Raimy, V. C. (Ed.). (1950). *Training in clinical psychology.* Englewood Cliffs, NJ: Prentice Hall.

Rancurello, A. C. (1968). *A study of Franz Brentano: His psychological standpoint and his significance in the history of psychology.* New York: Academic Press.

Reese, H. W. (2010). Regarding Little Albert. *American Psychologist, 65*, 300–301.

Reid, T. (1785). *Essays on the intellectual powers of man.* Edinburgh: Bell and Robinson.

Richards, G. (2004). "It's an American thing": The "race" and intelligence controversy from a British perspective. In A. Winston (Ed.), *Defining difference: Race and racism in the history of psychology* (pp. 137–169). Washington, DC: American Psychological Association.

Ricord, E. (1840). *Elements of the philosophy of mind, applied to the development of thought and feeling.* Geneva, NY: John N. Bogert.

Rodkey, E. N. (2011). Last of the Mohicans? James McCosh and psychology "old" and "new." *History of Psychology, 14*, 335–355.

Roediger, H. L., III. (1985). Remembering Ebbinghaus. *Contemporary Psychology, 30*, 519–523.

Roediger, H. L., III. (2000). Sir Frederic Charles Bartlett: Experimental and applied psychologist. In G. A. Kimble & M. Wertheimer (Eds.), *Portraits of pioneers in psychology* (v. 4, pp. 149–161). Washington, DC and Mahwah, NJ: American Psychological Association and Lawrence Erlbaum Associates.

Roethlisberger, F. J., & Dickson, W. J. (1939). *Management and the worker: An account of a research program conducted by the Western Electric Company, Hawthorne Works, Chicago.* Cambridge: Harvard University Press.

Rogers, C. R. (1942). *Counseling and psychotherapy: Newer concepts in practice.* Boston: Houghton Mifflin.

Romanes, G. J. (1883). *Animal intelligence*. New York: D. Appleton and Co.

Rosenzweig, S. (1994). *The historic expedition to America (1909): Freud, Jung and Hall the king-maker*. St. Louis: Rana House.

Ross, D. (1972). *G. Stanley Hall: The psychologist as prophet*. Chicago: University of Chicago Press.

Rossiter, M. W. (1982). *Women scientists in America: Struggles and strategies to 1940*. Baltimore: Johns Hopkins University Press.

Rushton, J. P., & Jensen, A. R. (2005). Thirty years of research on race differences in cognitive ability. *Psychology, Public Policy, and Law, 11*, 235–294.

Rutherford, A. (2003). B. F. Skinner's technology of behavior in American life: From consumer culture to counterculture. *Journal of the History of the Behavioral Sciences, 39*, 1–23.

Rutherford, A. (2004). A "visible scientist": B. F. Skinner's writing for the popular press. *European Journal of Behavior Analysis, 5*, 109–120.

Rutherford, A. (2006). Mother of behavior therapy and beyond: Mary Cover Jones and the study of the "whole child." In D. A. Dewsbury, L. T. Benjamin, Jr., & M. Wertheimer (Eds.), *Portraits of pioneers in psychology* (v. 6, pp. 188–204). Washington, DC & Mahway, NJ: American Psychological Association and Lawrence Erlbaum.

Rutherford, A. (2009). *Beyond the box: B. F. Skinner's technology of behavior from laboratory to life, 1950s–1970s*. Toronto: University of Toronto Press.

Samelson, F. (1977). World War I intelligence testing and the development of psychology. *Journal of the History of the Behavioral Sciences, 13*, 274–282.

Samelson, F. (1978). From "race psychology" to "studies in prejudice": Some observations on the thematic reversal in social psychology. *Journal of the History of the Behavioral Sciences, 14*, 265–278.

Samelson, F. (1981). Struggle for scientific authority: The reception of Watson's behaviorism, 1913–1920. *Journal of the History of the Behavioral Sciences, 17*, 399–425.

Sanchez, G. I. (1934). Bilingualism and mental measures. *Journal of Applied Psychology, 18*, 765–772.

Scarborough, E. (1992). Mrs. Ricord and psychology for women, circa 1840. *American Psychologist, 47*, 274–280.

Scarborough, E., & Furumoto, L. (1987). *Untold lives: The first generation of American women psychologists*. New York: Columbia University Press.

Schiller, F. (1992). *Paul Broca: Founder of French anthropology, explorer of the brain*. New York: Oxford University Press.

Schmit, D. (2005). Re-visioning antebellum American psychology: The dissemination of Mesmerism, 1836–1854. *History of Psychology, 8*, 403–434.

Schultz, D. P., & Schultz, S. E. (1987). *A history of modern psychology* (4th ed.). San Diego: Harcourt, Brace, Jovanovich.

Scott, W. D. (1903). *The theory of advertising*. Boston: Small, Maynard.

Scott, W. D. (1908). *The psychology of advertising*. Boston: Small, Maynard.

Sealey, A. (2011). The strange case of the Freudian case history: The role of long case histories in the development of psychoanalysis. *History of the Human Sciences, 24(1)*, 36–50.

Shields, S. A. (1975). Functionalism, Darwinism, and the psychology of women: A study in social myth. *American Psychologist, 30*, 739–754.

Shields, S. A. (1982). The variability hypothesis: The history of a biological model of sex differences in intelligence. *Signs: Journal of Women in Culture and Society, 7*, 769–797.

Simon, H. A. (1991). *Models of my life*. New York: Basic books.

Simpson, J. A., & Weiner, E. S. C. (1989). *The Oxford English dictionary, Vol. 12* (2nd ed.). New York: Oxford University Press.

Sizer, N., & Drayton, H. S. (1890). *Heads and faces and how to study them: A manual of phrenology and physiognomy for the people*. New York: Fowler and Wells Co.

Skinner, B. F. (1938). *The behavior of organisms: An experimental analysis*. New York: Appleton, Century.

Skinner, B. F. (1945, October). Baby in a box. *Ladies' Home Journal*, 30–31, 135–136, 138.

Skinner, B. F. (1948). *Walden two*. New York: Macmillan.

Skinner, B. F. (1957). *Verbal behavior*. New York: Appleton-Century-Crofts.

Skinner, B. F. (1958). Teaching machines. *Science, 128*, 969–977.

Skinner, B. F. (1960). Pigeons in a Pelican. *American Psychologist, 15*, 28–37.

Skinner, B. F. (1967). B. F. Skinner. In E. G. Boring & G. Lindzey (Eds.), *A history of psychology in autobiography* (v. 5, pp. 387–413). New York: Appleton-Century-Crofts.

Skinner, B. F. (1971). *Beyond freedom and dignity*. New York: Alfred A. Knopf.

Skinner, B. F. (1983). *A matter of consequences: Part three of an autobiography*. New York: Alfred A. Knopf.

Skinner, B. F. (1987). Why are we not acting to save the world? In B. F. Skinner (Ed.), *Upon further reflection* (pp. 1–14). Englewood Cliffs, NJ: Prentice Hall.

Skinner, B. F. (1990). Can psychology be a science of mind? *American Psychologist, 45*, 1206–1210.

Snider, D. E., Jr., & Satcher, D. (1997). Behavioral and social sciences at the Centers for Disease Control and Prevention: Critical disciplines for public health. *American Psychologist, 52*, 10–142. (See the entire February, 1997 issue of this journal for articles on the work of psychologists in the CDC.)

Sokal, M. M. (1980). *Science* and James McKeen Cattell, 1894–1945. *Science, 209*, 43–52.

Sokal, M. M. (1981). *An education in psychology: James McKeen Cattell's journal and letters from Germany and England, 1880–1888*. Cambridge, MA: MIT Press.

Sokal, M. M. (1982). James McKeen Cattell and the failure of anthropometric mental testing, 1890–1901. In W. R. Woodward & M. G. Ash (Eds.), *The problematic science: Psychology in nineteenth-century thought* (pp. 322–345). New York: Praeger.

Sokal, M. M. (Ed.) (1987). *Psychological testing and American society, 1890–1930*. New Brunswick, NJ: Rutgers University Press.

Sokal, M. M. (1992). Origins and early years of the American Psychological Association, 1890–1906. *American Psychologist, 47*, 111–122.

Sokal, M. M. (2001). Practical phrenology as psychological counseling in the 19th-century United States. In C. D. Green, M. Shore, & T. Teo (Eds.), *The transformation of psychology: Influences of 19th-century philosophy, technology, and natural science* (pp. 21–44). Washington, DC: American Psychological Association.

Sokal, M. M. (2006). James McKeen Cattell: Achievement and alienation. In D. A. Dewsbury, L. T. Benjamin, Jr., & M. Wertheimer (Eds.), *Portraits of pioneers in psychology* (v. 6, pp. 18–35). Washington, DC & Mahwah, NJ: American Psychological Association and Lawrence Erlbaum Associates.

Sommer, A. (2012). Psychical research and the origins of American psychology: Hugo Münsterberg, William James, and Eusapia Palladino. *History of Human Sciences, 25(2)*, 23–44.

Stagner, R. (1988). *A history of psychological theories*. New York: Macmillan.

Stumpf, C. (2012). *The origins of music*. New York: Oxford University Press. (Originally published in 1911.)

Sturm, T., & Ash, M. G. (2005). Roles of instruments in psychological research. *History of Psychology, 8*, 3–34.

Terman, L. M. (1916). *The measurement of intelligence*. Boston: Houghton Mifflin.

Thacher, I., & Haynes, S. N. (2000). Health psychology: Assessments and interventions. In A. Kazdin (Ed.), *Encyclopedia of psychology* (v. 4, pp. 89–97). Washington, DC: American Psychological Association.

Thomas, J. L., Cummings, J. L., & O'Donahue, W. T. (Eds.) (2002). *The entrepreneur in psychology: The collected papers of Nicholas A. Cummings*. Vol. 2. Phoenix, AZ: Zeig, Tucker, & Theisen.

Thomas, R. K. (2007). Recurring errors among recent history of psychology textbooks. *American Journal of Psychology, 120*, 477–495.

Thomas, R. K., & Young, C. D. (1993). A note on the early history of electrical stimulation of the human brain. *Journal of General Psychology, 120*, 73–81.

Thompson, H. B. (1903). *The mental traits of sex*. Chicago: University of Chicago Press.

Thorndike, E. L. (1914). *Educational psychology. Vol. III: Mental work and fatigue and individual differences and their causes*. New York: Teachers College, Columbia University.

Tinker, M. A. (1932). Wundt's doctoral students and their theses, 1875–1920. *American Journal of Psychology, 44*, 630–637.

Titchener, E. B. (1896). *An outline of psychology*. New York: Macmillan.

Titchener, E. B. (1898a). The postulates of a structural psychology. *Philosophical Review, 7*, 449–465.

Titchener, E. B. (1898b). A psychological laboratory. *Mind, 7*, 311–331.

Titchener, E. B. (1901–1905). *Experimental psychology: A manual of laboratory practice – Vol. 1: Qualitative experiments, Vol. 2: Quantitative experiments* (2 parts each). New York: Macmillan.

Titchener, E. B. (1910a). *A textbook of psychology*. New York: Macmillan.

Titchener, E. B. (1910b). The past decade in experimental psychology. *American Journal of Psychology, 21*, 404–421.

Titchener, E. B. (1914). Psychology: Science or technology. *Popular Science Monthly, 84*, 39–51.

Titchener, E. B. (1928). *A text–book of psychology*. New York: Macmillan.

Titchener, E. B. (1929). *Systematic psychology: Prolegomena*. New York: Macmillan.

Tolman, E. C. (1932). *Purposive behavior in animals and men*. New York: D. Appleton.

Tolman, E. C. (1948). Cognitive maps in rats and men. *Psychological Review, 55*, 189–208.

Tolman, E. C. (1951). *Collected papers in psychology*. Berkeley: University of California Press.

Triplett, H. (2004). The misnomer of Freud's "seduction theory." *Journal of the History of Ideas, 65*, 647–665.

Upham, T. C. (1827). *Elements of intellectual philosophy*. Portland, ME: William Hyde.

Upham, T. C. (1831). *Elements of mental philosophy*. Portland, ME: Hilliard Gray and Co.

Vande Kemp, H. (1992). G. Stanley Hall and the Clark school of religious psychology. *American Psychologist, 47*, 290–298.

Van Wyhe, J. (2004). *Phrenology and the origins of Victorian scientific naturalism*. Burlington, VT: Ashgate Publishing Co.

Viney, W., & Burlingame-Lee, L. (2003). Margaret Floy Washburn: A quest for the harmonies in the context of a rigorous scientific framework. In G. A. Kimble & M. Wertheimer (Eds.), *Portraits of pioneers in psychology* (v. 5, pp. 73–88). Washington, DC & Mahwah, NJ: American Psychological Association and Lawrence Erlbaum.

von Mayrhauser, R. T. (1989). Making intelligence functional: Walter Dill Scott and applied psychological testing in World War I. *Journal of the History of the Behavioral Sciences, 25*, 60–72.

Washburn, M. F. (1908). *The animal mind*. New York: Macmillan.

Watson, J. B. (1913). Psychology as the behaviorist views it. *Psychological Review, 20*, 158–177.

Watson, J. B. (1914). *Behavior: An introduction to comparative psychology*. New York: Henry Holt.

Watson, J. B. (1928). *Psychological care of the infant and child*. New York: W. W. Norton.

Watson, J. B. (1936). John Broadus Watson. In. C. Murchison (Ed.), *A history of psychology in autobiography* (v. 1, pp. 271–281). Worcester, MA: Clark University Press.

Watson, J. B., & Morgan, J. J. B. (1917). Emotional reactions and psychological experimentation. *American Journal of Psychology, 28*, 163–174.

Watson, J. B., & Rayner, R. (1920). Conditioned emotional reactions. *Journal of Experimental Psychology, 3*, 1–14.

Watson, R. I., & Evans, R. B. (1991). *The great psychologists: A history of psychological thought* (5th ed.). New York: Harper Collins.

Weber, E. H. (1834). De Tactu. Translated by E. B. Titchener. (1905). *Experimental psychology* (Vol. 2, Part 2). New York: Macmillan.

Webster, S., & Coleman, S. R. (1992). Contributions to the history of psychology: LXXXVI. Hull and his critics: The reception of Clark L. Hull's behavior theory, 1943–1960. *Psychological Reports, 70*, 1063–1071.

Wells, S. (1866). *New physiognomy or signs of character as manifested through temperament and external forms and especially in the human face divine.* New York: Fowler and Wells.

Wertheimer, M. (1912). Experimentelle studien über das Sehen von Bewegung, *Zeitschrift für Psychologie, 61*, 161–265. English translation appears in T. Shipley (Ed.), (1961). *Classics in psychology.* New York: Philosophical Library.

Wertheimer, M. (1938). Gestalt theory. In W. D. Ellis (Ed.), *A source book of Gestalt psychology.* London: Kegan Paul, Trench, Trubner.

Wertheimer, M. (1945). *Productive thinking.* New York: Harper and Bros.

White, S. H. (1992). G. Stanley Hall: From philosophy to developmental psychology. *Developmental Psychology, 28*, 25–34.

Williams, J. (1998). *Thurgood Marshall: American revolutionary.* New York: Times Books.

Windholz, G. (1990). Pavlov and the Pavlovians in the laboratory. *Journal of the History of the Behavioral Sciences, 25*, 64–74.

Winston, A. S. (1990). Robert Sessions Woodworth and the "Columbia Bible": How the psychological experiment was redefined. *American Journal of Psychology, 103*, 391–401.

Winston, A. S. (Ed.) (2004). *Defining difference: Race and racism in the history of psychology.* Washington, DC: American Psychological Association.

Winston, A. S. (2006). Robert S. Woodworth and the creation of an eclectic psychology. In D. A. Dewsbury, L. T. Benjamin, Jr., & M. Wertheimer (Eds.), *Portraits of pioneers in psychology* (v. 6, pp. 50–66). Washington, DC & Mahwah, NJ: American Psychological Association and Lawrence Erlbaum Associates.

Wissler, C. (1901). The correlation of mental and physical tests. *Psychological Review Monograph Supplements, 3*, no. 6.

Witmer, L. (1897). The organization of practical work in psychology. *Psychological Review, 4*, 116–117.

Witmer, L. (1907). Clinical psychology. *The Psychological Clinic, 1*, 1–9. (reprinted in *American Psychologist*, 1996, *51*, 248–251)

Wolfle, D. (1946). The reorganized American Psychological Association. *American Psychologist, 1*, 3–6.

Wong, W-C. (2009). Retracing the footsteps of Wilhelm Wundt: Explorations in the disciplinary frontiers of psychology and in Völkerpsychologie. *History of Psychology, 12*, 229–265.

Woodworth, R. S. (1918). *Dynamic psychology.* New York: Columbia University Press.

Woodworth, R. S. (1921). *Psychology: A science of mental life.* New York: Henry Holt.

Woodworth, R. S. (1929). *Psychology* (revised edition). New York: Henry Holt.

Woodworth, R. S. (1938). *Experimental psychology.* New York: Henry Holt.

Woodworth, R. S. (1958). *Dynamics of behavior.* New York: Henry Holt.

Woolley, H. T. (1910). Psychological literature: A review of the recent literature on the psychology of sex. *Psychological Bulletin, 7*, 335–342.

Wundt, W. (1902). *Outlines of psychology* (trans. C. H. Judd). New York: Gustav E. Stechert.

Wundt, W. (1904). *Principles of physiological psychology* (5th ed.) (trans. E. B. Titchener). New York: Macmillan. (First edition originally published in 1874.)

Wundt, W. (1912). *An introduction to psychology* (trans. R. Pintner). London: George Allen & Co.

Zeigarnik, B. (1938). On finished and unfinished tasks. In W. D. Ellis (Ed.), *A source book of Gestalt psychology.* London: Kegan Paul, Trench, Trubner.

Index

Lightning Source UK Ltd.
Milton Keynes UK
UKOW06f1818140715

255192UK00011B/56/P